June 2012

Lleyton —

A book you and Dad can enjoy together.

Love —
Grams and Grandad

THE ULTIMATE GUIDE
WORLD CUP 2010

THE ULTIMATE GUIDE
WORLD CUP 2010

KEIR RADNEDGE

igloo

igloo

Published in 2011
by Igloo Books Ltd
Cottage Farm
Sywell
NN6 0BJ
www.igloo-books.com

Copyright © 2008 Igloo Books Ltd

All rights reserved. No part of this publication may be reproduced, stored in a retrieval system, or transmitted in any way or by any means, electronic, mechanical, photocopying, recording, or otherwise, without the prior written permission of the publisher.

10 9 8 7 6 5 4 3 2 1

B044 0811

ISBN: 978-0-85780-124-1

Printed and manufactured in China

The publisher would like to thank the following for permission to reproduce the following copyright material:

Endpapers: Istock. Mirrorpix: 17, 18 (tl, tr, and br), 19 (tl, tc, c, bl, tr, br), 34 (tl, c, bl, tr, and br), 108 (c, tr), 109 (tl, bc, br), 124 (tl, bl, tr, br), 125 (tl, bl, c, br), 65, 136 (b, tr, cr), 137 (tl, cl, tr,), 152, 153, 157, (l and r), 159, 160 (tl, bl, c, tr, br), 161 (tl, bl, c, tr, br), 162, 167, 169, 178, 181, 183, 186, 189, 192 (tr, br,), 193 (tr), 197, 202(t), 204, 205 (t), 206, 207, 210 (tr, cr, br), 211 (tl), 212, 213, 214, 215, 218, 219, 220, 221, 223(r).

Cover images: Action Images/Getty Images

Getty Images: 2, 3, 6, 7, 8, 10, 11, 12, 13, 14, 15, 16, 18 (c and bl), 20, 21, 22, 23, 25, 26, 27, 28, 29, 30, 31 (t and b), 33 (t and b), 35 (tl, cl, b, tr, and br), 36, 37, 38, 39 (t and b), 40, 41 (t and b), 42, 43 (t and b), 44, 45 (t and b), 46, 47 (t and b), 48, 49(t and b), 50, 51 (t and b), 52, 53 (t and b), 54 (t and b), 55, 56, 57 (t and b), 58, 59, 60 (t and b), 61, 62 (t and b), 63, 64, 65, 66 (t and b), 67 68, 69, 70, 71, 72, 73, 74 (t and b), 75, 76, 77, 78 (t and b), 79, 80 (tl, bl, c, tr, br), 81 (tl, bl, cl, cr, bl, br), 82 (t and b), 83, 84, 85, 86, 87, 88, 89, 90, 91, 92 (t and b), 93, 94 (t and b), 95, 96, 97 (t and b), 98, 99 (t and b), 100, 101, 103 (t and b), 105, 106, 107, 108 (tl, bl ,br), 109 (bl, tc, tr,), 111, 112, 113, 114, 115, 116, 117, 118 (t and b), 119, 120, 121, 122, 123, 124 (c), 125 (tr), 126, 127, 128 (r and l), 131 (t and b), 132, 133, 134, 135, 136 (tl, cl,), 137 (bl, cr, br), 138, 139, 140, 141 (l and r), 142, 143, 144 (tl, bl, c, tr, br), 145 (tl, bl, tc, c, tr, br), 146, 147, 149 (t and b), 150, 151, 154, 155, 156, 161(cr), 163, 164, 165, 168, 170, 171, 172, 173, 174, 175, 176, 177, 179, 180, 182, 184, 185, 187, 188, 190, 191, 192 (tl, bl, c), 193 (tl, bl, tc, ,tr, cr, br), 194, 195, 196, 198, 199, 200, 201, 202 (b), 203 (t and b), 205 (b), 208, 209, 210 (tl, bl,), 211 (cl, tc, tr, cr, b), 216, 217, 222, 223 (l), and Istock: 4,5.

Every effort has been made to obtain permission to reproduce copyright material, but there may be cases where we have been unable to trace a copyright holder. The publisher will be happy to correct any omissions in future printings.

CONTENTS

THE ORIGINS OF THE GAME	6

THE WORLD CUP	**10**
FOUNDATION & 1930s	12
1950s	14
1960s	16
MOMENTS	18
1970s	20
1980s	22
1990	24
1994	26
1998	28
2002	30
2006	32
MOMENTS	34

WORLD CUP 2010	**36**
ARGENTINA	38
BRAZIL	40
ENGLAND	42
FRANCE	44
GERMANY	46
ITALY	48
NETHERLANDS	50
PORTUGAL	52
SPAIN	54
USA	56
ALGERIA	58
AUSTRALIA	59
CAMEROON	60
CHILE	61
DENMARK	62
GHANA	63
GREECE	64
HONDURAS	65
IVORY COAST	66
JAPAN	67
KOREA DPR	68

MEXICO	69
NEW ZEALAND	70
NIGERIA	71
PARAGUAY	72
SERBIA	73
SLOVAKIA	74
SLOVENIA	75
SOUTH AFRICA	76
SOUTH KOREA	77
SWITZERLAND	78
URUGUAY	79
MOMENTS	80
CRISTIANO RONALDO	82
DIDIER DROGBA	83
DIEGO FORLÁN	84
FERNANDO TORRES	85
FRANCK RIBÉRY	86
GIANLUIGI BUFFON	87
IKER CASILLAS	88
KAKA	89
LANDON DONOVAN	90
LIONEL MESSI	91
MICHAEL BALLACK	92
MICHAEL ESSIEN	93
MIROSLAV KLOSE	94
ROBIN VAN PERSIE	95
SAMUEL ETO'O	96
THIERRY HENRY	97
TIM CAHILL	98
WAYNE ROONEY	99

EUROPEAN CHAMPIONSHIP	**100**
FOUNDATION & 1960s	102
1970s	104
1980s	106
MOMENTS	108
1990s	110
2000s	112

REGIONAL CUPS	**114**
COPA AMERICA	116
AFRICAN NATIONS CUP	118
OTHER NATIONAL TEAM COMPETITIONS	120
CLUB WORLD CHAMPIONSHIPS	122
MOMENTS	124

INTERNATIONAL CLUB COMPETITIONS	**126**
FOUNDATION & 1950s	128
EUROPE 1960s	130
EUROPE 1970s	132
EUROPE 1980s	134
MOMENTS	136
EUROPE 1990s	138
EUROPE 2000s	140
UEFA CUP & CUP WINNERS CUP	142
MOMENTS	144
SOUTH AMERICA	146
REST OF THE WORLD	148

GREAT NATIONS	**150**
BRAZIL	152
ARGENTINA	154
ITALY	156
NETHERLANDS	158
MOMENTS	160
ENGLAND	162
FRANCE	164
GERMANY	166
PORTUGAL	168
SPAIN	170
RUSSIA	172
REST OF THE WORLD	174

GREAT CLUBS	**184**
EUROPE	186
MOMENTS	192
AMERICAS	196
REST OF THE WORLD	198

GREAT PLAYERS & MANAGERS	**200**
MANAGERS	202
EUROPEAN PLAYERS	206
MOMENTS	210
EUROPEAN PLAYERS	212
AMERICAS' PLAYERS	216
MOMENTS	220
REST OF THE WORLD	222
INDEX	224

THE ORIGINS OF THE GAME

Modern football is only a century-and-a-half old, but competitive ball-kicking games can be traced back much earlier. FIFA recognizes the ancient Chinese game *tsu-chu* (or *cu-ju*) as modern football's oldest ancestor.

Tsu-chu was popularized around 200–300BC as an exercise in the army. In one variation, players kicked a feather-filled ball into a 12–16 inch (30–40cm) net hung between two 30 foot (9m) high bamboo poles. In AD600, the Japanese game *kemari* was invented. Players passed a small, grain-filled ball between themselves without letting it touch the ground.

Early versions of football in Europe came from the Greek and Roman Empires. These games were more similar to rugby than modern football, with players able to use their hands as well as their feet. The Roman version, known as *harpustum*, grew into *calcio*, a notoriously violent Renaissance game, which gives its name to modern Italian football.

MEDIEVAL FOOTBALL

Records of medieval football (called fute-ball) in France and Britain tell of violent mobs charging through towns, using anything from a pig's bladder

RIGHT Gabriele Bella's painting of a game of football in Venice in the eighteenth century

LEFT Members of Harrow School's Soccer Eleven, 1867

to the head of a defeated Danish prince as a ball. Football was so competitive, popular, and disruptive that it caused riots. Both the Lord Mayor of London in 1314 and Henry VIII in 1540 attempted to ban the sport, despite Henry having his own pair of football boots.

RULES AND REGULATIONS

By the 19th century, football—or soccer, as it was also known from its earliest years—had started to take a more recognizable shape as part of British public school curriculums. Two unofficial sets of rules, one from Cambridge University and another developed by clubs in the north east of England, were established to govern the game.

The English Football Association (FA) was formed in 1863 and published the first consolidated set of formal laws. Rebel schools, which wanted to permit running while holding the ball, abandoned association football and launched rugby football.

AN INTERNATIONAL GAME

Football quickly spread around the world as sailors, engineers, bankers, soldiers, and miners introduced it wherever they went. Clubs were formed in Copenhagen, Vienna, and Genoa, with British colonial outposts further aiding the spread of the game. In 1891, Argentina became the first nation outside the UK to establish a football league and British sailors helped to popularize the game in Brazil. Even the United States had its own "soccer" teams as far back as the 1860s. By the end of the century, leagues—albeit not necessarily national ones at this early stage—were running in England, Scotland, Italy, Holland, and pre-communist Russia.

The first international match took place the year after the inaugural FA Cup, when England played Scotland in 1872, at Hamilton Crescent, Partick, Glasgow. The British Home Internationals quickly became a fixture.

THE ORIGINS OF THE GAME

THE CREATION OF FIFA

By the start of the 20th century, national football associations had been formed in countries across Europe and South America, including Uruguay, Chile, Paraguay, Denmark, Sweden, Italy, Germany, Holland, Belgium, and France.

Carl Anton Wilhelm Hirschman of Holland suggested convening an international meeting of football associations to the English FA's secretary, F. J. Wall. The English FA was initially positive, but left the call unanswered. Robert Guerin from the French Sports Association didn't want to wait indefinitely and, at a match between France and Belgium in 1904, he invited the European associations to join together.

This time the English FA made it clear it was not interested. However, the others agreed and FIFA (Fédération Internationale de Football Associations) came into being on 21 May 1904, in Paris, when representatives agreed a list of regulations, including playing matches according to the English Football Association's law book. Represented at the meeting were France, Belgium, Denmark, Holland, Spain, Sweden, and

FOOTBALL FACTS

300–200BC *tsu-chu* popularized in China
AD600 *kemari* developed by the Japanese aristocracy
12th century both women and men took part in huge games in England
1314 "football" banned by the Lord Mayor of London
1530 a famous *Calcio* game takes place during the siege of Florence
1848 "Cambridge Rules" published by Cambridge University
1863 English Football Association founded with a set of codified laws for modern football

RIGHT Crowds build at the 1923 FA Cup "White Horse Final" between West Ham United and Bolton Wanderers

Switzerland. The seeds were sown for the World Cup, with Article Nine stipulating that FIFA would be the only body with the authority to organize such an international tournament.

Although none of the British nations attended the founding meeting of FIFA, they joined two years later and England's D. B. Woodfall became president.

ENGLAND'S INFLUENCE

The English game remained revered around the world in those days, proof of which is to be found in the English clubs names which survive far and wide. Clubs named after Arsenal are to be found in countries as far apart as Ukraine and Argentina and the famous amateur team, the Corinthians, saw their title adopted by what is now one of Brazil's greatest clubs.

In Italy, the English legacy is still evident in the names of clubs such as Milan and Genoa—not the Italian "Milano" and "Genova"—while the fervent Basque supporters of Athletic Bilbao in northern Spain maintained a private insistence on "Atleti" despite the Franco dictatorship imposing the Spanish-language "Atletico" label.

Students who came to England for an education also took home with them more than the latest developments in engineering, finance, and commerce. One such was Charles Miller, whose Scottish father, a railway engineer in Sao Paulo, had sent his son "home" for an English boarding school education. Young Miller returned to Brazil in 1894 with two footballs in his baggage—and sparked a passion which resulted in a record five World Cup triumphs.

Jimmy Hogan, William Garbutt, and Arthur Pentland were outstanding among English football coaches who taught the finer points of the game on the continent in the first half of the 20th century. Hogan worked in Hungary and then in Austria whose national team he coached in their famously narrow 4-3 defeat by England at Stamford Bridge in 1932.

THE ORIGINAL LAWS OF THE GAME
(as adopted by the Football Association on December 8, 1863)

1. The maximum length of the ground shall be 200 yards, the maximum breadth shall be 100 yards, the length and breadth shall be marked off with flags; and the goal shall be defined by two upright posts, eight yards apart, without any tape or bar across them.

2. A toss for goals shall take place, and the game shall be commenced by a place kick from the center of the ground by the side losing the toss for goals; the other side shall not approach within 10 yards of the ball until it is kicked off.

3. After a goal is won, the losing side shall be entitled to kick off, and the two sides shall change goals after each goal is won.

4. A goal shall be won when the ball passes between the goal-posts or over the space between the goal-posts (at whatever height), not being thrown, knocked on, or carried.

5. When the ball is in touch, the first player who touches it shall throw it from the point on the boundary line where it left the ground in a direction at right angles with the boundary line, and the ball shall not be in play until it has touched the ground.

6. When a player has kicked the ball, any one of the same side who is nearer to the opponent's goal line is out of play, and may not touch the ball himself, nor in any way whatever prevent any other player from doing so, until he is in play; but no player is out of play when the ball is kicked off from behind the goal line.

7. In case the ball goes behind the goal line, if a player on the side to whom the goal belongs first touches the ball, one of his side shall be entitled to a free kick from the goal line at the point opposite the place where the ball shall be touched. If a player of the opposite side first touches the ball, one of his side shall be entitled to a free kick at the goal only from a point 15 yards outside the goal line, opposite the place where the ball is touched, the opposing side standing within their goal line until he has had his kick.

8. If a player makes a fair catch, he shall be entitled to a free kick, providing he claims it by making a mark with his heel at once; and in order to take such kick he may go back as far as he pleases, and no player on the opposite side shall advance beyond his mark until he has kicked.

9. No player shall run with the ball.

10. Neither tripping nor hacking shall be allowed, and no player shall use his hands to hold or push his adversary.

11. A player shall not be allowed to throw the ball or pass it to another with his hands.

12. No player shall be allowed to take the ball from the ground with his hands under any pretence whatever while it is in play.

13. No player shall be allowed to wear projecting nails, iron plates, or gutta-percha on the soles or heels of his boots.

THE WORLD CUP

The World Cup is the planet's greatest sports event. In terms of competing nations, television viewers, and finance, it dwarfs every other tournament. Uruguay were the first hosts—and first winners—in 1930, but the worldwide game is perfectly balanced: South American nations have won nine cups and so have Europe's finest. Brazil have carried off the golden trophies a record five times, followed by Italy (four) and Germany (three).

THE WORLD CUP
FOUNDATION & 1930s

After a string of false starts, the World Cup was launched in 1930. The inaugural international tournament was the British Home Championship, but FIFA's first attempt to launch a truly international championship in 1906 had fallen flat. Switzerland agreed to host the tournament and even made a trophy, but no-one turned up.

PAGE 10 Italy score the first goal in the 1982 World Cup final

PAGE 11 Italy's Fabio Cannavaro lifts the 2006 trophy

THE RESULT 1930
Location: Montevideo
Final: Uruguay 4 Argentina 2
Shirts: Uruguay white, Argentina light blue-and-white stripes
Scorers: Dorado, Cea, Iriarte, Castro; Peucelle, Stabile

England, now a member of FIFA, organized the first large-scale international football tournament as part of the 1908 London Olympic Games.

FIFA became a genuinely international body as countries from North and South America started to join. The Olympic football tournament continued, and from 1914 FIFA took a lead role, officially designating it the "world championship of amateur football."

Yet FIFA still harbored ambitions of launching its own tournament. Not only was the status of football in the Olympics insecure—it was almost dropped entirely from the 1932 Games at Los Angeles—but interest was hampered by the sudden spread of professionalism.

URUGUAY WIN ON HOME TERRITORY

In the 1920s, two Frenchmen, FIFA President Jules Rimet and French Federation Secretary Henri Delaunay, set up a steering committee. In 1928, the FIFA Congress in Amsterdam voted to support a first world championship and Uruguay's bid to host

RIGHT Czech goalkeeper Planicka punches clear in the 1934 final

the event easily beat off European competition. As part of the country's centenary celebrations, the event was guaranteed financially by the government. The Uruguayans boasted an impressive pedigree as double Olympic champions—in 1924 they won in France and four years later they triumphed in Amsterdam—and built the massive Centenario Stadium in Montevideo.

Lucien Laurent of France scored the first-ever World Cup goal in the 4-1 victory over Mexico, but Uruguay's generosity in hosting the tournament was rewarded with ultimate victory, when 80,000 fans packed the Centenario Stadium to witness their 4-2 win over Argentina in the final.

WORLD CUP 1934

Italy were both hosts and winners of the first finals to be staged in Europe. Dictator Benito Mussolini wanted to put on a show to impress his international visitors. But World Cup title holders Uruguay stayed away because they feared their top players would remain in Europe.

Vittorio Pozzo, Italy's manager, included three Argentinian-born players in his squad, while his best home-grown players were forwards Giuseppe Meazza and veteran Angelo Schiavio.

Spain became Italy's most awkward opponents. The heroics of the legendary Spanish goalkeeper Ricardo Zamora held the hosts to a 1-1 draw in the quarter-finals. However, Zamora took such a battering from Italy's over-physical forwards that he was not fit enough to play in the replay.

Italy won 1-0 and then defeated Austria, Europe's other top nation, by the same score. In the final they beat Czechoslovakia 2-1, but only after extra time, with Schiavio scoring the winner.

ABOVE Leonidas (left) leads Brazil to their victory over Sweden in 1938

WORLD CUP 1938

Four years later, Italy won a second time, this time in France. The atmosphere was very different compared to 1934, when Pozzo's team had benefited from home advantage, generous referees, and home support. In France they were jeered by fans angered by Italy's fascist politics.

England, despite being outside FIFA, were invited to compete at the last minute in place of Austria—which had been swallowed up by Adolf Hitler's Germany. However, England's Football Association declined the invitation, even though they had thrashed Germany 6-3 in Berlin shortly before the finals.

The favorites included Brazil, following their astonishing first round match against Poland. Brazil won 6-5 in extra time: Brazil's Leonidas and Poland's Ernst Wilimowski both scored hat-tricks.

Brazil were so confident of beating Italy in the semi-finals that they rested Leonidas to keep him fresh for the final, but their gamble misfired because they lost 2-1. Italy went on to defeat Hungary 4-2 in the final to become the first-ever back-to-back World Cup winners.

THE RESULT 1934
Location: Rome
Final: Italy 2 Czechoslovakia 1 (after extra time)
Shirts: Italy blue, Czech red
Scorers: Orsi, Schiavio; Puc

THE RESULT 1938
Location: Paris
Final: Italy 4 Hungary 2
Shirts: Italy blue, Hungary cherry red
Scorers: Colaussi 2, Piola 2; Titkos, Sarosi

FOUNDATION & 1930s | 13

THE WORLD CUP
1950s

> "All I remember was everyone in tears."
>
> PELÉ RECALLS THE 1950 FINAL

A nation was traumatized when the host, and one of the favorites, Brazil lost to Uruguay in the climax of the first postwar World Cup. The competition ended not with a one-off final but a four-team group, a format not used since.

1950

The closing match, in front of a record crowd of nearly 200,000 in Rio's Maracana Stadium, proved decisive as Uruguay claimed their second title.

Free-scoring Brazil needed only a draw to win their first World Cup, and looked to be on their way when Friaça fired them into the lead. But underdogs Uruguay, captained and marshaled by center half Obdulio Varela, stunned the hosts with late goals by Juan Schiaffino and Alcides Ghiggia. Brazilian fans were furious with their team's failure, with much of the blame heaped on unfortunate goalkeeper Barbosa.

The defeat marked the very last time that Brazil wore an all-white uniform, which was believed to be so unlucky that it was replaced by the now famous yellow shirts. Because of the result, the Uruguay players remained in their dressing room for hours after the final whistle until it was safe to emerge.

The final was not the only shock of the tournament—England had been humbled in the first round by the United States. England lost 1-0 at Belo Horizonte, courtesy of a goal from Haiti-born Joe Gaetjens.

1954

When runaway favorites Hungary thrashed under-strength West Germany 8-3 in their opening round group game, no one expected these sides to meet again in the final—let alone for the West Germans to triumph.

West Germany's coach Sepp Herberger rested several key players for their first game, while Hungary's captain Ferenc Puskás suffered an ankle injury that was meant to rule him out of the rest of the tournament. Yet Puskás, as the star player, was controversially brought back for the final and even gave his Magical Magyars a sixth-minute lead. Left winger Zoltan Czibor scored again almost immediately, with another rout looking likely.

But the Germans made a spirited comeback. Led by captain Fritz Walter and two-goal hero Helmut Rahn, the Germans battled back for what is known in footballing history as "Das Wunder von Bern"—the miracle of Berne.

Hungary entered the tournament as Olympic champions and overwhelming favorites, but remarkably the final would be their only defeat between 1950 and early 1956.

RIGHT 1954 souvenir postcard featuring the Maracana Stadium and views over Rio de Janerio

THE RESULT 1950
Location: Rio
Final: Uruguay 2 Brazil 1
Shirts: Uruguay light blue, Brazil white
Scorers: Schiaffino, Ghiggia; Friaça

14 THE WORLD CUP

They thought they had done enough to take the match into extra time, only for an 88th-minute Puskás strike to be controversially disallowed for offside by Welsh linesman Mervyn Griffiths.

The competition produced an amazing 140 goals over 26 matches, including the World Cup's highest-scoring match during Austria's thrilling 7-5 triumph over Switzerland.

1958

Brazil finally ended their wait for their first World Cup crown, with a little help from their latest superstar, Pelé, in Sweden. The 17-year-old Santos prodigy had to wait until Brazil's final group game to make Vicente Feola's starting line-up, with mesmerizing winger Garrincha also given his first opportunity at the finals.

The pair proved irresistible by setting up Vavá for both goals to beat the Soviet Union, before Pelé grabbed a hat-trick in the 5-2 semi-final success over France. Brazil defeated hosts Sweden by the same score in the final, including two goals by Pelé, who broke down in tears at the end.

Yet Brazil were not the only ones to impress. French striker Just Fontaine scored 13 goals, a record for a single World Cup tournament that no one has since come close to emulating. The 1958 finals were also the only time that all four of the UK's Home Nations qualified, although England had lost Duncan Edwards and several other international players in the Munich air disaster.

West Germany lost a bitter and violent semi-final to Sweden. Captain Fritz Walter was fouled out of the game and could not be replaced because substitutes were not allowed at the time.

BELOW Brazil's 17-year-old Pelé shoots for goal in the 1958 final

THE RESULT 1954
Location: Berne
Final: West Germany 3 Hungary 2
Shirts: West Germany white, Hungary cherry red
Scorers: Morlock, Rahn 2; Puskás, Czibor

WEST GERMANY / HUNGARY lineup

THE RESULT 1958
Location: Stockholm
Final: Brazil 5 Sweden 2
Shirts: Brazil blue, Sweden yellow
Scorers: Vavá 2, Pelé 2, Zagallo; Liedholm, Simonsson

BRAZIL / SWEDEN lineup

1950s 15

THE WORLD CUP
1960s

Even without Pelé at the helm, Brazil were unstoppable as they comfortably retained their title in South America. Pelé scored in Brazil's first game but was injured in the next match, so he played no further part in the tournament.

RIGHT Garrincha (left) and Amarildo celebrate Brazil's equalizer against Czechoslovakia in the 1962 final

THE RESULT 1962
Location: Santiago
Final: Brazil 3 Czechoslovakia 1
Shirts: Brazil yellow, Czechoslovakia red
Scorers: Amarildo, Zito, Vavá; Masopust

1962

Pelé's deputy was Amarildo from Botafogo of Rio de Janeiro. Known as "the white Pelé," he made an immediate impact by scoring two goals in the 2-1 win over Spain in their decisive concluding group match. Amarildo also notched an equalizer in the final, but the undisputed star of the tournament was Garrincha, nicknamed "the Little Bird." Garrincha, the world's greatest-ever dribbler, was the two-goal man of the match as Brazil saw off England 3-1. He even overcame the embarrassment of being sent off in the 4-2 semi-final win over hosts Chile.

Brazil managed to persuade the disciplinary panel not to ban their star player, so he played in the final. The defending champions suffered an early shock when midfielder Josef Masopust shot the Czechoslovakians into an early lead. However, mistakes by goalkeeper Vilem Schroif helped Brazil hit back to register a 3-1 victory. Masopust's consolation, months later, was to be voted as the European Footballer of the Year.

Chile's preparations had been marred by an earthquake two years earlier, yet they surpassed expectations not only off the pitch but on it as they clinched a deserved third place.

The Chileans caused a quarter-final upset by knocking out the highly rated Soviet Union, despite the outstanding efforts of legendary goalkeeper Lev Yashin.

1966

A historic hat-trick hero, a Soviet linesman, and a dog named Pickles were all made famous by the World Cup hosted in England.

West Ham's Geoff Hurst, who started the finals as a reserve striker, became the only man ever to score three goals in a World Cup final as the hosts beat West Germany 4-2 at Wembley Stadium.

But his second strike was one of the most controversial in football history. West Germany leveled through Wolfgang Weber's 89th-minute goal to take the final into extra time. In the first-half of extra time, Hurst produced an angled shot that struck the underside of the crossbar and went down behind the goal line before bouncing back out again for the Germans to clear it to safety.

England claimed they had scored and, despite West Germany's protests, linesman Tofik Bakhramov told Swiss referee Gottfried Dienst that the ball had indeed crossed the line.

Hurst, who fell while shooting at goal, was unsighted. However, fellow striker Roger Hunt was so certain that the ball had crossed the line that he did not bother even following up to put it back into the net. The controversial goal left the Germans deflated and Hurst capped his performance by claiming his hat-trick—and England's greatest footballing triumph—with virtually the last kick of the contest.

Alf Ramsey's hard-working side, nicknamed the "Wingless Wonders," had edged past Uruguay, Mexico, France, Argentina, and Portugal en route to the final. However, there were some complaints that England had been able to play all their matches in their stronghold of Wembley Stadium.

Their quarter-final against Argentina proved to be the most bitter. Visiting captain Antonio Rattin was sent off for dissent by German referee Rudolf Kreitlein but initially refused to leave the pitch and eventually had to be escorted by police.

The tournament had been boycotted by African nations, who were unhappy at their "winner" having to qualify via a play-off with the champions of Asia or Oceania.

BRAZIL MISS PRESENCE OF PELE

For the second successive World Cup finals, Pelé limped out of the tournament early on after being the victim of relentlessly tough tackling. His aging team-mates were unable to raise their game without their star player, and Brazil surprisingly crashed out in the first round.

It was also a story of woe for former champions Italy, whose squad were pelted with rotten vegetables on their return home. They suffered a 1-0 defeat to the minnows of North Korea, whose winner was drilled home by dentist Pak Doo Ik. The Koreans raced into a 3-0 quarter-final lead over Portugal, before Mozambique-born Eusébio inspired the Portuguese to a 5-3 comeback and slotted home four goals.

Eusébio, dubbed the "Black Panther" for his goal scoring prowess, ended the tournament as top scorer with nine goals but was denied a place in the final by Bobby Charlton's two goals, which guided England to a 2-1 semi-final success.

Less than four months before England captain Bobby Moore accepted the Jules Rimet trophy from Queen Elizabeth II, it had been stolen from a London exhibition. Fortunately, a mongrel dog called Pickles dug up the trophy from a South London garden and was promptly rewarded with a lifetime's supply of pet food.

THE RESULT 1966
Location: London
Final: England 4 West Germany 2
Shirts: England red, West Germany white
Scorers: Hurst 3, Peters; Haller, Weber

ABOVE Pickles, the dog who found the stolen World Cup

LEFT England captain Bobby Moore holds aloft the Jules Rimet trophy

WORLD CUP MOMENTS

1938

ABOVE Just Fontaine parades his top-scoring golden boot

RIGHT France striker Fontaine on the way to his record 13 goals

1958

ABOVE Czech forward Jan Riha outwits Brazil's Domingos da Guia

1966

ABOVE Portugal's Eusébio is floored for a penalty against North Korea

BELOW Geoff Hurst rises above the West German defense at Wembley

1970

LEFT Romania and England line up in the first round in Mexico

BELOW Brazil's Jairzinho is sent flying by a Uruguayan defender

ABOVE England left back Terry Cooper outwits West German captain Uwe Seeler

LEFT Weary England await extra time in their quarter-final in Leon

1974

ABOVE Top-scoring Gerd Müller eludes Yugoslav keeper Enver Maric

BELOW Franz Beckenbauer (white) breaks up a Dutch attack

MOMENTS 19

THE WORLD CUP
1970s

"Brazil on that day were on a different planet."

ITALY'S GIACINTO FACCHETTI

This was the first World Cup to be broadcast in sun-soaked color around the world. Nothing could match Brazil's famous yellow shirts as Mario Zagallo showcased arguably the most dazzling attacking side in footballing history.

1970

Spearheaded by Pelé, Jairzinho, Rivelino, and Tostão, Brazil were allowed to keep the Jules Rimet trophy after becoming the first country to win three World Cups. Pelé became the only player with a hat-trick of victories, although in 1962 he had been injured very early in the tournament.

Brazil featured in a classic first round contest, when they defeated England 1-0. However, both sides qualified for the quarter-finals. England's title defense came to a dramatic end when West Germany avenged their 1966 final defeat to bounce back from a two-goal deficit to register an extra time 3-2 win over Sir Alf Ramsey's men. The effort of overcoming England undermined the Germans in their semi-final against Italy, and West Germany ran out of steam and lost another epic, to be edged out 4-3.

Brazil wrapped up the tournament with a 4-1 triumph over Italy in Mexico City. Brazil's fourth goal was the finest of the tournament, and one of the most memorable ever scored in a final. A smooth passing move, the length of the pitch, was finished off by captain Carlos Alberto. Manager Mario Zagallo became the first man to win the World Cup both as a player and a manager.

THE RESULT 1970
Location: Mexico
Final: Brazil 4 Italy 1
Shirts: Brazil yellow, Italy blue
Scorers: Pelé, Gerson, Jairzinho, Carlos Alberto; Boninsegna

RIGHT Jairzinho scores Brazil's third goal against Italy

1974

Franz Beckenbauer achieved the first half of his own leadership double when he captained hosts West Germany to victory over Holland. The final was played in Munich's Olympic Stadium, the footballing home to Beckenbauer and his FC Bayern team-mates—goalkeeper Sepp Maier, defenders Hans-Georg Schwarzenbeck and Paul Breitner, and strikers Uli Hoeness and Gerd Müller.

Yet the dominant personality of the finals was Holland's center forward Johan Cruyff who, as captain, epitomized their revolutionary style of total football, characterized by a high-speed interchange of playing positions.

Hosts West Germany surprisingly stuttered in the first round but managed to qualify despite suffering a shock defeat to East Germany, who had emerged through the Berlin Wall for the first and last time in World Cup history. Jürgen Sparwasser made a name for himself with an historic strike in the 77th-minute to secure a slender 1-0 success.

West Germany topped their second round group ahead of Poland—qualifying victors over England—while Holland topped the other group ahead of an over-physical Brazil.

English referee Jack Taylor awarded the first World Cup final penalty—Cruyff had been fouled in the opening minute at Munich. Johan Neeskens stepped up to put the Dutch ahead before the hosts had even touched the ball.

West Germany soon leveled matters through a penalty kick and went ahead decisively, courtesy of Müller, just before the half-time interval.

1978

Holland had to settle for second best again, this time without the inspirational Cruyff, who refused to travel to Argentina, amid kidnap fears.

Cruyff's absence was particularly missed in the final as the hosts clinched their inaugural World Cup 3-1 after extra time. Argentina's only European-based player, Mario Kempes, finished as top scorer, with six goals, including two goals in the final.

A ticker-tape assisted storm of home support carried manager César Menotti's Argentina through the first round and to the second group with a tricky meeting against Peru. Needing to win by at least four clear goals, Menotti's men ran out contentious 6-0 winners to deny Brazil a final berth. Instead, Brazil settled for a 2-1 win over Italy in the third place play-off.

In the final, Holland went behind to a Kempes strike before half-time and equalized through substitute striker Dick Nanninga. On the verge of the full-time whistle, Rob Rensenbrink's effort was denied by the post and proved a costly miss as Argentina pulled away in extra time with further goals from Kempes and Daniel Bertoni.

Scotland failed to progress beyond the first round and were shamed by Willie Johnston being kicked out of the tournament after failing a dope test. The dazzling left winger protested his innocence, insisting he was taking Reactivan tablets to treat a cold, but he was banned from internationals and his playing career fizzled out.

THE RESULT 1974
Location: Munich
Final: West Germany 2 Holland 1
Shirts: West Germany white, Holland orange
Scorers: Breitner (pen), Müller; Neeskens (pen)

THE RESULT 1978
Location: Buenos Aires
Final: Argentina 3 Holland 1
Shirts: Argentina blue and white, Holland orange
Scorers: Kempes 2, Bertoni; Nanninga

LEFT Holland's Johan Cruyff holds off a West German defender

THE WORLD CUP
1980s

The competition swelled to 24 sides in 1982, as Spain played hosts for the first time. Italy ended a 44-year wait for their third title, with captain Dino Zoff becoming the oldest player to win a World Cup at the grand age of 40.

1982

Toni Schumacher, West Germany's goalkeeper, was fortunate to have been playing in the final. Despite having knocked unconscious France's Patrick Battiston with a brutal foul during a thrilling semi-final in Seville, he somehow escaped punishment.

In the final, Schumacher faced a spot kick from Antonio Cabrini and the Italian left back made history by becoming the first player to miss a penalty in the title decider. In the same match, German Paul Breitner wrote himself into the annals of history when he became the first player to score a penalty in two separate finals.

But second half goals from Paolo Rossi, Marco Tardelli, and Alessandro Altobelli handed Enzo Bearzot's attacking side the trophy. Rossi's hat-trick in a 3-2 win had earlier knocked out a Brazil team that included Falcao, Socrates, and Zico.

Rossi finished up as the tournament's six-goal leading marksman to claim the Golden Boot. This was an astonishing achievement because the Juventus striker had returned to top-class football only six weeks earlier, following a two-year suspension for his role in a match-fixing scandal.

Holders Argentina struggled from the outset and they introduced their new hero, 21-year-old Diego Maradona, who had narrowly missed out on a place in their previous World Cup squad. Yet Maradona was stifled in the opening match, beaten 1-0 by Belgium, and then sent off for retaliation during a second round defeat by Brazil.

Spain were one of the more disappointing World Cup hosts out on the pitch, sensationally beaten by Northern Ireland in their opening match and later eliminated after finishing bottom of a three-nation second round group behind West Germany and England.

THE RESULT 1982
Location: Madrid
Final: Italy 3 West Germany 1
Shirts: Italy blue, West Germany white
Scorers: Rossi, Tardelli, Altobelli; Breitner

ITALY
Zoff
Scirea Gentile Bergomi Collovati Cabrini
Conti Oriali Tardelli
Rossi Graziani
(Altobelli) (Causio)
Rummenigge Fischer Littbarski
(H Müller)
Dremmler Breitner B Förster
(Hrubesch)
Briegel K Förster Stielike Kaltz
Schumacher
WEST GERMANY

RIGHT Claudio Gentile and skipper Dino Zoff celebrate in Madrid

A further change of format saw the knockout semi-finals restored. Italy defeated Poland 2-0 in Barcelona to make the final, then West Germany saw off France in Seville, courtesy of the first penalty shoot-out in World Cup history. A magical match swung one way, then the other: Germany opened the scoring but trailed 3-1 before battling back with two goals to force extra time. Schumacher went from villain to hero by stopping the crucial last French penalty from Maxime Bossis.

1986

After his previous World Cup disgrace, Maradona jumped into the spotlight when, virtually single-handedly, he won Argentina their second World Cup by combining audacious skills with equally audacious law-breaking.

The world saw the best and worst of Maradona in a five-minute spell of Argentina's quarter-final contest against England. Although the Argentinian captain punched the ball into the back of the net, Tunisian referee Ali bin Nasser allowed the goal to stand (this was his first and last World Cup game as a referee).

Maradona claimed the goal was "a little bit of Maradona, a little bit the hand of God," a boast that accompanied him for years to the delight of a nation that considered the trick a belated answer to Argentina's military and naval defeat by Britain in the 1982 Falkland Islands conflict.

However, no one could dispute the majesty of Maradona's second strike. A solo slalom took him the full length of the England half, before he swept the ball past embattled goalkeeper Peter Shilton with his left foot, for one of the best-ever goals. Just to prove this had been no accident, maverick Maradona scored a similar solo goal in the 2-0 semi-final victory over Belgium.

Despite being closely marked by West Germany's Lothar Matthäus in the final, Maradona escaped long enough to provide the defense-splitting pass that set up Jorge Burruchaga's late goal to once more clinch World Cup success. The Germans had clawed their way back from a two-goal deficit and looked to be heading toward extra time, before the glittering run and pass from match-winner Maradona.

Franz Beckenbauer, a World Cup winner with West Germany in 1974, was in charge of the national team. Yet even his magic touch off the pitch was simply no match for the genius of Maradona on it.

England's consolation was that striker Gary Lineker went on to win the Golden Boot as the tournament's leading scorer with six goals. His tally included a hat-trick in England's first round defeat of Poland, which sent them to the quarter-finals against Paraguay. England had struggled initially, losing their opening game 1-0 to Portugal, and in the scoreless draw against Morocco they lost key players—Ray Wilkins was sent off and captain Bryan Robson was helped off with an injury.

European champions France sneaked past Brazil on penalties in their quarter-final, but for the second successive World Cup fell in the semi-final to West Germany. The Germans simply cruised into the final against Argentina, courtesy of goals from Andreas Brehme and Rudi Völler.

THE RESULT 1986

Location: Mexico City
Final: Argentina 3 West Germany 2
Shirts: Argentina blue and white, West Germany green
Scorers: Brown, Valdano, Burruchaga; Rummenigge, Völler

ARGENTINA

Pumpido
Cuciuffo Brown Ruggeri
Giusti Burruchaga Batista Olarticoechea Enrique
(Trobbiani)
Valdano Maradona
Rummenigge Allofs
(Völler)
Brehme Eder Magath Matthäus
(Hoeness)
Briegel K Förster Jakobs Berthold
Schumacher

WEST GERMANY

BELOW Diego Maradona sends Peter Shilton the wrong way

THE WORLD CUP 1990

"It was simple: we worked hard and we deserved it."

GERMANY'S LOTHAR MATTHÄUS

West Germany overcame Diego Maradona and Argentina, gaining revenge for their 1986 final defeat, which meant Franz Beckenbauer joined Brazil's Mario Zagallo as the only other man to win a World Cup as player and coach.

Victory in the Stadio Olimpico saw history made as Franz Beckenbauer became the first man to have won separate World Cups as coach and captain (Zagallo had not captained Brazil), while Argentina saw red and paid the penalty for their negative tactics in the final. Beckenbauer stepped down after the triumphant return home and was promptly succeeded by his former assistant Berti Vogts. However, the Germans have not won a World Cup since.

Unlike four years earlier, the final showdown of Italia '90 was a dull defensive game. Settled by Andreas Brehme's controversial late penalty, it was marred by red cards for Argentina's Pedro Monzon and Gustavo Dezotti. This was the first time that a player had been sent off in a World Cup final.

The 1990 finals were later considered as one of the poorest tournaments in the event's history, partly because of the inferior quality of refereeing. Sepp Blatter, then the general secretary of world governing body FIFA and later its president, decided then and there to launch a campaign to improve refereeing standards.

CAMEROON BRING AN AFRICAN BEAT

Argentina were not a patch on the team who had won the World Cup for the second time in their history just four years earlier. Inspirational captain Diego Maradona was carrying a knee injury and in their showpiece opening match they were pulled apart by nine-man Cameroon, the African surprise package. The Africans, making their debut in the World Cup finals, beat the holders 1-0, thanks to a historic strike from François Omam Biyik.

Cameroon's secret weapon was veteran striker Roger Milla. He provided some of the tournament's highlights but Cameroon were let down by their indiscipline. The Africans led England, managed by Bobby Robson, 2-1 in their quarter-final contest in Naples, but slack defending opened up gaps, which prompted them into conceding two penalties. Both were converted by Gary Lineker, who helped drive England through to their first semi-final appearance for 24 years.

But England's fortune with penalties ran out when they faced West Germany. England finished 1-1 after extra time, but lost the penalty shoot-out 4-3 after Stuart Pearce and Chris Waddle missed their spot-kicks.

England, managed for the last time by Robson, who was moving to PSV Eindhoven, lost to hosts Italy in the third place play-off. By then, the Tottenham midfielder Paul Gascoigne had become a national icon, both for his performances as well as for the tears he shed after being shown a yellow card in the semi-final defeat by the Germans. The card was Gascoigne's second of the tournament, which meant he would have missed the final had England reached that grand stage. Later, Gascoigne returned to Italy to play for Lazio.

THE RESULT 1990

Location: Rome
Final: West Germany 1 Argentina 0
Shirts: West Germany white, Argentina blue
Scorers: Brehme (pen)
Sent Off: Monzón, Dezotti

WEST GERMANY
Illgner
Augenthaler
Berthold (Reuter), Kohler, Buchwald, Brehme
Hässler, Matthäus
Littbarski, Völler, Klinsmann

ARGENTINA
Maradona, Dezotti
Lorenzo, Basualdo, Troglio, Burruchaga (Calderón)
Sensini, Serrizuela, Ruggeri (Monzón), Simon
Goycochea

England were not the only nation to suffer the pain of penalty punishment. In the second round, Romania fell in the shoot-out to the Irish Republic, who were making an impressive debut under manager Jack Charlton, and Argentina edged past both Yugoslavia in the quarter-finals and hosts Italy in the last four through penalty kicks.

The finest match in the tournament was arguably the second round duel between old rivals Holland and West Germany. Tension surrounding the game was exacerbated in the first half by the expulsions of Holland midfielder Frank Rijkaard and German striker Rudi Völler. Ultimately, West Germany won 2-1, thanks to a sensational performance by striker Jürgen Klinsmann—possibly the best of his career—who scored and made the other goal.

Argentina's new hero, especially in the shoot-outs, was goalkeeper Sergio Goycochea. The first choice, Nery Pumpido, was injured in Argentina's opening group game against the former Soviet Union, so Goycochea played instead.

MARADONA AT HOME IN NAPLES

The duel between Italy and Argentina was staged in Naples, where Maradona was plying his trade at club level. His appeal for Napoli fans to cheer for Argentina backfired, yet they still won.

The downside for Argentina was that their outstanding winger, Claudio Caniggia, received a yellow card for a second time in the tournament and so was suspended from playing in the final.

Maradona had played remarkably throughout Italia '90, considering his injury. But in the final his luck ran out, and he pointed the blame at everyone except himself, including FIFA's Brazilian president João Havelange.

The final straw for Maradona was the controversial award of a late penalty to West Germany for a foul on striker Völler. Lothar Matthäus was the designated German penalty taker. But, citing a muscle strain, the captain handed over the responsibility to Brehme, who made no mistake in shooting past Goycochea.

ABOVE Andy Brehme celebrates his World Cup-winning penalty against Argentina

1990

THE WORLD CUP 1994

After missing out to Mexico in 1986, the United States finally hosted a World Cup and proved better than expected on the pitch by reaching the second round before bowing out to the eventual champions—Brazil.

RIGHT Diana Ross launches the World Cup party in Chicago

The Americans had set themselves a goal of staging the event back in the late 1960s. They had failed with a bid to host the finals in 1986, but won FIFA approval through both their commercial potential and a promise to build a solid professional league.

Bora Milutinovic, a freelance Yugoslav coach, was hired to build a national team on the strength of his work in guiding Mexico, as hosts, to the quarter-finals in 1986. His "Team America" reached the second round before narrowly losing to Brazil, the eventual winners.

The finals proved surprisingly successful, with the average attendance for the tournament reaching its highest-ever figure of 69,000. The total attendance of 3.6 million became the then highest attendance in World Cup history.

The tournament was also the most attended single sport sporting event in US history, and featured the first-ever indoor match in the World Cup finals, when the US hosted Switzerland in the Pontiac Silverdome in Michigan, Detroit.

The competition kicked off at Soldier Field Stadium in Chicago with another penalty miss, when veteran pop star Diana Ross rolled a pretend spot-kick wide during a glitzy opening ceremony in front of US President Bill Clinton.

The opening match saw holders Germany edge past Bolivia 1-0, courtesy of Jürgen Klinsmann's strike on the hour mark. Ultimately, the Germans, playing for the first time as a unified team since the collapse of the Berlin Wall, were dethroned 2-1 by Bulgaria in the quarter-finals.

One of the favorites to win overall had been Colombia, led by their maverick frizzy-haired playmaker Carlos Valderrama, who was dubbed "El Pibe"—the kid. The Colombians had been tipped for great things by no less a judge than Pelé, after an incredible 5-0 win away to Argentina during the qualifying competition, in which winger Faustino Asprilla exploded onto the international scene. Unfortunately, their campaign proved both short-lived and tragic. They failed to progress beyond the first group stage, when central defender Andrés

THE RESULT 1994
Location: Los Angeles
Final: Brazil 0 Italy 0 (after extra time; Brazil 3-2 on penalties)
Shirts: Brazil yellow, Italy blue

BRAZIL
- Taffarel
- Jorginho (Cafu), Aldair, Márcio Santos, Branco
- Mazinho II, Dunga, Mauro Silva, Zinho (Paulo Viola)
- Romário, Bebeto

ITALY
- R Baggio, Massaro
- D Baggio (Evani), Albertini, Berti, Donadoni
- Maldini, Baresi, Mussi (Apolloni), Benarrivo
- Pagliuca

26 THE WORLD CUP

Escobar scored an own goal in their 2-1 defeat by the United States.

Colombia's squad returned home to a furious reception from fans and media. The furore was cut short within days, after Escobar was shot dead after an argument near his home. His killer was later jailed for 43 years, but served only 11 years of the sentence before being paroled.

MARADONA MAKES HASTY EXIT

Diego Maradona's final World Cup also proved controversial and short-lived. In 1991 he had fled Italy in disgrace after failing a dope test for cocaine and was banned for 15 months while playing for Napoli. He made a comeback in Spain and then Argentina, playing his way back into the national squad in time for the World Cup finals.

However, after scoring and starring in an opening win against World Cup newcomers Greece, Maradona then failed a further dope test for the stimulant ephedrine, following Argentina's 2-1 win over Nigeria, and was immediately expelled from the tournament. Maradona later blamed the dope test failure on the weight-loss drugs he had been taking prior to the World Cup finals.

His shocked team-mates were not long in following him home to Buenos Aires after their unexpected 3-2 exit at the hands of Romania in the last 16 knockout stage. The Romanian side was built around the creative midfield talents of Gheorghe Hagi, known as the "Maradona of the Carpathians."

For the first time since the four British Home Nations returned to the FIFA fold after World War II, none of them qualified for the finals. However, the Republic of Ireland—largely built around English league players—emerged impressively from a first round group that featured Italy, Mexico, and Norway. They fell at the next hurdle, soundly beaten 2-0 in the last 16 by Holland at the Citrus Bowl Stadium in the midday humidity of Orlando, Florida.

BRAZILIAN BLEND FAITH AND FLAIR

Brazil, despite lacking the flair of some of their previous sides, boasted the most effective strike partnership of the tournament in the European-based pair of Bebeto and Romario.

But a disappointing final against Italy ended scoreless, making it the first in the history of the World Cup to be settled by a penalty shoot-out.

The decisive kick was missed by Italian forward Roberto Baggio, whose goals had been crucial in taking his country all the way to the final at the Rose Bowl Stadium in Los Angeles, California.

Mario Zagallo, the assistant manager of Brazil to Carlos Alberto Parreira, became the first man to be involved in four World Cup winning teams, 20 years after his first attempt at gaining this distinction. Zagallo had been an invaluable outside left in Brazil's victorious teams at Sweden in 1958 and four years later in Chile. He successfully managed Brazil in 1970, but four years later his side crashed out to finish fourth.

ABOVE Consolation for Italy's Roberto Baggio after his decisive penalty miss

THE WORLD CUP 1998

Zinedine Zidane's distinctive balding head won France their first World Cup. The midfielder's headed goals, either side of half-time, was overshadowed by a Brazilian side subdued by striker Ronaldo's pre-match collapse.

THE RESULT 1998
Location: Paris
Final: France 3 Brazil 0
Shirts: France blue, Brazil yellow
Scorers: Zidane 2, Petit
Sent Off: Desailly

FRANCE
Barthez
Thuram Leboeuf Desailly Lizarazu
Petit Deschamps Karembeu Zidane
(Boghossian)
Djorkaeff
(Vieira)
Guivarc'h
(Dugarry)

Ronaldo Bebeto
Leonardo Rivaldo Dunga César Sampaio
(Denilson)   (Edmundo)
Carlos Baiano Aldair Cafu
Taffarel
BRAZIL

Internazionale striker Ronaldo had been a member of the 1994 Brazil squad, but did not play a game. Yet, by 1998 he was the team's key player and goal scorer. But crucially, on the morning of the World Cup final, he collapsed in the hotel room that he shared with Roberto Carlos, and was taken to hospital for an emergency check-up.

Manager Mario Zagallo, not expecting Ronaldo to be available to play, named an official line-up that featured Edmundo in Ronaldo's place. Surprisingly, Ronaldo appeared in the line-up after being given the medical all clear. Zagallo swiftly obtained FIFA clearance to alter the team line-up and later denied that he had been pressured into including Ronaldo by FIFA officials and/or sponsors. Although Ronaldo did play the entire match, he was never a force in the game and rarely threatened to add to his personal tally of four goals scored during the previous rounds.

Zidane's double and a last-minute third goal from midfielder Emmanuel Petit provided France with a comfortable victory in Saint-Denis, north of Paris. The 3-0 triumph was astonishing because the French side were reduced to ten men after defender Marcel Desailly was sent off.

Desailly's red card cost Thierry Henry an opportunity to make an appearance in the final. The striker had played in all the previous games and as a substitute was expected to play a part. But manager Aimé Jacquet opted to bring on a replacement defender for Desailly instead.

ABOVE Referee Kim Milton Nielsen sends off England's David Beckham

An earlier red card, in England's second round loss to Argentina, had already made David Beckham notorious. England had reached the finals by qualifying from a tough group that included Italy. Under the management of former international midfielder Glenn Hoddle, England had beaten Tunisia and Colombia in their first round group but finished in second spot because of a 2-1 reversal to Romania. It proved a costly slip up because it meant England had to tackle old rivals Argentina in the second round instead of Croatia.

England's Michael Owen, the outstanding new Liverpool striker, scored a superb solo goal, but early in the second half Manchester United midfielder Beckham was sent off by Danish referee Kim Morten Nielsen for flicking a retaliatory foot at the Argentinian midfielder Diego Simeone. England, without the influential Beckham, fought bravely and even had a potential winning "goal" by defender Sol Campbell contentiously disallowed before they eventually succumbed in the lottery of a penalty shoot-out.

Argentina's midfielder Ariel Ortega was given his marching orders during their next game against Holland. Being reduced to ten men meant the same ultimate outcome of defeat. Holland progressed to the finals with a 2-1 win, courtesy of a superb winning goal from Arsenal striker Dennis Bergkamp—later voted the best goal of the finals.

FRANCE FIND WINNING FORMULA

Dutch luck finally ran out. In their semi-final they lost on a penalty shoot-out to Brazil while hosts France, gathering speed and confidence, sneaked past Croatia thanks to the first and second goals of defender Lilian Thuram's international career. France won despite finishing with ten men after Laurent Blanc was sent off after a tussle with Slaven Bilic.

Croatia went on to finish third on their debut at the finals, less than a decade after the country had gained independence out of the wreckage of the former Yugoslavia. Star striker Davor Suker ended up as the tournament's six-goal leading marksman to crown a remarkable season and win the coveted Golden Boot. Less than two months earlier, Suker had became a European club champion with Real Madrid following their slender 1-0 victory over Juventus in the Champions League final.

France went on to defeat Brazil and duly celebrate the triumph for which they had been waiting since fellow countryman Jules Rimet had launched the inaugural World Cup 68 years earlier.

Thousands of delirious fans poured into central Paris to celebrate, and the victorious team undertook an open-top bus parade the following day down the Champs-Elysées. Manager Aimé Jacquet, a former international midfielder, was delighted with the manner of victory because he had been subjected to a barrage of relentless criticism for his tactics and team selection by the daily sports newspaper *L'Equipe*.

Jacquet stepped down after the finals and handed over to assistant Roger Lemerre. The new manager proved that the World Cup triumph had been no fluke by leading France to a further international victory at the subsequent European Championships two years later with a 2-1 success over Italy.

BELOW Team-mates join Zinedine Zidane in celebrating his second goal against Brazil

1998

THE WORLD CUP 2002

> *"We proved the World Cup belongs to everyone."*
>
> JAPAN'S HIDETOSHI NAKATA

Although the trophy went to hot favorites Brazil, the tournament was full of upsets. Holders France made a swift exit, while co-hosts South Korea stunned Portugal, Italy, and Spain to reach the semi-finals.

RIGHT Park Ji-sung of South Korea enjoys that winning feeling against Portugal

South Korea were beaten to third place by Turkey, who had previously never progressed beyond the first round.

This was the first World Cup to be played in Asia. Japan had long been campaigning for the right to stage the finals, and one major step in their bid to impress the world authority FIFA had been the launch of the professional J.League in 1993.

Less than two years before the hosting decision, in 1996, the Japanese were challenged in the bidding race by neighbors South Korea. A major political battle within FIFA ended with a compromise that resulted in both countries being awarded the finals jointly. This decision meant that not only was the 2002 event the inaugural Asian finals but the first, and so far the only, World Cup finals to be co-hosted.

The co-hosting proved highly expensive for FIFA and highly complex in logistical terms. The match schedule for the finals had to be especially organized to ensure that each co-host played all matches in their country. In the end, the tournament organization ran remarkably smoothly.

FRANCE FAIL TO SCORE A GOAL

Out on the pitch, the first of many shocks kicked off with the tournament's grand opening match. Defending champions France were narrowly beaten 1-0 by Senegal, who were making their debut in the finals. Midfielder Papa Bouba Diop scored the goal for the impressive and organized Senegal side.

France may have been reigning world and European champions but, in a disastrous defense of their World Cup, they were knocked out in the first round without even scoring a goal in their three group games. It was the worst record of any defending nation in the tournament's history, although they were handicapped by the initial absence of Zinedine Zidane. The key midfielder had been injured in a warm-up friendly against South Korea on the eve of the finals. Manager Roger Lemerre, who had guided France, or "Les Bleus," to victory in the European Championship two years earlier, was fired on France's return home, despite having been awarded a contract extension before the finals.

The once-mighty Argentina also failed to make the second round, after finishing third in their group behind England and table-topping Sweden.

THE RESULT 2002
Location: Yokohama
Final: Brazil 2 Germany 0
Scorers: Ronaldo 2
Shirts: Brazil yellow, Germany white

BRAZIL
Marcos
Cafu   Lúcio   Roque Júnior   R Carlos
Ronaldinho   Edmilson   Silva   Kléberson
(Paulista)
Ronaldo   Rivaldo
(Denilson)
Klose   Neuville
(Bierhoff)
Bode   Hamann   Jeremies   Schneider
(Ziege)   (Asamoah)
GERMANY
Metzelder   Ramelow   Linke   Frings
Kahn

30 THE WORLD CUP

With memories of the 1998 World Cup penalty shoot-out still fresh in their memories, Argentina tackled England indoors at Tokyo's Sapporo Dome. England emerged as 1-0 winners courtesy of a penalty converted by David Beckham, who avenged his 1998 World Cup expulsion against the South Americans.

England were guided by Swede Sven-Göran Eriksson, their first foreign manager, and beat Denmark surprisingly easily 3-0 in the second round but then lost 2-1 to Brazil in the quarter-finals. The decisive goal was a long-range fluke shot from Ronaldinho that drifted over the head of helpless England keeper David Seaman. Ronaldinho was sent off in the 57th minute, but Brazil held onto their lead without the influential midfielder for both the rest of this contest and for their semi-final 1-0 victory over Turkey.

SEMI-FINAL SLOTS FILLED BY UNDERDOGS

Japan reached the second round before being eliminated 1-0 by Turkey, while South Korea made the most of their fervent home support to race into the semi-finals and finish fourth overall. South Korea were astutely organized by the Dutch coach Guus Hiddink and inspired by attacking players such as Ahn Jung Hwan, whose extra time goal beat Italy in a dramatic second round tie. Turkey had rarely appeared before in the finals of any major tournament, let alone the World Cup. But they made the most of this opportunity by reaching the semi-final stage. Veteran striker Hakan Sükür scored the fastest-ever goal in the World Cup by taking just 10.8 seconds to give Turkey the lead in a 3-2 win over South Korea in the third place play-off.

The final, played at the International Stadium Yokohama in Japan, belonged to Brazil's prolific striker Ronaldo. He scored twice against a competitive but uninspired German team that clearly missed their key midfielder Michael Ballack, who was suspended after collecting a second yellow card of the tournament in the semi-final.

Ronaldo finished the tournament as its eight-goal leading marksman to not only pick up the Golden Boot but to equal Pelé's Brazilian record of 12 goals overall in World Cup finals.

Oliver Kahn, Germany's captain, became the first goalkeeper to be voted as the best player of the tournament despite making a crucial error to concede the first goal in the final.

Cafu, Brazil's captain, also made history by becoming the first footballer to play in the final of three consecutive World Cups.

BELOW David Seaman is fooled by Ronaldinho's long shot

BELOW Ronaldo scores Brazil's first goal after a mistake by goalkeeper Oliver Kahn

2002 31

THE WORLD CUP 2006

Italy collected their fourth World Cup, although the final shall always be associated with Zinedine Zidane's violent act. The French master was aiming for a fairytale ending to his illustrious career, but instead bowed out disgracefully.

The final pitched France against Italy in Berlin's Olympic Stadium and saw Real Madrid midfielder Zinedine Zidane give France the lead with a cheeky penalty, in what was to be his final game before retiring from the sport.

Italy equalized through a header from rugged central defender Marco Materazzi, which sent the game into extra time. With ten minutes of extra time and the contest still at stalemate, Zidane suddenly launched his head into Materazzi's chest and was sent off for violent conduct by the Argentinian referee Horacio Elizondo.

Subdued France had no Zidane to help them in the penalty shoot-out. Italy, coached by Marcello Lippi, became the second side to win the World Cup on penalties after the French striker David Trezeguet hit the bar with his attempt.

Despite such a disgraceful end to his career, Zidane was voted player of the tournament because of his efforts in masterminding victories over Spain, Brazil, and Portugal to reach the final.

Italy proved to be the tournament's most consistent team, largely thanks to the contributions of the outstanding goalkeeper Gianluigi Buffon, center back and captain Fabio Cannavaro, and influential midfielder Andrea Pirlo.

Their success was all the more dramatic since it occurred at the same time as a trial in Italy, in which senior figures in club football were being accused and found guilty of systemic match-fixing. Juventus official, Luciano Moggi, was the controversial central figure in the corruption scandal. Five of Italy's successful squad and seven other World Cup players returned to Italy after the tournament to find that their club had been relegated to Serie B as punishment. The once mighty trio of Juventus, Lazio, and Fiorentina were demoted.

Italy had beaten Germany 2-0 during extra time at the semi-final stage. The hosts had been one of the most exciting teams to watch under the guidance of former striker Jürgen Klinsmann.

KLINSMANN LEADS GERMAN REVIVAL

The German federation had appointed Klinsmann, a World Cup winner in 1990, as coach in the summer of 2004, following their nation's disappointing showing at the UEFA European Championship. Klinsmann demanded a free hand, which included the right to continue to live in California and bring in his choice of new staff—coaches, assistants, and fitness experts. His approach drew initial skepticism among other coaches and fans. By the time the World Cup finals started, it became clear that Klinsmann was winning fans with his tactics and approach to matches.

Germany made an adventurous—and, crucially, winning—start, by defeating Costa Rica 4-2 in the opening game. New heroes included young striker Lukas Podolski and defender Philipp Lahm. Ultimately, the German effort was halted in a semi-final in Dortmund by Italy in what was

THE RESULT 2006
Location: Berlin
Final: Italy 1 France 1 (after extra time, Italy 5-3 penalties)
Shirts: Italy blue, France white
Scorers: Materazzi; Zidane (pen)
Sent Off: Zidane

arguably the finest game of the tournament. Italy snatched victory through last-gasp goals in extra time from Fabio Grosso and Alessandro Del Piero.

The Germans scored a 3-1 third place play-off win over Portugal, resulting in a far better finish to their campaign than many home fans had feared.

DULL ENGLAND SUFFER ON SPOT-KICKS

In contrast to the Germans, England's World Cup performances were dreary, in Sven-Göran Eriksson's third and last tournament as national coach. The quarter-finals were once again the end of the road as England lost on penalties for the second time in three World Cups, beaten by Portugal in a shoot-out for the second time in a row—after a similar finish in the 2004 UEFA European Championship held in Portugal.

England's hopes had been hindered by a pre-tournament foot injury to star striker Wayne Rooney, which delayed his arrival. Then fellow striker Michael Owen was seriously injured during a freak accident in a group game against Sweden.

Rooney was sent off for stamping on defender Ricardo Carvalho during the quarter-final contest. Cristiano Ronaldo, Rooney's Manchester United team-mate, endured a hate campaign on his return to English football after having been caught smiling and winking at the Portuguese bench following Rooney's expulsion.

Portugal's progress was ended by France, who inflicted a 1-0 semi-final defeat in a lackluster match through Zidane's 33rd-minute penalty.

South America's challenge ended in the quarter-finals. In the group stage, a surprisingly adventurous Argentina had contributed the goal of the tournament against Serbia & Montenegro, a 24-pass move finished by Esteban Cambiasso. But they lost to Germany on penalties in the quarter-finals while Brazil lost their hold on the trophy at the same stage by a 1-0 reversal to France.

German striker Miroslav Klose finished top scorer with five goals, the lowest tally since 1962, for the winner of the Golden Boot.

BELOW Italy's Marco Materazzi acclaims his equalizer in the final

BOTTOM Zinedine Zidane beats Gigi Buffon to open the score for France

WORLD CUP MOMENTS

1978

ABOVE Keeper Jan Jongbloed comes to Holland's rescue

RIGHT Dutch defender Ruud Krol foils Scotland's Asa Hartford

BELOW Argentina's fans hail Daniel Passarella

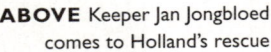

1986

ABOVE Diego Maradona celebrates victory over England

BELOW Gary Lineker pulls one goal back for England

1990   **1994**   **1998**   **2002**   **2006**

ABOVE Andy Brehme converts Germany's penalty winner in the final

ABOVE Romario celebrates a quarter-final goal against Holland

RIGHT Dennis Bergkamp fires the final's best goal past Carlos Roa

ABOVE David Beckham scores England's winner against Argentina

BELOW Sent-off Zinedine Zidane makes an exit

MOMENTS 35

THE WORLD CUP 2010

Football fans all over the world have one ultimate goal: to watch their country's team qualify, compete and win the Jules Rimet trophy – the symbol of football supremacy. The grueling hours of practice, the hard-fought matches, the injuries and the disappointments are all forgotten when teams secure that place to compete. Hopes ride high. With stats, stunning photographs, details on players, managers and teams' history, this is the place to follow that dream.

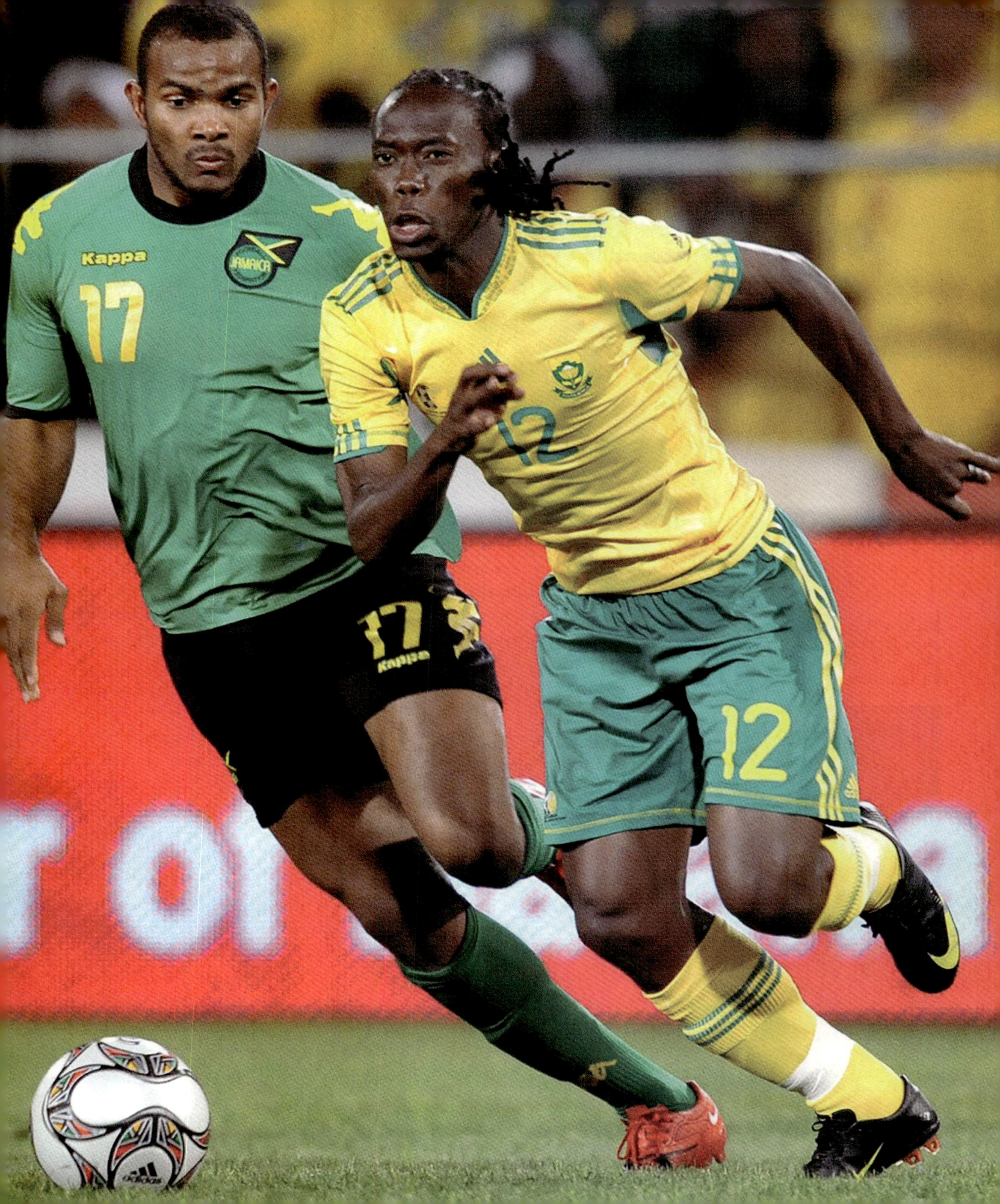
Kappa
17
JAMAICA
12
17
Kappa
12
adidas

WORLD CUP 2010, TEAMS
ARGENTINA

Argentina began their qualification marathon with some degree of fear as veteran coach Alfio Basile returned to lead the side.

PAGE 36 Jackson Martinez of Columbia celebrates his team's first goal during their qualifying match against Chile in October 2009.

PAGE 37 Reneilwe Letsholonyane (right), of World Cup 2010 hosts South Africa in action during a pre-tournament friendly match.

BELOW Head coach Diego Armando Maradona celebrates the victory over Uruguay that qualified Argentina for World Cup 2010.

Basile had guided the team to the 1994 World Cup where they finished third in their group, barely scraping through to the knockout stages when Romania immediately eliminated them. A repeat performance would not be tolerated, but they had to make it there first.

Basile had been invited back after José Pekerman resigned following the quarter-final defeat to host nation Germany in 2006. Having lost stalwarts such as Ayala and Crespo, it was down to the new breed of players like Carlos Tevez and Lionel Messi to make their mark, having both won trophies at club level.

Argentina got off to a good start in Buenos Aires, a disciplined performance that saw off Chile with two first-half goals from Juan Román Riquelme. Another 2-0 win with goals from Gabriel Milito and Lionel Messi away to Venezuela meant that Argentina topped the group and memories of USA '94 were beginning to fade. Riquelme hit another brace against Bolivia the following month, after Sergio Agüero had put them one-up in a 3-0 victory. Argentina were flying, having not yet conceded one goal, and scoring seven.

Despite Carlos Tevez receiving a red card early on in the match, Messi's goal after half an hour made it seem like another romp was probable against Colombia. But, when the home side hit two in the final 30 minutes, it handed the group leaders a shock defeat despite ending 2007 ranked number one in the world. Another defeat looked certain when the team returned to action in June against Ecuador. But substitute Rodrigo Palacio equalized with the last kick of the game.

Having suffered heavy losses in their last two matches, Argentina were desperate for a positive result against Brazil, and could have sealed the match had Messi not squandered two late chances. The 0-0 draw left them within touching distance of Paraguay at the top of the group, and they were up next.

The opportunity to lead the group was dashed after Gabriel Heinze scored an own goal after 13 minutes. The task was made harder when Tevez received his second red card of the campaign. It took a goal from substitute Sergio Agüero to salvage a point and keep Paraguay from running away with the group.

September 2008 proved frustrating as the team threw away two points with the last kick of the game in Peru. Esteban Cambiasso put the visitors ahead with just eight minutes left, but Johan Fano's last-gasp leveler left Argentina third. Nothing less than victory against Uruguay at home would be acceptable for coach Basile, and the team delivered; goals from Messi and Agüero in the first 15 minutes were enough to withstand a second-half goal from Fenerbahçe defender Diego Lugano.

But it was the calm before the storm. A 1-0 loss away to Chile four days later would see Basile hand in his resignation. Javier Mascherano slammed his teammates for the form that led to Basile leaving his job. "It has to do with the players that the coach has resigned; it has to do with the weak level we showed. We are all responsible."

Though former Boca Juniors coach Carlos Bianchi was the bookie's favorite, the AFA decided to take a chance on Argentina's favorite son, one Diego Maradona—but the jury was out on his abilities. He was certainly set up for success; Basile had left the team third in the table and in an automatic qualification spot. Maradona had eight games to keep them there.

An inspired 4-0 thrashing of Venezuela in March 2009 got his competitive reign off to the best possible start, but the next result shocked the world. Minnows Bolivia inflicted Argentina's equal heaviest defeat, wiping them out 6-1 in La Paz, with Maradona claiming, "Every Bolivia goal was a stab in my heart." Riquelme declared he would never again play while Maradona was in charge—it appeared his reign was already falling apart.

Victory over Columbia in June was followed by another defeat to Ecuador. Despite the team's patchy form, Maradona signed a one-year contract extension, and issued a rallying cry ahead of the Brazil clash: "We're going to win because we have better players."

They went down 3-1, Napoli winger Jesús Dátolo grabbing their only goal. Another defeat to Paraguay days later left Argentina facing the real possibility of missing out on qualification.

Two games remained for them to save themselves. Gonzalo Higuaín and a last-minute Martín Palermo goal gave Argentina a dramatic 2-1 victory over Peru and set up a make-or-break game against Uruguay; the winner would proceed to South Africa automatically, while the loser would have to settle for the playoffs.

After Mario Bolatti became a national hero as he came off the bench to hit a late winner, Maradona launched an expletive-laden tirade at the world's press, saying "I want to say that all the people that criticized me and treated me as garbage can eat their words!" The tournament would certainly be more interesting for Argentina's inclusion.

ABOVE Argentina's Carlos Tevez (left) battles for the ball with Bolivia's Rivero Kuhn (right).

ROAD TO WORLD CUP 2010

Argentina	2-0	Chile
Venezuela	0-2	Argentina
Argentina	3-0	Bolivia
Columbia	2-1	Argentina
Argentina	1-1	Ecuador
Brazil	0-0	Argentina
Argentina	1-1	Paraguay
Peru	1-1	Argentina
Argentina	2-1	Uruguay
Chile	1-0	Argentina
Argentina	4-0	Venezuela
Bolivia	6-1	Argentina
Argentina	1-0	Columbia
Ecuador	2-0	Argentina
Argentina	1-3	Brazil
Paraguay	1-0	Argentina
Argentina	2-1	Peru
Uruguay	0-1	Argentina

LEFT Argentina's Martin Palermo (left) heads the ball next to Peru's defender Alberto Rodriguez (middle).

ARGENTINA 39

WORLD CUP 2010, TEAMS
BRAZIL

With governing body CONMEBOL placing South American teams in a group of 10, former champions Brazil faced a demanding 18-game campaign, starting a year before other confederations.

ROAD TO WORLD CUP 2010

Columbia	0-0	Brazil
Brazil	5-0	Ecuador
Peru	1-1	Brazil
Brazil	2-1	Uruguay
Paraguay	2-0	Brazil
Brazil	0-0	Argentina
Chile	0-3	Brazil
Brazil	0-0	Bolivia
Venezuela	0-4	Brazil
Brazil	0-0	Columbia
Ecuador	1-1	Brazil
Brazil	3-0	Peru
Uruguay	0-4	Brazil
Brazil	2-1	Paraguay
Argentina	1-3	Brazil
Brazil	4-2	Chile
Bolivia	2-1	Brazil
Brazil	0-0	Venezuela

RIGHT Brazil's Kaká (left) controls the ball in front of Venezuela's Gerzon Chacon (right).

Under ex-player Dunga Brazil were going back to basics rather than relying on the reputation of their larger stars.

This strategy saw the emergence of players such as Juventus midfielder Felipe Melo, with strikers Nilmar and Luís Fabiano returning after years out of the side.

After victory in the 2007 Copa América, the most successful team in World Cup history were expected to qualify with ease. The team got off to a poor start, 0-0 away to Columbia, before returning to Rio to thump Ecuador 5-0. Vágner Love scored the first goal, Ronaldinho the second, and Elano squeezed a goal in between a brace from Kaká.

The hot-and-cold form continued in November 2007 when Brazil let a one-goal lead slip against Peru; Kaká's third in two games just before half time was canceled out by Juan Vargas. Three days later, there were concerns as Uruguay took an early lead in São Paolo before a Fabiano double salvaged Brazil's unbeaten start.

It would be seven months before Brazil resumed play in the group but it was not a happy restart; goals from Roque Santa Cruz and Salvador Cabañas ensured Paraguay replaced Brazil at the summit. Another 0-0 three days later, this time against archrivals Argentina, proved frustrating for Dunga.

There was an improved performance in September 2008 as Brazil cruised to a 3-0 victory over Chile; another brace from Fabiano and a first for new Manchester City signing Robinho secured the away win. But, once more plagued by inconsistency, Brazil failed to find the net again against Bolivia; another two points lost.

Ronaldinho was dropped for the October matches against Venezuela and Columbia, but Dunga stressed it was not irreversible: "He needs more practice time, more rhythm. He will improve."

Brazil coped without him, hammering four past Venezuela in San Cristóbal. Kaká marked his return from injury with a goal, and Robinho continued his fine form for club and country. Adriano made it three in the first 20 minutes before Robinho sent Brazil home with the points. In what was becoming the theme of their campaign, Brazil once again failed to win the following match, playing out another 0-0 draw against Columbia.

40 WORLD CUP 2010, TEAMS

As 2008 ended, Dunga was under pressure for his side's inability to string two wins together, Brazil were joint second in the group with Argentina behind leaders Paraguay. With seven games left, it was time to cut out the mistakes.

Roma midfielder Julio Baptista struck against Ecuador with just 20 minutes left, but Christian Noboa equalized with one minute left to ensure Brazilian frustration continued. Peru at home was earmarked a must-win game, and Fabiano eased any early fears with an 18th-minute penalty. He followed up with a second and, when Melo scored a third in the second half, fans were hoping the inconsistency had ended.

Goals were again no problem against Uruguay, as Brazil recorded a four-goal haul. Dani Alves and Juan netted the first two, before Luis Fabiano got his seventh goal in 13 games and Kaká capped an emphatic victory.

When Paraguay struck first four days later, fans would be forgiven for fearing another draw, but a Robinho volley and a scrappy winner from Nilmar made it three victories in a row. Now top of the group, a win against Argentina in September 2009 would secure a place in South Africa.

However, the Confederations Cup was just four days away. Victory in South Africa strengthened Dunga's position and meant confidence in the camp was again high, particularly for tournament top scorer Fabiano. He added another two to his tally in a 3-1 victory over Argentina after Benfica captain Luisão put Brazil one-up.

The win sent them to the World Cup but fans would argue the party should have begun far earlier. The samba celebrations began with a 4-2 win against Chile in their next game, Nilmar scoring a hat trick and Baptista adding a fourth.

As the final two fixtures approached, the team's desire to win seemed to trail off. They were 2-0 down to second-bottom Bolivia, and not even a Nilmar goal in the second half could spark a comeback. It was Brazil's first loss in 19 matches. The defeat was followed by yet another 0-0 draw, against Venezuela.

Brazil still managed to hold on to top spot, just one point in front of Chile and Paraguay.

Top scorer Luis Fabiano insisted, "This is a group that can win, that breaks records. Brazil are on the right path and we have to maintain this unity. Of course we will have to correct some things, but we are following the right path." They certainly needed Fabiano firing if they were to win their sixth World Cup.

ABOVE Gilberto Silva (left) of Brazil jumps above Matias Fernandez of Chile to win the ball.

LEFT Luis Fabiano (left) scores the first goal against Argentina during Brazil's 3-1 victory.

BRAZIL 41

WORLD CUP 2010, TEAMS
ENGLAND

England kicked off their qualifying campaign for South Africa with a point to prove after failing to reach Euro 2008. The taste of defeat to Croatia was still fresh as the team traveled to Barcelona to face minnows Andorra.

The venue was switched to Spain in order to accommodate a large crowd, as was the case when the two teams met in 2006. England had become a better side under former Real Madrid and Juventus manager Fabio Capello; the Italian, appointed in December 2007, was known for his discipline and tactical mind, and it appeared to be paying off.

England had lost only once with Capello at the helm—a 1-0 friendly defeat to France in his second game. No such mistake was repeated as, with John Terry once again leading, Chelsea teammate Joe Cole bagged both goals as Andorra were soundly beaten.

All thoughts were already on the next game. After England were drawn with Croatia in their qualifying group, David Beckham revealed his wounds from their last encounter had not yet fully healed: "All players like to get their own back on a team who've beaten them and we'll be no different…we have to go there and perform better than we did in the Euros."

The battle lines were drawn as the team arrived in Zagreb. Croatia's home record was very impressive—they had lost just one competitive fixture at the Maksimir Stadium in nearly two decades—so heads were turned when Theo Walcott blasted England ahead within half an hour. It was the beginning of a rout, the Arsenal winger going on to grab a hat trick, with Wayne Rooney compounding the Croats' misery.

While Croatia would regain some measure of pride, thrashing Andorra in their next game, it just got better for England. As the new Wembley hosted its first World Cup qualifier, the Three Lions turned on the style against Kazakhstan, crushing them 5-1 in front of nearly 90,000. Kuchma scored an own goal while Ferdinand and Defoe grabbed their first goals of the campaign. Rooney struck twice, sending out a message to the rest of Group Six—England had won three out of three, scoring an impressive 11 and conceding just two.

Four days later, Rooney bagged another brace against Belarus in Minsk. Gerrard put England one-up before Pavel Sitko equalized on 28 minutes. With Capello's men bulldozing the group, and Wayne Rooney unstoppable, it was unfortunate there was a five-month break between qualifiers.

England picked up where they left off in April 2009, defeating Ukraine 2-1. Crouch had put the whites ahead, before Andriy Shevchenko equalized with 15 minutes left. It was left to captain John Terry to score a rare goal with his feet on 85 minutes to send Ukraine home empty-handed.

As the midway point of qualifying approached, England hit their peak, hitting an incredible 10 goals in two games with no reply. First to be put to the sword were the Kazakhs, falling to a 4-0 home defeat with Gareth Barry, Emile Heskey, and Rooney putting England three-up before a

BELOW Wayne Rooney (left) and Fabio Capello (right) in discussion during England's 1-0 loss to Ukraine.

Lampard penalty completed the victory.

A return to home turf saw Andorra hit for six; Rooney and Defoe notched a brace apiece, with Lampard and Crouch also getting in on the action. Rooney, lauded as England's talisman in the run-up to Euro 2004, was now living up to the title.

The final stretch beckoned and England had a 100% record in the group. It was equally fitting and inevitable that qualification for the World Cup would be secured with a result over Croatia at Wembley. It was a businesslike performance, Lampard netting a penalty within 10 minutes and Gerrard sending England in 2-0 up. The style was turned on in the second half as the Chelsea and Liverpool midfielders bagged a second goal each. Arsenal striker Eduardo hit back but it was Rooney who ended the display with an incredible ninth goal of the campaign.

England were on the plane to South Africa with three games still to play. Their 100% record had finally put to bed the events of two years earlier.

Capello insisted the team would not rest on their laurels as they prepared to face Ukraine, who still had it all to play for. But England put in an uninspiring performance, compounded by Robert Green's sending-off in the first half. A second-half Nazarenko goal handed England their first defeat, and marked the first time they had failed to score.

The team prepared to end the campaign on a high in front of the Wembley faithful against Belarus. With Capello inviting all current England representatives to the game there was a real sense of occasion as Peter Crouch put the hosts in front in just four minutes. Shaun Wright-Phillips added the second and Crouch completed a personal double 15 minutes from time to stake his claim for a place in the squad for the finals.

With only one blot on their qualifying copybook, England accepted that the expectations of the nation had once again been considerably raised as they prepared to try to win the World Cup for the second time in their history.

ROAD TO WORLD CUP 2010

Andorra	0-2	England
Croatia	1-4	England
England	5-1	Kazakhstan
Belarus	1-3	England
England	2-1	Ukraine
Kazakhstan	0-4	England
England	6-0	Andorra
England	5-1	Croatia
Ukraine	1-0	England
England	3-0	Belarus

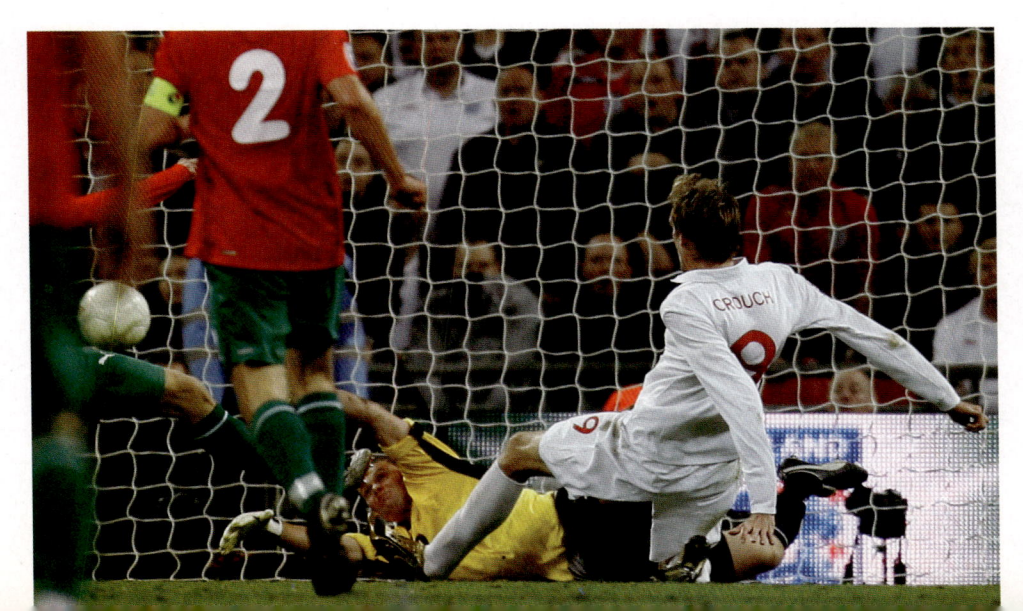

ABOVE Danijel Pranjic of Croatia (left) is unable to stop Theo Walcott of England (right) scoring.

LEFT Peter Crouch (right) scores his second goal against Belarus during England's 3-0 victory.

WORLD CUP 2010, TEAMS
FRANCE

"Les Bleus" had a World Cup qualifying campaign peppered with controversy and criticism, and one which came just 20 minutes from, possibly, being derailed.

The 1998 champions still had a team considered one of the best in the world, and would certainly be among the favorites in South Africa. But qualifying was not to prove a straightforward task.

Coach Raymond Domenech had been in charge of France since 2004. His predecessor Jacques Santini had resigned, unable to emulate the success of World Cup and European Championship winners Aimé Jacquet and Roger Lemerre respectively.

A stuttering qualifying campaign for the 2006 World Cup put Domenech under immediate scrutiny. But a run to the final, including victories over Spain, Brazil, and Portugal, won some doubters over, even though France eventually lost to Italy.

Domenech's team selection frequently baffled fans and media alike, although the recall of previously retired players such as Lilian Thuram and Claude Makelele appeared to pay off, as both were instrumental in Germany.

The team had a disastrous Euro 2008, exiting at the group stages despite a team that was strong in all departments. The international experience of William Gallas in defense complemented the tenacity of young full-backs Bacary Sagna and Patrice Evra. The team had attacking flair in the form of wingers Florent Malouda and Sidney Govou and goal-scoring potential in strikers Nicolas Anelka and Thierry Henry.

The pressure was on for the players and manager to succeed. But their first qualifying game in Vienna was nothing less than a disaster as France lost 3-1 to Austria, Govou hitting their only goal. Domenech attacked the world's media after the match: "I'm happy the guillotine no longer exists, otherwise some of you would have been delighted to send me there."

A 2-1 victory over Serbia days later did little to appease the doubters, Henry and Anelka notching two goals in 10 minutes at the beginning of the second half. The year ended on a worrying note for France as Romania held them to a 2-2 draw in Constanta. The hosts raced to a 2-0 lead after 20 minutes and it took Franck Ribery and Bordeaux midfielder Yoann Gourcuff to spare French blushes.

Successive 1-0 victories against Lithuania were anything but convincing, but nevertheless gave France a much-needed six-point boost. Franck Ribery grabbed the only goal in both matches, contributing to his rising stock.

The trend of narrow victories over smaller countries continued as they edged past the Faroe Islands in August 2009, a first international goal from André-Pierre Gignac collecting the points. But 1-1 draws against Romania and Serbia meant France had to face up to the possibility of the playoffs instead of automatic qualification. Serbia were four points ahead after their draw, with just two games left to play.

France showed their desire to qualify automatically with a 5-0 thumping of the Faroe Islands—Gallas, Anelka, and Real Madrid striker Karim Benzema among the scorers. Unfortunately, Serbia recorded the same scoreline against Romania; participation in the playoffs was now reality.

ABOVE Bacary Sagna beats Serbia forward Nikola Zigic during their 1-1 draw in Belgrade.

LEFT William Gallas is mobbed after his controversial playoff winner against the Republic of Ireland.

There was controversy, however, as replays showed Thierry Henry had handled the ball before crossing it to Gallas, an incident likened to Maradona's "Hand of God" goal against England at the 1986 World Cup. "I didn't deliberately do it," said Henry, "but it was handball. The ball bounced off my hand, the referee did not see it and I played on… I'm happy we have qualified."

A clearly relieved Domenech echoed his captain's sentiments. "I am very happy for the players and the staff and the people here. The only word we need to say tonight is that we are very happy at the qualification."

France had stumbled over the line to qualify for the World Cup. But they had reached their fourth consecutive World Cup finals, and hope was running high for a repeat, or better, of their 2006 performance.

ROAD TO WORLD CUP 2010

Austria	3-1	France
France	2-1	Serbia
Romania	2-2	France
Lithuania	0-1	France
France	1-0	Lithuania
Faroe Islands	0-1	France
France	1-1	Romania
Serbia	1-1	France
France	5-0	Faroe Islands
France	3-1	Austria
Republic of Ireland	0-1	France
France	1-1	Republic of Ireland (AET)

BELOW Nicolas Anelka hits the winner in the first leg of France's playoff against the Republic of Ireland.

A 3-1 victory at home to Austria coupled with a Serbian defeat meant France only finished one point below the leaders, but still had to beat the Republic of Ireland in the playoffs to secure a place at the tournament. France had at least avoided meeting "stronger" opponents in Portugal, Russia or Greece thanks to FIFA controversially seeding the draw.

Domenech was bullish ahead of the tie. "The advantage is that we all know the Irish team, it's like another England. All the (French) players know them. We even have some players who play alongside them, so there won't be too many surprises."

The first leg in Dublin was a close affair, a deflected goal from Nicolas Anelka deciding the tie. But confidence was shattered 30 minutes into the second leg in Paris when Ireland leveled the tie on aggregate. The game looked set for penalties before William Gallas headed in from a yard out.

WORLD CUP 2010, TEAMS
GERMANY

Germany began their qualifying schedule with only one aim—to target their first World Cup triumph in nearly two decades.

ROAD TO WORLD CUP 2010

Liechtenstein	0-6	Germany
Finland	3-3	Germany
Germany	2-1	Russia
Germany	1-0	Wales
Germany	4-0	Liechtenstein
Wales	0-2	Germany
Azerbaijan	0-2	Germany
Germany	4-0	Azerbaijan
Russia	0-1	Germany
Germany	1-1	Finland

The progression started under Jürgen Klinsmann, who had taken the national team to third place in the 2006 World Cup and was very popular with fans after his exploits as a player. Despite Germany's commendable finish he resigned immediately afterward, with assistant Joachim Löw promoted to the top job.

Löw decided to stay at the helm after defeat to Spain in the final of Euro 2008. He was buoyed by the prospect of a winnable qualification group, Russia being the only rival with any real international pedigree.

Germany made the short trip to Liechtenstein for their opening fixture and cruised to a 6-0 victory. Two Lucas Podolski goals either side of half time were followed up by a blitz in the final 30 minutes, Rolfes, Schweinsteiger, Hitzlsperger, and Westermann's first international strike completing the rout.

The next game would not prove so easy. Germany had to fight back three times to take a point against Finland in Helsinki, thanks to Miroslav Klose, who completed his hat trick with just seven minutes remaining. It was a wake-up call, but Löw was happy with his side's spirit. "If you draw 3-3 then you can't say that everything went really well, but we can say that it was a point gained."

Germany continued rotating their games around the stadia built for the 2006 World Cup as they took on Russia in Dortmund. The game was a straightforward affair, Podolski and captain Michael Ballack ensuring they were two-up before half time, before a strike from Andrei Arshavin for the Russians.

A 1-0 defeat of Wales four days later ensured Germany were on course for the finals as 2008 ended. Hamburg midfielder Piotr Trochowski scored the only goal in Mönchengladbach against

RIGHT Michael Ballack of Germany scores past goalkeeper Wayne Hennessey of Wales during Germany's 2-0 victory.

a Welsh side that had won two of their previous three games.

However, all was not well in the camp. Michael Ballack, an outspoken critic of previous administrations, turned his attention to Löw, blasting the coach for dropping Werder Bremen midfielder Torsten Frings to the bench, claiming it showed a lack of respect to the 31 year-old who had amassed 78 caps for his country.

Although the player later said sorry, the in-fighting had exposed Germany as seemingly ripe for the picking. This proved not to be the case as 2009 began in Leipzig, Germany blowing away Liechtenstein with four goals in less than an hour. They went two-up through Ballack and Marcell Jansen, while Schweinsteiger and Podolski grabbed a further brace within five minutes of the restart. The victory strengthened Germany's position at the top spot of Group Four with five games to play.

A professional performance against Wales at the Millennium Stadium in April brought a 2-0 victory, thanks to Ballack and Wales defender Ashley Williams who scored an own goal. Although it seemed Ballack had put his recent troubles behind him, a bust-up with teammate Podolski in the second half once again showed German frailties.

Off the pitch wasn't proving any easier. The international retirement of Oliver Kahn and Jens Lehmann, who held the monopoly on the position for years, left Löw with little international experience to call upon. Lehmann announced his desire to return, but Werder Bremen keeper Tim Wiese blasted. "He is absolutely over-rated and out of touch with reality. It is a real pity."

Despite the continued sniping, Germany rolled over Azerbaijan in August 2009. Schweinsteiger maintained Germany's penchant for early goals with an 11th-minute strike, while Klose returned to the score sheet in the second half. More had been expected against the minnows, especially with former Germany coach Berti Vogts at the helm.

A stronger message was sent to their old boss a month later with the return game in Hannover.

An early Ballack penalty set the tone as Klose added two more in 10 minutes in the second half. Ballack's sparring partner Podolski completed the 4-0 romp, leaving just Germany and Russia to battle it out for top spot in the group.

The game in Moscow was tense, the only goal arriving after 35 minutes when Klose got his seventh of the campaign. The disciplined display ensured Germany qualified for the World Cup with one game to spare. Löw was overjoyed with his side after their calm display. "We came here with no intention of playing for a draw. We only wanted to win."

Germany's chances looked good; the flair of Schweinsteiger and Lahm coupled with the experience and quality of veterans Ballack and Klose seemed to provide the perfect balance for a strong campaign in South Africa.

First, however, the team that gathered in Hamburg for their final match against Finland was inexperienced and it required a Podolski goal in the final minute to deny the Finns victory.

It didn't take the gloss off a solid, unbeaten campaign for the Germans, who were already looking to South Africa and the possibility of a fourth World Cup win.

ABOVE Miroslav Klose (right) celebrates scoring the winning goal with midfielder Mesut Oezil (left) during Germany's 1-0 victory over Russia.

BELOW German midfielder Piotr Trochowski (right) tackles Finland's Kasper Haemaelaeinen (left) during the 1-1 draw in Hamburg.

WORLD CUP 2010, TEAMS
ITALY

Current holders Italy found themselves in the peculiar position of having to qualify for the World Cup in South Africa. A FIFA ruling in 2002 denied them a guaranteed place, even though the host nation were spared the task of qualifying.

After high expectations were dashed in Euro 2008 under former player Roberto Donadoni, Marcelo Lippi, the architect of Italy's success in Germany, was re-appointed. The chance to retain the trophy in 2010 proved too tempting for the 61-year-old tactician, as he took charge for a second time in June 2008.

The core of Lippi's champions was still intact, but players such as Gianluigi Buffon and Gennaro Gattuso were now into their 30s. But with striker Alberto Gilardino and midfielder Daniele De Rossi hitting their peak, many hoped Italy could find the right mix.

The team got off to a winning start, though were lucky to leave Cyprus with three points; Antonio Di Natale scored his second of the game two minutes into injury time. Success against Georgia later that week was more convincing. De Rossi bagged both goals at Udinese's Stadio Friuli, and the Azzurri had a 100% record after their opening fixtures. Lippi was content with his side's start to the campaign. "We finished with two good results and now we can go home and get five or six [domestic] games under our belts before the next matches."

The return to domestic action did not appear to sharpen the strikers' instincts as Italy drew a blank against Bulgaria with the likes of Buffon and Andrea Pirlo missing. With winless Montenegro up next, Lippi demanded improvement. "If we win, then the draw in Sofia will become a good result but, if we don't, then they will become two bad matches."

The 2-1 victory with two goals from midfielder Alberto Aquilani ensured Italy topped Group Eight as 2009 beckoned, but fans were hoping the new year would bring more goals.

Lippi's first squad of the year was hampered by injury and age, with veterans Alessandro Del Piero and Filippo Inzaghi again left out, as well as first-team regulars Gilardino and Gattuso. Despite this, they were too much for Montenegro; a Pirlo penalty and

BELOW Alberto Gilardino (center) slides in to score Italy's dramatic, late equalizer against the Republic of Ireland.

LEFT Head Coach Marcello Lippi celebrates during Italy's 2-2 draw with the Republic of Ireland.

ABOVE Alberto Aquilani (left) of Italy battles for the ball with Zurab Menteshashvili (right) of Georgia.

a Giampaolo Pazzini header ensured the minnows were glad to see the back of the world champions.

A showdown with second-place Ireland beckoned in Bari. Disaster struck when Italy were reduced to 10 men within five minutes; Pazzini received his marching orders after an elbow on John O'Shea. But it was the home side that took the lead just six minutes later; Fabio Grosso threaded a ball to Vicenzo Iaquinta who finished coolly. The one-man deficit proved costly, however, as Ireland bossed the game and grabbed a deserved equalizer three minutes from time.

The team had five months until their next qualifier, and the Confederations Cup in South Africa offered some respite from the pressure. After a disappointing tournament saw them finish third in their group, including a shock 1-0 defeat to Egypt, confidence was low in the Italian camp. Following a 2-0 victory over Georgia, a return to the Stadio Olimpico in Turin spelt trouble for visitors Bulgaria; Italy were going back to basics.

A thoroughly professional performance saw Italy break away from Ireland at the top, four points ahead with two to play. Grosso struck early with a volley after 10 minutes, and Iaquinta set up a comfortable second half by grabbing the second goal just before the half-time whistle. Only one point was needed against Ireland in October to ensure the holders were able to defend their crown.

Seventy thousand crammed into Croke Park, most hoping Ireland could pull off the victory. And it was the home side that took the lead early on, before Mauro Camoranesi leveled the score 15 minutes later.

Ireland looked to have sealed victory with just three minutes left to play; Sean St. Ledger wheeled away to celebrate the goal that left Italy's automatic qualification far from guaranteed. But it was not to be, as Gilardino secured the point needed in the last minute.

With just a game against Cyprus left, Italy had booked their place in the finals, but it was far from convincing. The victories were never comprehensive, and the lack of goals was cause for concern with free-scoring sides such as Brazil and England having already qualified.

An under-strength side started out in Parma with their place in South Africa secured, and it looked like the minds of the players were already there as the Cypriots took a shock 2-0 lead. Quality shone through in the second half, though, as Gilardino struck three times in 14 minutes to secure the three points.

Though unbeaten in the group, Lippi issued a rallying call to his team: "We want to defend our title and that means doing a lot better. If we want to win the World Cup again, we have to step up the tempo now. Italy, like all the big nations, never goes to these tournaments just to take part."

ROAD TO WORLD CUP 2010

Cyprus	1-2	Italy
Italy	2-0	Georgia
Bulgaria	0-0	Italy
Italy	2-1	Montenegro
Montenegro	0-2	Italy
Italy	1-1	Republic of Ireland
Georgia	0-2	Italy
Italy	2-0	Bulgaria
Republic of Ireland	2-2	Italy
Italy	3-2	Cyprus

WORLD CUP 2010, TEAMS
NETHERLANDS

The Netherlands were placed in the smallest of the UEFA qualifying groups. Playing against some perceived minnows, they were out to make a statement.

The Netherlands' record in World Cups had been less than satisfactory, despite two final appearances in the 1970s.

Like Spain coach Luis Aragonés, Marco Van Basten chose the end of Euro 2008 to announce his resignation, deciding instead to manage Ajax. He was replaced by Feyenoord manager Bert Van Marwijk, who had a high standard to maintainl; Van Basten was revered for his illustrious playing career.

Hopes were high the new crop of Dutch players could match expectations. Players such as Arjen Robben, Klaas-Jan Huntelaar, and Rafael Van Der Vaart were all mid-20s and playing at Europe's top clubs.

The team kicked off solidly with a 2-1 away victory at Macedonia through Atletico Madrid defender John Heitinga and Van Der Vaart. There was controversy surrounding the match as striker Dirk Kuyt hit out at Van Marwijk's decision to leave him on the bench for the game, opting instead to bring him on for the final 20 minutes in place of Van Persie. "I will never accept my role as 12th man. Being a substitute is unacceptable to me."

His coach defused the situation, claiming, "Dirk just looks in the mirror and wants to get more out of his career. He demands a starting place from himself, not from me. That only means that he is a good sportsman."

Kuyt was restored to the starting XI for the October 2008 match against Iceland in Rotterdam, as was record cap holder Edwin Van Der Sar. Injuries to both first-choice goalkeepers Maarten Stekelenburg and Henk Timmer caused Van Der Sar to come out of retirement.

Hamburg center-back Joris Mathijsen opened the scoring for the hosts after just 15 minutes before Huntelaar grabbed his first of the campaign. It was two wins out of two for the Netherlands as they headed to Oslo to face Norway. Mark Van Bommel struck after an hour to ensure the points and Van Der Sar got the send-off he hoped, keeping two clean sheets during his brief return.

Stekelenburg returned between the sticks for Holland's first game of 2009 when Scotland visited the Amsterdam Arena, despite Van Marwijk's best efforts to coax Van Der Sar back permanently; Huntelaar and Van Persie put them two-up by half time before Kuyt hit a late third.

Another four goals without reply crushed Macedonia, and the coach chose to express his confidence in his keeper amid all the talk of

BELOW Nigel de Jong of The Netherlands (left) scores while compatriot Robin van Persie (center) and Gretar Steinsson of Iceland (right) look on.

nostalgia. "I will stick by Stekelenburg. He has the most potential of all [my goalkeepers] and is the best available." Kuyt continued where he left off with a first-half double either side of a 25th-minute Huntelaar strike, and Van Der Vaart wrapped up proceedings with two minutes to go.

The Dutch were flying, and needed a victory against Iceland to become the first UEFA team to qualify for the finals. Another goal avalanche looked on the cards as a header from Nigel De Jong and Van Bommel's strike put them 2-0 up within 15 minutes, but it stayed that way until defender Kristján Sigurðsson pulled one back with three minutes to go.

Six wins out of six meant Holland were unchallenged, but the coach would not allow thoughts to wander until the campaign was over. This was proved with a 2-0 defeat of Norway, André Ooijer and Arjen Robben ensured the perfect sequence continued in Rotterdam ahead of their last game against Scotland.

On the eve of the game and the Oranje still without an established number one, Van Der Sar started the next chapter of his "will he won't he" saga while recovering from a broken hand: "The rehabilitation of my injury is the most important thing right now. After that, I will focus on [Manchester] United and then we will see what is happening with the national team."

Meanwhile Van Marwijk was quick to play down any thoughts of complacency, instead keen to be the first manager to lead the Dutch through qualifying with a 100% record. "Winning all eight games is an extra motivation for me. The players also have that extra motivation."

There was less than 10 minutes on the clock when Hamburg winger Eljero Elia came off the bench to secure the perfect qualifying campaign. It was only Elia's second international appearance, showing the future was bright for the team as the tournament approached.

With the likelihood that Group Nine would not receive a playoff place, most of the media attention turned elsewhere, leaving a certain understated orange team to conduct their business and hope that it would be third time lucky in South Africa.

ABOVE Dutch forward Klaas-Jan Huntelaar slots the ball past Macedonian goalkeeper Tome Pacovski.

ROAD TO WORLD CUP 2010

Macedonia	1-2	Netherlands
Netherlands	2-0	Iceland
Norway	0-1	Netherlands
Netherlands	3-0	Scotland
Netherlands	4-0	Macedonia
Iceland	1-2	Netherlands
Netherlands	2-0	Norway
Scotland	0-1	Netherlands

LEFT Dirk Kuyt (number 9) of the Netherlands wins the ball against Steven Naismith of Scotland.

NETHERLANDS

WORLD CUP 2010, TEAMS
PORTUGAL

Portugal had long been seen as underachievers on the world footballing stage.

Despite improved performances at Euro 2004 and World Cup 2006, it was widely believed that nothing short of a trophy for Portugal would do, given their current crop of players.

The Portuguese FA brought in a man who knew all about nurturing player potential; Carlos Queiroz was appointed manager in July 2008, despite a less than successful spell in the early 1990s where Portugal failed to qualify for both Euro 1992 and the 1994 World Cup.

He was, however, in charge of the Portuguese side that won the 1989 and 1991 FIFA Youth Championships, with teams that included future stars Paulo Sousa and, latterly, Luis Figo and Rui Costa.

That, coupled with a stint as Real Madrid manager, and two spells as assistant to Alex Ferguson at Manchester United, meant hopes were high Queiroz could get the best out of the national team and inspire them to their first ever World Cup win.

The new generation of Portuguese stars was promising. In Bruno Alves, Pepe, and José Bosingwa they had three defenders at their peak, while players such as Deco and Simão had a wealth of European experience as well as killer instinct in front of goal.

But the jewel in the crown was undoubtedly Cristiano Ronaldo. The player named the world's best was both captain and inspiration for the team. Many thought the World Cup would be diminished without him, so the pressure was on for Portugal to top a group containing tough opposition in both Sweden and Denmark.

A 4-0 hammering of Malta gave them a dream start; an own goal in the first half was followed up by three second-half goals from Werder Bremen striker Hugo Almeida, Simão, and Manchester United's Nani.

Portugal were devastated in Lisbon days later when they thought victory was assured after Deco scored against Denmark with four minutes remaining, but two late goals from the visitors left Portugal with nothing.

It would be the start of a barren run that would threaten Portugal's chances of making it past the group stage. Three successive 0-0 draws—two against Sweden and another against Albania—

BELOW José Bosingwa keeps Sweden striker Kim Kallstroem at arm's length.

would leave them in critical condition. They only had six points from five matches.

They were heading for another draw against Albania until Bruno Alves snatched victory with a header in injury time. Many were hoping it would kick-start Portugal's qualification challenge, but it was not to be as, days later, they drew 1-1 with group leaders Denmark, leaving it late again, with Sporting Lisbon striker Liédson scoring with four minutes left.

As teams entered the final stretch, things did not bode well for Portugal, and failure to qualify looked a real possibility. They had to win their last three games and hope Sweden slipped up along the way. It was no longer in their own hands. A Pepe goal in the 10th minute won the game against Hungary in Budapest—a vital away win but, with Sweden winning as well, games were fast running out.

Hungary visited Lisbon days later in the second match of their double-header. This time Portugal were far more comfortable, running out 3-0 winners with a Simão brace either side of a Liédson goal. With Denmark toppling Sweden, Portugal's playoff place was theirs to lose, with just Malta left to play.

The downside to the victory was Ronaldo's substitution after just 27 minutes. A later scan showed he would be out for a month, missing Portugal's final group match and the playoffs—if they reached them.

But the team showed they could cope without their talisman as they crushed Malta 4-0 in Lisbon, their desire to reach the finals showing just in time.

Portugal were seeded in the playoff draw and were paired with Bosnia & Herzegovina, who had impressed in a group that included Spain.

Striker Simão called on his teammates to perform in the absence of Ronaldo. "It would have been important to have him, but we have top-quality players who will do their best. The perfect Saturday would be a win for Portugal without conceding goals."

He got his wish; a Bruno Alves header gave them a narrow victory in the Estadio da Luz, despite the visitors hitting the woodwork a number of times. The second leg in Zenica was equally tense, but the tie was put beyond doubt after 56 minutes when Porto midfielder Raul Meireles struck from a Nani cross.

Portugal had come into form at precisely the right time. Despite only losing once in qualification, their inability to find the goal caused too many draws but, when it mattered, they had players all over the pitch who hit the goals to send them through, even without Cristiano Ronaldo. That would be enough to worry other teams, if and when they reached their top level in South Africa.

ABOVE It was a frustrating qualifying campaign for the Portuguese, and Cristiano Ronaldo in particular.

ROAD TO WORLD CUP 2010

Malta	0-4	Portugal
Portugal	2-3	Denmark
Sweden	0-0	Portugal
Portugal	0-0	Albania
Portugal	0-0	Sweden
Albania	1-2	Portugal
Denmark	1-1	Portugal
Hungary	0-1	Portugal
Portugal	3-0	Hungary
Portugal	4-0	Malta
Portugal	1-0	Bosnia & Herzegovina
Bosnia & Herzegovina	0-1	Portugal

LEFT Raul Meireles celebrates his goal against Bosnia that confirmed Portugal's passage to South Africa.

PORTUGAL 53

WORLD CUP 2010, TEAMS
SPAIN

Spain began the qualifying process as perhaps the most feared team on the planet. Victory at Euro 2008 placed them as kings of Europe, and they began their road to South Africa ranked number one in the world by FIFA, despite never having won a World Cup.

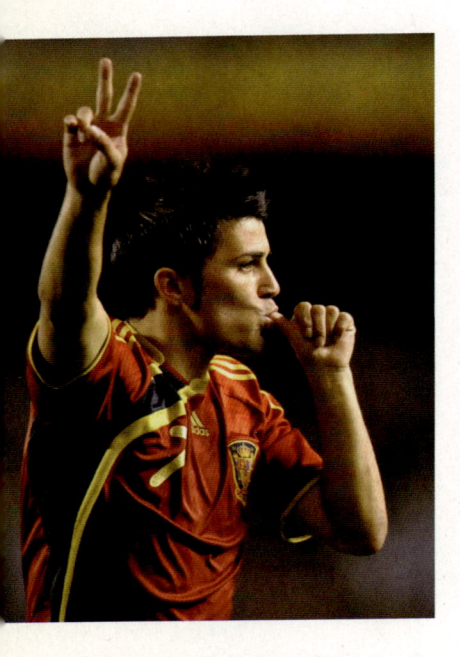

Manager Luis Aragonés left his post after the summer's triumph to return to club management. Former Real Madrid boss Vincente Del Bosque was charged with carrying the expectations of an ambitious nation.

The form of strikers David Villa and Fernando Torres led many in Spain and beyond to believe qualification would be a foregone conclusion. The pressure was on for Del Bosque to deliver.

The squad was largely the same as 2006, but youngsters such as Torres and Cesc Fabregas had matured. The campaign got off to a low-key start in Murcia; a solid performance saw them squeeze past Bosnia & Herzegovina, Villa getting the only goal of the game just before the hour. With Bosnia & Herzegovina going on to thrash Estonia 7-0 in their next game, it would be seen as a good result.

Spain made the short trip to Albacete for their second fixture against Armenia. This time, the goals rained as Joan Capdevila opened the scoring after seven minutes, before Villa grabbed a brace either side of the break. Villarreal midfielder Marcos Senna topped off a magnificent performance with a fourth on 83 minutes.

October 2008 saw Spain travel to Estonia where they achieved their third win out of three under Del Bosque. Real Betis defender Juanito opened the scoring with a header with 34 minutes played, before Torres was felled in the box and Villa put away the resulting penalty just four minutes later. Carlos Puyol made it three in the second half and ensured Spain continued their 100 percent record in style.

Wesley Sonck shocked the Spanish with an early strike for Belgium in their next match, a lead that would last just half an hour before Andrés Iniesta leveled the scores. Villa ensured the three points with his fifth goal in four games.

Spain began the New Year at the Bernabéu where they welcomed unbeaten Turkey in the first

ABOVE David Villa celebrates after scoring his second goal in Spain's 5-0 win against Belgium.

RIGHT Gerard Piqué of Spain (center) climbs high to win the ball from Bosnia's Miralem Pjanic (right).

54 WORLD CUP 2010, TEAMS

of a double-header over just five days. Barcelona defender Gerard Piqué settled the game on the hour mark in a low-key affair. The return fixture in Istanbul was not as easy, as Fenerbahçe striker Semih put the home side ahead in the first half. It was left to Liverpool pair Xabi Alonso and Albert Riera to salvage the three points, the latter scoring two minutes into injury time. Spain were proving they could win ugly—albeit with a bit of luck.

As summer approached, the Confederations Cup beckoned; Spain continued their incredible form, including breaking the world record of 15 consecutive victories. A shock defeat in the semi-finals to the United States meant they had to settle for third place after victory over the hosts South Africa, though they still had four players in FIFA's team of the tournament.

The defeat in South Africa only served as inspiration for further success as they returned to action in September 2009, scoring eight goals in two games without reply. The first team they defeated was Belgium at the Estadio Riazor. David Silva and Villa nabbed a brace apiece while Piqué also got on the scoresheet in a 5-0 crushing.

"It seems incredible that we are not yet qualified" said an exasperated Torres after the game. Indeed, it was the team's seventh victory in a row in the group, but victory against Estonia in Mérida would seal the deal. Cesc Fabregas got the ball rolling before young wingers Santi Cazorla and Juan Mata added a goal each later on to ensure the celebrations began in earnest.

Spain had brushed aside all before them in qualifying, with two games left to play. They could be forgiven for not concentrating fully when they journeyed to Armenia four days later but Del Bosque insisted there would be none of that. "We only have five games before the tournament—we have to profit from them to the max."

Playing for their World Cup futures, the players impressed. Despite an equalizer from Arzumanyan after Fabregas had put the visitors ahead, Mata continued his fine start to his international career with the winner from the penalty spot.

Spain's campaign came full circle as they lined up against Bosnia in Zenica for their final game, their hosts already guaranteed a playoff place. Piqué and Silva put the table-toppers two-up within 15 minutes before a second-half brace from Alvaro Negredo in his first international start made it four. A last-minute fifth from Mata made it 5-2.

The result was the perfect finish to the perfect qualifying campaign; 10 wins from 10 games, with 28 scored and only five conceded meant every team was looking over their shoulders at Spain, who were looking to justify their place at the top of the world rankings.

ROAD TO WORLD CUP 2010

Spain	1-0	Bosnia & Herzegovina
Spain	4-0	Armenia
Estonia	0-3	Spain
Belgium	1-2	Spain
Spain	1-0	Turkey
Turkey	1-2	Spain
Spain	5-0	Belgium
Spain	3-0	Estonia
Armenia	1-2	Spain
Bosnia & Herzegovina	2-5	Spain

BELOW The ball on its way to the net as Cesc Fabregas scores for Spain against Estonia.

WORLD CUP 2010, TEAMS
USA

The United States had to play an incredible seven games just to contest the final CONCACAF qualifying group. After crushing Barbados 9-0 over two legs in June 2008, they entered a third-round group consisting of Trinidad & Tobago, Guatemala, and Cuba.

It was the beginning of a tough schedule for coach Bob Bradley, who had moved up from assistant to Bruce Arena following a disastrous World Cup in Germany.

The US national team had long been considered a force for the future, with football rising in popularity. Tim Howard was a worthy successor to Kasey Keller in goal, while Landon Donovan had experience far beyond his 27 years, racking up over 100 caps. The emergence of young striker Jozy Altidore and form of attacking midfielder Clint Dempsey meant hopes were high.

BELOW Clint Dempsey (right) of the United States vies for the ball with Salvadorean Alfredo Pacheco (left).

A 69th-minute Bocanegra goal was enough to ensure a winning start away to Guatemala. The following month Dempsey made it two from two in Havana against Cuba. Eleven thousand at Toyota Park, Illinois, saw Bradley's son Michael score the first against Trinidad & Tobago before Dempsey continued his form with a second. Houston Dynamo striker Brian Ching scored the third.

It rained goals in Washington as the US destroyed Cuba 6-1 in October. DeMarcus Beasley struck twice in the first 30 minutes before the visitors replied. Any disappointment was quickly dispelled as Donovan, Ching, Altidore, and Oguchi Onyewu sent Cuba packing.

The win meant the team had qualified for the fourth and final round of qualifying, but there were still two games to go. Defeat to Trinidad & Tobago followed; 40-year-old Russell Latapy hit the first for the home side, before Charlie Davies equalized. But a penalty from Dwight Yorke just four minutes later ended matters. A 2-0 US victory over Guatemala ended the round on a high with Kenny and Freddy Adu grabbing the goals.

The United States kicked off 2009 and their final qualifying group with victory over Mexico in Columbus. The 2-0 success came courtesy of a brace from Michael Bradley. It was the first of 10 matches in a group of six, the top three heading to the World Cup automatically.

In March, late goals from Altidore and Columbus Crew captain Frankie Hejduk ensured a share of the spoils against El Salvador. The team bounced back with victory over Trinidad & Tobago in Nashville. Altidore grabbed a hat trick in front of 30,000 fans.

June was a busy month. A 3-1 away defeat to Costa Rica was not the best preparation, with only a Donovan penalty in the 92nd minute preventing a heavier loss. He scored from the spot again against Honduras en route to a 2-1 victory as the team headed to their summer tournament.

The US surprised fans and critics alike by reaching the Confederations Cup final, even leading Brazil by two goals before losing 3-2. The hangover was evident as they lost to Mexico on their return to qualifying action; Davies helped them start brightly with a goal on nine minutes, but it was canceled out by Israel Castro before Miguel Sabah wrapped up the points at the Estadio Azteca.

Not a team to lose two in a row, the US took their frustrations out on El Salvador in Utah, Dempsey and Altidore scoring in the last five minutes of the first half after the visitors had taken the lead.

Ricardo Clark scored the only goal of the game four days later as they overcame Trinidad & Tobago in Port of Spain, their first away victory of the fourth round.

The team traveled to Honduras knowing victory would secure qualification. Julio de León put the home side ahead before Donovan and a Conor Casey double seemed to put the game out of sight. De León's second produced a nervy last 10 minutes but the US hung on to clinch a spot at the finals.

The team's homecoming looked set to be spoiled when Costa Rica's Bryan Ruiz hit a quick-fire double. Michael Bradley's second-half goal made it a nervy finish for the visitors. It was the 94th minute when left-back Jonathan Bornstein headed in from a corner to leave the US top of the group with the last move of the campaign.

ABOVE United States goalkeeper Tim Howard (right) and midfielder Michael Bradley (left) celebrate after drawing 2-2 with Costa Rica.

ABOVE Jozy Altidore of the United States runs with the ball during the United States 3-0 win against Trinidad & Tobago.

ROAD TO WORLD CUP 2010

USA	2-0	Mexico
El Salvador	2-2	USA
USA	3-0	Trinidad & Tobago
USA	2-1	Honduras
Costa Rica	3-1	USA
Mexico	2-1	USA
USA	2-1	El Salvador
Trinidad & Tobago	0-1	USA
Honduras	2-3	USA
USA	2-2	Costa Rica

USA

WORLD CUP 2010, TEAMS
ALGERIA

Algeria wanted to qualify for their first World Cup in 24 years to right the injustice suffered in Spain in 1982.

In 1982 Algeria were controversially eliminated when Germany played out a 1-0 victory over Austria to ensure both teams progressed at Algeria's expense.

The wounds were still raw for a country that had only had its own recognized international side since 1962. They turned to Rabah Saadane, the man who led them in the last World Cup finals they had reached in 1986. Saadane was appointed in 2007 for his fifth spell as Algeria manager.

He had, arguably, the strongest group of internationals since Algeria's 1990 African Cup of Nations' triumph. Players with top-flight European experience included defenders Madjid Bougherra and Nadir Belhadj, who played for Glasgow Rangers and Portsmouth respectively. And goals were never far away with attacking players such as Wolfsburg's Karim Ziani and striker Rafik Saifi.

Algeria eased to the third round of CAF qualifying, finishing top of a group including Gambia, Senegal, and Liberia. Algeria then stumbled with a surprising 0-0 draw away to Rwanda, but quickly compensated with a 3-1 success over rivals Egypt in Blida. A 2-0 victory over Zambia two weeks later ensured they topped their group.

After a narrow 1-0 win in the return match against Zambia, they cruised past Rwanda 3-1, with Ziani and Belhadj among the scorers. With just Egypt left to play, Algeria were in the position of knowing anything better than a 2-0 defeat would guarantee them a place in South Africa.

If Algeria lost by two it would leave them equal on points, goal difference and head-to-head results with Eqypt, meaning that a one-off playoff match would be required to determine the winner.

Algerians were ready to celebrate qualification with Egypt leading by one goal, but their opponents scored again with the last kick of the game to force a playoff. The momentum was firmly with Egypt. Sudan was chosen as the neutral venue and a volley from VfL Bochum defender Antar Yahia just before half time proved decisive in a tense and scrappy affair.

Despite the last-minute slip-up, Algeria had managed to progress in a high-pressure atmosphere, and looked forward to a possible revenge match with Germany in South Africa.

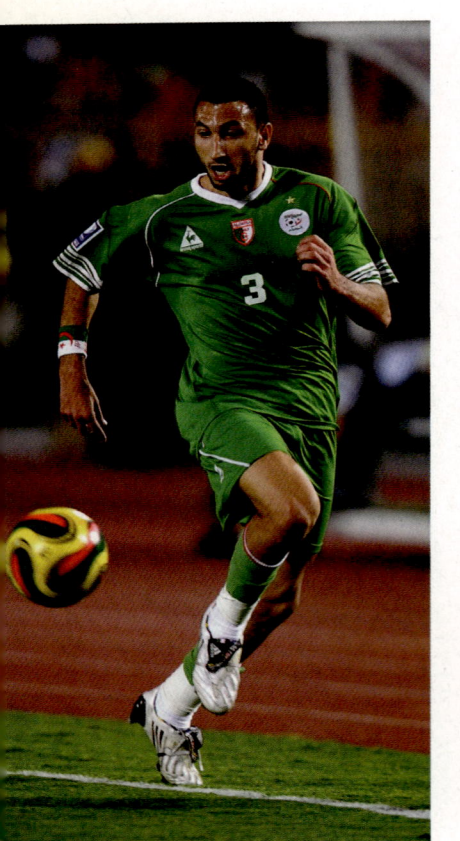

ABOVE Nadir Belhadj leads the array of Algerian stars in Europe.

ROAD TO WORLD CUP 2010

Senegal	1-0	Algeria
Algeria	3-0	Liberia
Gambia	1-0	Algeria
Algeria	1-0	Gambia
Algeria	3-2	Senegal
Liberia	0-0	Algeria
Rwanda	0-0	Algeria
Algeria	3-1	Egypt
Zambia	0-2	Algeria
Algeria	1-0	Zambia
Algeria	3-1	Rwanda
Egypt	2-0	Algeria
Algeria	1-0	Egypt

WORLD CUP 2010, TEAMS
AUSTRALIA

Australia were finally realizing their potential as a national team and had their sights set on a third World Cup finals appearance.

Since switching confederations to AFC in 2005 had eased Australia's task of qualifying, and they were keen to make their mark on the world stage.

A last-minute penalty had seen them eliminated by eventual-winners Italy in 2006, and the Australians were determined to take this second chance. Coach Pim Verbeek continued the trend of Dutch managers after fellow countryman Guus Hiddink's success at the last tournament.

The squad was strong, with key players in veteran goalkeeper Mark Schwarzer and midfielders Harry Kewell and Tim Cahill. The latter was an important source of goals, with prolific strikers John Aloisi and Archie Thompson both winding down their careers.

Australia topped their group when they entered the third round of qualifying, despite suffering defeats to Iraq and the People's Republic of China. Scott Chipperfield got the only goal against Uzbekistan to ensure a winning start in round four. A 4-0 crushing of Qatar in Brisbane meant this continued.

A win over Bahrain in November 2008, courtesy of a last-minute Mark Bresciano goal showed resilience and, with Japan up next, they would need to show their dominance. The two teams drew a blank in Yokohama, but Australia were still well placed to win the group.

Another victory over the Uzbeks in Sydney—goals from Kewell and Joshua Kennedy sealing Australia's fourth win in five qualification games so far—meant only one point was needed to become one of the first teams to qualify for the tournament behind the hosts. This was secured after an uneventful match in Qatar. Verbeek had been criticized for his brand of football, but the results spoke for themselves. Australia had qualified after only six matches.

The team returned home to Sydney four days later to continue the celebrations, victory over Bahrain securing first place in the group. Wingers Mile Sterjovski and David Carney provided the goals in front of 39,000 jubilant fans. The party continued a week later, victory over second-place Japan ensuring that Australia had beaten all their rivals at least once. Two second-half goals from Cahill settled the match after the visitors had gone ahead through Tulio.

Australia went into their third World Cup finals with belief they could defeat anyone, and hopes of bringing home the trophy for the first time.

ROAD TO WORLD CUP 2010

Australia	3-0	Qatar
China PR	0-0	Australia
Australia	1-0	Iraq
Iraq	1-0	Australia
Qatar	1-3	Australia
Australia	0-1	China PR
Uzbekistan	0-1	Australia
Australia	4-0	Qatar
Bahrain	0-1	Australia
Japan	0-0	Australia
Australia	2-0	Uzbekistan
Qatar	0-0	Australia
Australia	2-0	Bahrain
Australia	2-1	Japan

LEFT Harry Kewell is first to the ball against Uzbekistan's Timur Kapadze.

WORLD CUP 2010, TEAMS
CAMEROON

Cameroon aimed to continue their run as Africa's most successful World Cup nation by qualifying for their sixth finals.

Otto Pfister, Cameroon's seasoned coach, had good international experience. He also had a lot of talent to work with: record cap holder Rigobert Song, now with Trabzonspor, Tottenham's Benoît Assou-Ekotto at the back, and Barcelona striker and national captain Samuel Eto'o.

The Indomitable Lions entered CAF qualification at the second round stage, and eased to the top of their group, winning five games and drawing one in a group containing minnows Cape Verde, Tanzania, and Mauritius.

The next stage started off disastrously for Cameroon. They lost their first match to Togo before drawing 0-0 at home with Morocco. This led to Pfister being sacked and replaced by former Glasgow Rangers and Paris Saint-Germain coach Paul Le Guen.

Le Guen's impact was instant, with Cameroon picking up two victories over Gabon in four days; the first was a 2-0 win away from home. In the return match, the home side came out on top with a 2-1 win. Eto'o furthered his impressive international goal tally with a strike in both games.

Revenge over Togo was secured via a 3-0 drubbing in October 2009. But, despite their fast-improving fortunes, Cameroon had to win on the final matchday away against Morocco and hope that Gabon failed to secure victory in Togo.

They came out 2-0 winners in Morocco. Then wild celebrations began as news came through that Togo had beaten Gabon 1-0.

The country that became the first ever African nation to reach the World Cup quarter-finals and took England to extra time in Italia 1990, was dreaming of a repeat performance in South Africa.

RIGHT Midfielder Achille Emana, (center), of Cameroon fights for the ball against Morocco.

ABOVE Benoît Assou-Ekotto shields the ball from Gabon's Roguy Meye during a 2-0 victory.

ROAD TO WORLD CUP 2010

Cameroon	2-0	Cape Verde
Mauritius	0-3	Cameroon
Tanzania	0-0	Cameroon
Cameroon	2-1	Tanzania
Cape Verde	1-2	Cameroon
Cameroon	5-0	Mauritius
Togo	1-0	Cameroon
Cameroon	0-0	Morocco
Gabon	0-2	Cameroon
Cameroon	2-1	Gabon
Cameroon	3-0	Togo
Morocco	0-2	Cameroon

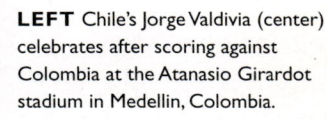

WORLD CUP 2010, TEAMS
CHILE

Chile have a checkered World Cup history; they were banned in 1990 and 1994 and have failed to win a match in the finals since their third-place finish in 1964.

Drawing on the experience of former Argentina coach Marcelo Bielsa, Chile had a tough task in a group requiring 18 games, and including Brazil and Argentina. A first-match defeat against Argentina was proof of the task ahead.

After a 2-0 victory over Peru, Chile had a 2-2 draw against Uruguay where top scorer Marcelo Salas scored the last goals of his international career before retirement.

Defeat to group leaders Paraguay in November 2007 was followed up by successive victories against Bolivia and Venezuela.

Bielsa had a young team; the first XI that were in their 20s. The veteran was goalkeeper Claudio Bravo, who had gathered 40 caps. But goals were coming from attacking midfielder Matías Fernández and striker Humberto Suazo.

They were taught a footballing lesson in September 2008 when Brazil cruised to a 3-0 victory, but hammered Colombia a few days later.

The win-loss pattern continued into October, where defeat to Ecuador preceded their most famous result of the campaign—a 1-0 victory over Argentina. The win had an impact on both teams, with Argentina coach Alfio Basile sacked after the defeat.

For Chile, it sparked a five-game unbeaten streak that saw victories registered against Peru, Paraguay, and Bolivia. Brazil ended it with a 4-2 victory, 11 months after Chile's run began, but now Chile required only three points to qualify. They got six; a 4-2 triumph away to Colombia and a 1-0 success over Ecuador.

It was a job well done for the team, now in its first World Cup finals in 12 years.

ROAD TO WORLD CUP 2010

Argentina	2-0	Chile
Chile	2-0	Peru
Uruguay	2-2	Chile
Chile	0-3	Paraguay
Bolivia	0-2	Chile
Venezuela	2-3	Chile
Chile	0-3	Brazil
Chile	4-0	Colombia
Ecuador	1-0	Chile
Chile	1-0	Argentina
Peru	1-3	Chile
Chile	0-0	Uruguay
Paraguay	0-2	Chile
Chile	4-0	Bolivia
Chile	2-2	Venezuela
Brazil	4-2	Chile
Colombia	2-4	Chile
Chile	1-0	Ecuador

LEFT Chile's Jorge Valdivia (center) celebrates after scoring against Colombia at the Atanasio Girardot stadium in Medellin, Colombia.

WORLD CUP 2010, TEAMS
DENMARK

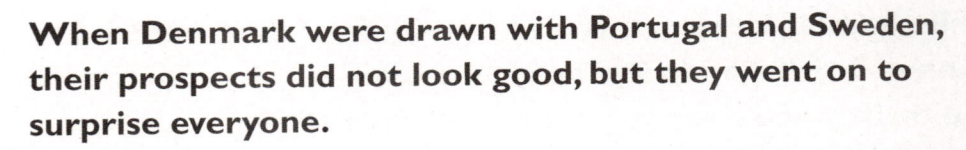

When Denmark were drawn with Portugal and Sweden, their prospects did not look good, but they went on to surprise everyone.

Success had proved hard to come by for the Danes, since they shocked the football world in 1992 by capturing the European Championship.

Manager Morten Olsen, in his ninth year with the national side, was hoping to spring another surprise by qualifying for the World Cup. An opening stalemate against Hungary preceded a famous 3-2 victory over favorites Portugal in Lisbon.

After Nani ensured Portugal led at half time, Nicklas Bendtner looked to have secured a point with a strike six minutes from time. Deco then slotted home a penalty, but injury-time goals from Christian Poulsen and Werder Bremen's Daniel Jensen snatched victory for Denmark.

Three successive 3-0 victories over Malta (twice) and Albania ensured the Danes topped their group at the beginning of 2009. A 22nd-minute strike from Wolfsburg midfielder Thomas Kahlenberg ensured victory over Sweden before they cemented their position with a draw against Portugal.

Only a goal from substitute Liédson denied Denmark another famous victory over Portugal, but they were still keeping competitors at arm's length after their blistering start. A 1-1 draw with Albania did little to derail their qualification charge, and victory over Sweden would secure their passage to South Africa.

A goal from Jakob Poulsen with just 12 minutes to go confirmed this in front of 38,000 fans in Copenhagen and condemned once-fancied Portugal to the lottery of the playoffs. Not even defeat to Hungary in their final match could detract from Danish celebrations, Buzáky hitting the only goal of a game that had no bearing on the group.

Though a surprise, Danish success was testament to the players who were regularly performing in the top leagues. Experienced Premier League goalkeeper Thomas Sorensen provided the foundation for a stable defense that included Liverpool's Daniel Agger, while creative players such as Dennis Rommedahl and Arsenal's Nicklas Bendtner meant that goals were never far away.

LEFT Nicklas Bendtner proves he's as good with his head as with his feet.

ABOVE Daniel Jensen (left) shows his elation at hitting the winner against Portugal.

ROAD TO WORLD CUP 2010

Hungary	0-0	Denmark
Portugal	2-3	Denmark
Denmark	3-0	Malta
Malta	0-3	Denmark
Denmark	3-0	Albania
Sweden	0-1	Denmark
Denmark	1-1	Portugal
Albania	1-1	Denmark
Denmark	1-0	Sweden
Denmark	0-1	Hungary

WORLD CUP 2010, TEAMS
GHANA

Ghana were hoping to continue their rapid ascent as a global footballing force by qualifying for their second World Cup in a row.

The CAF qualification groups required teams to compete also for a place at the 2010 African Cup of Nations, so there was all to play for.

Many were surprised when Ghana appointed Serbian Milovan Rajevac in August 2008—limited top-level experience had made him an outsider for the position, but the success of predecessor and countryman Ratomir Dujkovic, who'd left in 2006 to manage China, convinced the Ghanaian FA he could lead them to South Africa.

Rajevac had a wealth of talent at his disposal, with many of the national team plying their trade at the highest level in Europe. Lyon center-back John Mensah and Fulham right-back John Pantsil were stars of the back-four, while midfielders Michael Essien and Sulley Muntari had plenty of European experience despite being only 25 and 26 respectively.

Although not playing for a club side, captain Stephen Appiah still featured regularly, with stints at Juventus and Fenerbahçe proof of his quality. There were also high hopes for young Rennes forward Asamoah Gyan.

It was Prince Tagoe who got Ghana's campaign off to a winning start, however, with the only goal of the game against Benin. Strike partner Matthew Amoah got three goals in two games as they defeated Mali and Sudan by the same 2-0 scoreline. It was a blistering start for the team known as the Black Stars.

When the team reconvened after a summer break, Ghana needed just one more victory to qualify after playing just four games. It was midfield duo Muntari and Essien who combined once again to put Sudan to the sword and ensure Ghana's participation in the World Cup, less than six months after they began their group.

Perhaps understandably, the campaign tailed off in the last two games; with qualification assured, a mid-strength team lost 1-0 to Benin before a 2-2 home draw with Mali ended proceedings on a subdued note. Nevertheless, Ghana were just the eighth team to reach the World Cup finals, a blistering (for the most part) campaign having deservedly sent them racing up the football world rankings.

ABOVE Prince Tagoe pictured on the ball during a match with Sudan, against whom Ghana clinched qualification.

ROAD TO WORLD CUP 2010

Ghana	1-0	Benin
Mali	0-2	Ghana
Sudan	0-2	Ghana
Ghana	2-0	Sudan
Benin	1-0	Ghana
Ghana	2-2	Mali

WORLD CUP 2010, TEAMS
GREECE

In recent years, Greece have shown how stability and hard work can bring success to a small footballing nation.

ROAD TO WORLD CUP 2010

Luxembourg	0-3	Greece
Latvia	0-2	Greece
Greece	3-0	Moldova
Greece	1-2	Switzerland
Israel	1-1	Greece
Greece	2-1	Israel
Switzerland	2-0	Greece
Moldova	1-1	Greece
Greece	5-2	Latvia
Greece	2-1	Luxembourg
Greece	0-0	Ukraine
Ukraine	0-1	Greece

Since manager Otto Rehhagel took the reins in 2001 Greece have become European champions. They had their sights on their second World Cup finals.

The famous victory over Portugal in the Euro 2004 final saw Greece's stock rise dramatically and, despite failing to qualify for the 2006 World Cup and a disastrous Euro title defense in 2008, they were still considered well-placed to top their group.

Greece still had in their team Angelos Basinas, Giorgos Karagounis, and Angelos Charisteas, who scored in the final in 2004. With fellow strikers Georgios Samaras and Theofanis Gekas, goals were guaranteed.

Three wins against Luxembourg, Latvia, and Moldova displayed their credentials, with Gekas and Charisteas grabbing three goals apiece. The team had scored eight and had yet to lose one.

The run halted against Switzerland in October 2008 when Greece lost 2-1 at home. A 1-1 draw in Israel followed. Four days later, a Samaras penalty secured a 2-1 win.

Defeat to Switzerland in the last 10 minutes meant Greece had to contemplate the playoffs. A last-minute goal from Moldova in their next match meant the spoils were shared, and Greece's chances of automatic qualification were slim.

Gekas grabbed four goals in a 5-2 victory over Latvia. That, coupled with a Swiss win against Luxembourg, meant Greece had to win on the final day and hope that Switzerland lost.

Despite Greece beating Luxembourg 2-1, Switzerland got the point they needed to qualify, and a two-legged playoff match versus the Ukraine awaited.

The first leg ended goalless in Athens, setting up a winner-take-all showdown in Donetsk. It was settled with one goal from Panathinaikos striker Dimitris Salpingidis after half an hour, sending Greece to South Africa.

RIGHT The Greek players celebrate qualifying for the World Cup after their playoff match against Ukraine.

WORLD CUP 2010, TEAMS
HONDURAS

Honduras were desperate to reach only their second ever finals under former Colombia coach Reinaldo Rueda.

LEFT Wilson Palacios shoots for goal against the United States.

A number of players had broken into Europe's top sides in recent years, most notably David Suazo at Inter Milan, while Wigan Athletic had taken Maynor Figueroa, Hendry Thomas, and Wilson Palacios, before the latter secured a big-money transfer to Tottenham Hotspur.

Veteran striker Carlos Pavon provided the goals, with record cap-holder Amando Guevara the team leader. Pavon scored his first of the campaign in a draw against Trinidad & Tobago. It was a welcome point after a defeat in their opener against Costa Rica.

Pavon added another alongside Carlo Costly as they picked up their first three points against Mexico. Defeat against the United States days later inspired the team to a run of three consecutive victories against El Salvador, Costa Rica, and Trinidad & Tobago. They were halted 1-0 by Mexico, but were in a strong position with two games to go.

A brace from Torino midfielder Julio César de León was not enough to beat the Americans, whose victory secured their own qualification. Costa Rica were in pole position for the final qualification spot as the teams approached the last matchday, with Honduras two points behind.

Honduras had to win and hope that Costa Rica lost or drew against the US. Pavon came through once again, with the only goal of the game and, as Costa Rica drew, Honduras narrowly qualified for the finals on goal difference.

Pavon was the group's top scorer with seven.

ROAD TO WORLD CUP 2010

Costa Rica	2-0	Honduras
Trinidad & Tobago	1-1	Honduras
Honduras	3-1	Mexico
USA	2-1	Honduras
Honduras	1-0	El Salvador
Honduras	4-0	Costa Rica
Honduras	4-1	Trinidad & Tobago
Mexico	1-0	Honduras
Honduras	2-3	USA
El Salvador	0-1	Honduras

WORLD CUP 2010, TEAMS
IVORY COAST

The Ivory Coast were determined to qualify for a second successive World Cup after their first appearance in the finals in 2006 had ended in swift elimination.

ROAD TO WORLD CUP 2010

Ivory Coast	5-0	Malawi
Guinea	1-2	Ivory Coast
Burkina Faso	2-3	Ivory Coast
Ivory Coast	5-0	Burkina Faso
Malawi	1-1	Ivory Coast
Ivory Coast	3-0	Guinea

But the Elephants were one of a number of African teams on the rise, having entered FIFA's top 20 rankings for the first time in 2006.

Vahid Halilhodžic was charged with emulating former manager Henri Michel and ensuring the Ivorians once again graced the world stage. The team were certainly well equipped to do it, with many players regularly competing with the world's elite. Didier Drogba and Kolo Touré were stars of the Premier League, while Kolo's brother Yaya was a key player for Spanish giants Barcelona.

With results also counting towards 2010 African Cup of Nations qualification, a good start was imperative. The players were well aware of this as they eased to a 5-0 home success over Malawi, Drogba grabbing a brace. The match was overshadowed, however, by a stampede before kick-off, in which 19 people lost their lives.

June 2009 saw two crucial away victories and the Ivory Coast were beginning to impose themselves on the group. A 2-1 triumph in Conakry against Guinea was followed up by a 3-2 success in Burkina Faso. A close affair was settled by a Drogba strike on 70 minutes after the sides went in level at half time.

The two countries met again in September; this time the Ivory Coast breezed by with another five-goal haul in a not-so-close encounter and Drogba grabbed yet another double. The 100 percent record meant only one point was needed in Malawi to progress to the finals.

ABOVE Kolo Touré (left) and Souleymane Bamba pile on the pressure during a 5-0 victory over Burkina Faso.

ABOVE Ivorian players conduct muted celebrations against Malawi after the stampede that killed 19 Ivory Coast fans.

When defender Jacob Ngwira put the hosts ahead just after the hour, it looked like the Ivory Coast might have to wait until the final matchday for qualification. Enter Didier Drogba, who came off the bench to score in under two minutes and clinch the solitary point required. A brace from Lille striker Gervinho helped the Ivorians to a 3-0 thumping of Guinea in their final game, wrapping up a campaign that saw only two points dropped.

The Ivory Coast qualified with ease, proof of their dominance in CAF. But they would be hoping for a kind draw in South Africa, where all eyes would be on the mercurial yet enigmatic Drogba to fire his country to glory.

WORLD CUP 2010, TEAMS
JAPAN

Japan's emergence as a footballing force in the last decade had raised expectations as they began qualification.

But Brazilian legend Zico resigned as manager in 2006 and, after his replacement, Yugoslavian Ivica Osim, had his reign cut short due to ill health, Takeshi Okada was given the task of driving his national team toward South Africa.

Okada was no stranger to the task, having taken Japan to their first World Cup in 1998. There was a sense of both nostalgia and optimism in the air as Japan kicked off their campaign against Bahrain. But it turned to horror as they nearly squandered a three-goal lead, conceding two in the last five minutes.

Boasting a squad that played mainly in Japan, Okada had carried on the work of his predecessors, forging a hard-working unit of players. He preferred Seigo Narazaki to veteran goalkeeper Yoshikatsu Kawaguchi, while the tenacity of Celtic's Shunsuke Nakamura made Japan a force to be reckoned with in midfield.

Japan topped their third-round group, despite succumbing twice to Bahrain. They had their revenge in the next round, winning 3-2, but they couldn't overcome a stubborn Uzbekistan team in Saitama. They recovered with a 3-0 away drubbing of Qatar. Tatsuya Tanaka scored the first before second-half goals from Tamada and Tulio clinched victory.

2009 brought a showdown with Australia; both teams were vying for top spot and the honors were even after a goalless draw in Yokohama. Shunsuke Nakamura scored the only goal of the game in March to ensure that Bahrain would again come away with nothing and put Japan on the brink of qualification.

They became only the second team to qualify after hosts South Africa, by overcoming a potential tricky tie away to Uzbekistan. A Shinji Okazaki header in the ninth minute was enough to take the points. With two games left to play, Japan appeared to suffer from complacency against Qatar in Saitama, but a 1-1 draw did not dampen the celebrations of a fourth successive qualification.

Japan's final fixture was a showpiece match with also-qualified Australia. It took two second-half goals from Tim Cahill to win the match after Tulio had put Japan ahead. But the result was largely irrelevant. Fans were hoping Okada, the man who led them to their finest hour, could do so again in South Africa.

BELOW Shunsuke Nakamura (right) beats Qatar's Hamed Shami Zaher in Yokohama.

ROAD TO WORLD CUP 2010

Japan	4-1	Thailand
Bahrain	1-0	Japan
Japan	3-0	Oman
Oman	1-1	Japan
Thailand	0-3	Japan
Japan	1-0	Bahrain
Bahrain	2-3	Japan
Japan	1-1	Uzbekistan
Qatar	0-3	Japan
Japan	0-0	Australia
Japan	1-0	Bahrain
Uzbekistan	0-1	Japan
Japan	1-1	Qatar
Australia	2-1	Japan

WORLD CUP 2010, TEAMS
KOREA DPR

Despite only ever having qualified for one World Cup, Korea DPR—North Korea, as they were known on their sole finals appearance in 1966—had been the first Asian team to progress beyond the first round.

ROAD TO WORLD CUP 2010

Jordan	0-1	Korea DPR
Korea DPR	1-1	South Korea
Turkmenistan	0-0	Korea DPR
Korea DPR	1-0	Turkmenistan
Korea DPR	2-0	Jordan
South Korea	0-0	Korea DPR
United Arab Emirates	1-2	Korea DPR
Korea DPR	1-1	South Korea
Iran	2-1	Korea DPR
Korea DPR	1-0	Saudi Arabia
Korea DPR	2-0	United Arab Emirates
South Korea	1-0	Korea DPR
Korea DPR	0-0	Iran
Saudi Arabia	0-0	Korea DPR

Living in the shadow of their more successful neighbors, South Korea, only served as further inspiration for the team and for manager Kim Jong-Hun. His team had an uphill struggle ahead, with a lack of top-level experience; the majority of the squad played domestically in Asia, with only Hong Yong-Jo playing in Europe for Russian side FC Rostov.

They advanced from the third round level on points with South Korea, but their inexperience was highlighted in their first match of round four as none of their starting XI had amassed more than 50 caps. Despite this handicap, they grabbed the three points courtesy of second-half goals from Choe Kum-Chol and An Chol-Hyok.

A 1-1 draw against South Korea preceded a 2-1 reverse to Iran, leaving Korea DPR with just four points from their first three games as 2009 approached. Man In-Guk ensured their play picked up in the New Year, with the only goal of the game against Saudi Arabia in February; another win would mean qualification was back on track.

That win duly arrived the next month against United Arab Emirates in Pyongyang. Man In-Guk struck again in injury time to add to Pak Nam-Chol's earlier effort in a 2-0 victory.

Their run was brought to a halt after a late winner for South Korea in their second encounter, but they were still well placed to qualify with playoff rivals Iran and Saudi Arabia to face in their last two games. A goalless draw against the former set up a tense final day in which any one from three teams could secure a place.

Korea DPR could qualify with a point, providing archrivals South Korea prevented Iran from winning. They secured their point and Iran could not emerge victorious either, meaning the standings in the group table stayed as they were. Korea DPR had qualified on goal difference to their first tournament in over four decades.

BELOW Captain Hong Yong-Jo leads the charge on goal against Saudi Arabia.

WORLD CUP 2010, TEAMS
MEXICO

Mexico began the CONCACAF fourth round of World Cup qualification with former England manager Sven-Göran Eriksson in charge, despite unrest among the fans.

The Swedish manager was charged with continuing the team's solid record for qualifying for the tournament; Mexico had only missed one finals in nearly three decades, and that because of a FIFA ban.

Eriksson had inherited a promising youthful team, inspired by the experience of ageing forward Cuauhtémoc Blanco—and, with stars such as Arsenal's Carlos Vela and Giovanni Dos Santos, goals were always likely. But the team suffered from inconsistency both on and off the pitch, a fact that threatened to derail their hopes of qualification.

A 2-0 reverse to the United States was quickly canceled out by a 2-0 victory over Costa Rica. But defeat to Honduras in April 2009 would bring an abrupt end to Eriksson's reign of only 11 months. The timing was not ideal, but Mexico were hoping for an upturn in fortunes with the swift re-appointment of former manager Javier Aguirre.

There was no immediate impact, however, as the frustration continued. A late winner from El Salvador resulted in a 2-1 scoreline, leaving Mexico adrift of the pack. Goals from Guillermo Franco and Oscar Rojas secured victory over Trinidad & Tobago and, when Miguel Sabah hit a late winner to defeat the United States in August, qualification was once again being talked about.

Victories against Costa Rica and Honduras put Mexico in the surprising position of needing just one more win to qualify. The three points were secured in style with a 4-1 blasting of El Salvador, Blanco and Vela among the scorers.

In a stop-start campaign, Eriksson and Aguirre had used over 60 players, and the patchy sequence of results fully reflected that fact. Mexico came back twice to share the spoils in their last match with Trinidad & Tobago—their first and only draw of the group, offering proof of their inconsistency. Fans and manager alike would be hoping for greater stability if they were to challenge in South Africa.

ABOVE Striker Carlos Vela (right) bests El Salvador's Marvin Gonzalez during Mexico's 4-1 victory.

LEFT Sven-Göran Eriksson instructs Mexico veteran Cuauhtémoc Blanco.

ROAD TO WORLD CUP 2010

USA	2-0	Mexico
Mexico	2-0	Costa Rica
Honduras	3-1	Mexico
El Salvador	2-1	Mexico
Mexico	2-1	Trinidad & Tobago
Mexico	2-1	USA
Costa Rica	0-3	Mexico
Mexico	1-0	Honduras
Mexico	4-1	El Salvador
Trinidad & Tobago	2-2	Mexico

WORLD CUP 2010, TEAMS
NEW ZEALAND

New Zealand saw a golden opportunity to qualify for the World Cup after Australia switched to the AFC confederation in 2005.

ROAD TO WORLD CUP 2010

Fiji	0-2	New Zealand
Vanuatu	1-2	New Zealand
New Zealand	4-1	Vanuatu
New Caledonia	1-3	New Zealand
New Zealand	3-0	New Caledonia
New Zealand	0-2	Fiji
Bahrain	0-0	New Zealand
New Zealand	1-0	Bahrain

This left New Zealand as the only seeded side in a qualification group with very poor opposition. This increased the pressure on coach Ricki Herbert and his side.

New Zealand were granted entry directly to the final stage of qualification, the OFC Nations Cup. The four teams would be placed in a table, with the winner advancing to the playoffs.

Herbert's team lacked top-level football experience; only captain Ryan Nelsen played in the European top flight with Blackburn Rovers, while striker Rory Fallon played with Plymouth Argyle in the Coca-Cola Championship.

The All Whites kicked off with two away victories, 2-0 against Fiji and 2-1 against Vanuatu. Gold Coast United striker Shane Smeltz bagged a goal in each game.

Smeltz continued with a run of six goals in three games. He hit a first-half brace in the return against Vanuatu and scored another double in a 3-1 victory against New Caledonia. He once again hit two, as New Zealand cruised to a 3-0 win at home against New Caledonia.

Defeat in the final match against Fiji was inconsequential: New Zealand had set up a qualification playoff against a nation yet to be decided, but would have to wait 12 months.

They appeared at the 2009 Confederations Cup in South Africa but were eliminated in the group stage, failing to score a single goal, not good preparation for their World Cup decider against Bahrain.

The two-legged affair began with a 0-0 stalemate in Riffa. A goal in first-half injury time from Fallon decided the tie at the Westpac Stadium in Wellington, and sent New Zealand to only their second World Cup finals.

LEFT Rory Fallon secures New Zealand's first World Cup finals appearance in nearly three decades.

WORLD CUP 2010, TEAMS
NIGERIA

Nigeria began qualification with a point to prove. The team missed out on a place at the World Cup in 2006 on head-to-head encounters with Angola, despite having a better goal difference.

Coach Shaibu Amodu was brought in for a fourth time, having managed the side in 2002. The team had spent many years in the shadow of Cameroon, and had a strong team.

Established goalkeeper Vincent Enyeama was shielded by Joseph Yobo at center-back and Mikel John Obi in midfield, making up a strong spine. With attack-minded players such as Nwankwo Kanu, Obafemi Martins and Yakubu, they had a side with experience and style.

Nigeria proved this by topping their group in the second round of qualification, having had a bye through the first. They had a 100 percent record. Results also counted toward qualification for the 2010 African Cup of Nations.

Nigeria progressed to a four-team group, the winner qualifying automatically for the finals. A 0-0 draw against Mozambique was cause for concern and, while a 2-0 home victory against Kenya allayed those fears, there was a lot to do—especially with Tunisia winning two from two.

Two draws against Tunisia helped but, with two games left, Nigeria were still trailing by two points. Another goalless draw with Mozambique looked likely to end their hopes, but a last-minute winner by Malaga striker Victor Obinna set up a tense final day.

Nigeria had to win against Kenya in Nairobi and hope Mozambique won against Tunisia. Late goals in both matches altered the landscape of the group. Mozambique beat Tunisia, and an Obafemi Martins strike in the 83rd minute secured a 3-2 victory over Kenya, sending Nigeria fans into dreamland.

ROAD TO WORLD CUP 2010

Nigeria	2-0	South Africa
Sierra Leone	0-1	Nigeria
Equatorial Guinea	0-1	Nigeria
Nigeria	2-0	Equatorial Guinea
South Africa	0-1	Nigeria
Nigeria	4-1	Sierra Leone
Mozambique	0-0	Nigeria
Nigeria	2-0	Kenya
Tunisia	0-0	Nigeria
Nigeria	2-2	Tunisia
Nigeria	1-0	Mozambique
Kenya	2-3	Nigeria

LEFT Obafemi Martins takes on all comers against Mozambique.

WORLD CUP 2010, TEAMS
PARAGUAY

Paraguay set about qualifying, hoping continuity would see them through.

ROAD TO WORLD CUP 2010

Peru	0-0	Paraguay
Paraguay	1-0	Uruguay
Paraguay	5-1	Ecuador
Chile	0-3	Paraguay
Paraguay	2-0	Brazil
Bolivia	4-2	Paraguay
Argentina	1-1	Paraguay
Paraguay	2-0	Venezuela
Colombia	0-1	Paraguay
Paraguay	1-0	Peru
Uruguay	2-0	Paraguay
Ecuador	1-1	Paraguay
Paraguay	0-2	Chile
Brazil	2-1	Paraguay
Paraguay	1-0	Bolivia
Paraguay	1-0	Argentina
Venezuela	1-2	Paraguay
Paraguay	0-2	Colombia

RIGHT Paulo Cesar da Silva (left) and Dario Veron (right) of Paraguay battle for the ball with Nicolas Fedor (center) of Venezuela.

Argentinean coach Gerardo Martino was appointed in 2007 and intended to lead his settled team to a fourth successive World Cup finals.

Several key players retired, including goalkeeper José Luis Chilavert. New keeper and captain Justo Villar inspired a team built from the back, but Salvador Cabañas and Roque Santa Cruz promised goals up front.

Paraguay picked up four points from their first two matches—a goalless draw at Peru and a 1-0 victory at home to Uruguay. They then thrashed Ecuador 5-1, with Nelson Valdez and Santa Cruz among the scorers. A 3-0 victory over Chile ended 2007 on a high before Paraguay vanquished Brazil 2-0.

Defeat away to Bolivia and a draw against Argentina weakened Paraguay's grip on the top spot, but victories over Venezuela and Colombia ensured they still led the pack. Paraguay beat Peru by one goal to nil.

2009 started badly as Paraguay picked up just one point from four games; defeats to Uruguay, Chile, and Brazil meant they slipped to third. In September they got back on the winning trail, defeating Bolivia 1-0 courtesy of a Cabañas penalty in first-half injury time. Results elsewhere meant they could still guarantee qualification with victory over Argentina.

Valdez settled the game inside the first half-hour and Paraguay had made it. They eventually finished third in the group after a 2-1 victory away to Venezuela was followed by defeat against Colombia.

WORLD CUP 2010, TEAMS
SERBIA

Serbia were competing as an independent nation. No longer part of Yugoslavia or aligned with Montenegro, they appointed Radomir Antic to lead them to the World Cup.

LEFT Dejan Stankovic of Serbia holds his national flag after his team beat Romania in October 2009.

Antic had the pedigree for the job, one of only two men to manage both Real Madrid and Barcelona. His team included a wealth of top European experience. With Manchester United center-back Nemanja Vidic and Chelsea's Branislav Invanovic, and captain Dejan Stankovic from Inter Milan.

The team kicked off in Belgrade with a 2-0 win over the Faroe Islands. An own goal from the visitors got the ball rolling and Valencia forward Nikola Žigic hit a late second. Despite defeat against France in Paris days later, Serbia still believed in a playoff spot.

A 3-0 demolition of Lithuania in October 2008 helped. Three goals in nine first-half minutes sent Serbia on their way to another victory against Austria.

Another three-goal haul was enough for Serbia to take the points in Romania despite conceding two themselves. A 1-0 victory over Austria in June 2009 and two goals without reply against the Faroe Islands four days later, gave them their fifth consecutive victory.

France held them to a 1-1 draw in Belgrade. It was a crucial point, because Serbia only had to beat Romania at home to guarantee participation in the World Cup finals.

This they did, thumping Romania 5-0 in front of nearly 40,000 fans. A surprise loss to Lithuania in their final match was only their second of the campaign.

ROAD TO WORLD CUP 2010

Serbia	2-0	Faroe Islands
France	2-1	Serbia
Serbia	3-0	Lithuania
Austria	1-3	Serbia
Romania	2-3	Serbia
Serbia	1-0	Austria
Faroe Islands	0-2	Serbia
Serbia	1-1	France
Serbia	5-0	Romania
Lithuania	2-1	Serbia

WORLD CUP 2010, TEAMS
SLOVAKIA

Slovakia reached their first finals as an independent nation and finally emerged from the shadow of the Czech Republic.

ROAD TO WORLD CUP 2010

Slovakia	2-1	Northern Ireland
Slovenia	2-1	Slovakia
San Marino	1-3	Slovakia
Slovakia	2-1	Poland
Czech Republic	1-2	Slovakia
Slovakia	7-0	San Marino
Slovakia	2-2	Czech Republic
Northern Ireland	0-2	Slovakia
Slovakia	0-2	Slovenia
Poland	0-1	Slovakia

Despite the majority of Czechoslovakia's 1976 European Championship winning team being Slovaks, recent success had been considerably more difficult.

The two were paired in a group that also included Poland, Slovenia, and Northern Ireland. Slovakia got off to a solid start in a 2-1 defeat of Northern Ireland in Bratislava.

Defeat to Slovenia was followed by a 3-1 victory away to San Marino. A late home brace from Stanislav Šesták then snatched three points from Poland.

2009 brought the first long-awaited showdown with the Czech Republic, FC Kaiserslautern striker Erik Jendrišek's 82nd-minute winner ensuring a 2-1 victory.

Despite their position outside FIFA's top 20 teams, the Slovaks boasted names such as Liverpool defender Martin Škrtel and West Bromwich Albion's Marek Čech. Coach Vladimír Weiss's disciplined approach ensured they remained on course for qualification.

Slovakia beat San Marino 7-0—but this could not inspire a second win against their rivals. Despite going ahead twice, Slovakia had to settle for a point.

A 2-0 defeat of Northern Ireland in Belfast put Slovakia's qualification back on track, but another loss to Slovenia meant a nail-biting final match. A tense game was settled by an own goal after three minutes, Polish defender Seweryn Gancarczyk the guilty party.

Slovakia were going to the World Cup.

BELOW Erik Jendrišek is pictured after hitting a late winner against the Czech Republic.

ABOVE Defender Martin Škrtel outruns Martin Paterson of Northern Ireland during a 2-0 away win.

WORLD CUP 2010, TEAMS
SLOVENIA

Slovenia have made a habit of surprising everyone by qualifying for international tournaments since their split from Yugoslavia in the early 1990s.

They were hoping to cause another upset in their quest to reach their second ever World Cup.

Manager Matjaž Kek was a low-profile appointment, having worked his way up from managing Slovenia's Under 15 and 16 sides after an undistinguished playing career that saw him pick up just one cap for his country.

Kek had a side that relied on hard work. They had a solid goalkeeper in Udinese's Samir Handanovic who, at 25 years old, had established himself as number one for both club and country. In midfield Robert Koren had success in the Premier League with West Bromwich Albion, and FC Köln striker Milivoje Novakovic had scored regularly since his international debut in 2006.

Slovenia had a tough group that included Slovakia and the Czech Republic. They faced Poland in Wroclaw first, and a point was rescued in the first half.

Slovenia's solid start continued with a 2-1 victory over Slovakia. Slovenia topped their group after the first two rounds of games.

October 2008 saw Northen Ireland sent home with nothing after two late goals from Novakovic and Zlatan Ljubijankic.

One point from two meetings with the Czech Republic was followed by a 1-0 defeat to Northern Ireland in Belfast. Slovenia now had four games left to make a push for qualification.

A 5-0 home win over minnows San Marino helped, with Koren grabbing a brace, and, when Slovenia beat Poland, 3-0 a place in the playoffs was looking like a reality.

A 2-0 win against Slovakia confirmed that, while a 3-0 triumph over San Marino ended an impressive campaign. Russia in the playoffs was the reward for their efforts.

As the first leg was ending in Moscow, Slovenia were 2-0 down, but a late goal from C.D. Nacional midfielder Nejc Pecnik gave Slovenia a crucial away goal.

Striker Zlatko Dedic scored just before half time in Maribor to give Slovenia a shock victory on away goals and sent Russia out of the tournament. It was a remarkable achievement.

ABOVE The Slovenian players celebrate after beating Slovakia 2:0 during their World Cup 2010 qualifying campaign.

ROAD TO WORLD CUP 2010

Poland	1-1	Slovenia
Slovenia	2-1	Slovakia
Slovenia	2-0	Northern Ireland
Czech Republic	1-0	Slovenia
Slovenia	0-0	Czech Republic
Northern Ireland	1-0	Slovenia
Slovenia	5-0	San Marino
Slovenia	3-0	Poland
Slovakia	0-2	Slovenia
San Marino	0-3	Slovenia
Russia	2-1	Slovenia
Slovenia	1-0	Russia

WORLD CUP 2010, TEAMS
SOUTH AFRICA

Host nation South Africa were granted automatic qualification to their third World Cup. They did, however, enter the second phase of CAF qualification in an attempt to qualify for the African Cup of Nations.

It was a stern test for new coach Joel Santana, who had replaced fellow Brazilian Carlos Alberto Parreira who was forced to vacate the position for personal reasons. Many were hoping Santana's extensive experience in South America, where he had managed several teams including Fluminese and Vasco da Gama, would translate to the international stage. Unfortunately, his new team finished second to Nigeria in the first qualifying round.

After being banned by FIFA for nearly three decades due to apartheid, South Africa had not been past the World Cup group stages in two attempts in the 1990s. Now, expectation was at an all-time high, as the team prepared to do battle on home soil. Players such as Everton's Steven Pienaar and Blackburn's Aaron Mokoena offered experience at the highest level, while the emerging talents of young goalkeeper Itumeleng Khune gave South Africa stability at the back.

The Confederations Cup of 2009 was regarded as the dress rehearsal for the World Cup for both team and country as Santana could assess his squad in a competitive setting. The team got off to an uninspiring start, drawing 0-0 with Iraq before defeating New Zealand 2-0 with a brace from Red Star Belgrade striker Bernard Parker.

Despite losing 2-0 to Spain, the hosts joined Spain in the semi-finals where they faced Brazil. It was a spirited performance, and extra time beckoned before a late strike from Dani Alves meant that South Africa had to fight for third place. This meant a rematch with Spain, who had suffered a surprise loss to the United States.

It took an extra-time winner from Xabi Alonso to settle the game when it ended 2-2 after 90 minutes, three of the four goals coming in a frantic final five minutes.

It was a respectable fourth place for South Africa but, after the team endured a poor run of eight defeats in nine games, Santana was sacked and Parreira reinstated. With a World Cup winner at the helm the South Africans were hopeful of a good tournament.

BELOW Captain Aaron Mokoena leads by example, tackling the threat of Brazil's Robinho.

WORLD CUP 2010, TEAMS
SOUTH KOREA

South Korea surprised everyone with a fourth-place World Cup finish in 2002.

Despite faltering since, they were determined to put in a repeat performance in 2010.

After experimenting with Dutch coaches, countryman Huh Jung-Moo was appointed for a third time. The former midfielder had been intermittently involved with South Korea since 1989 as coach and manager, and was assistant to Dutchman Jo Bonfrere in 2004.

His side had European experience, none more than captain Park Ji-Sung, the first Asian to play in a Champions League final with Manchester United in 2009. The goals came from strikers Seol Ki-Hyeon and Lee Dong-Gook, who had experience in England's top flight with Fulham and Middlesbrough.

After progressing through round three in a group with rivals Korea DPR, they faced their neighbors again in round four. Teenage midfielder Ki Sung-Yong who got their opening goal in a 1-1 draw against rivals Korea DPR, his strike equalizing a penalty.

South Korea's first win came against the United Arab Emirates in Seoul, a brace from winger Lee Keun-Ho and goals from Ji-Sung and Kwak Tae-Hwi sealing a 4-1 victory. 2008 ended with a 2-0 triumph over Saudi Arabia, a last-minute goal coming from Monaco striker Park Chu-Young.

A free kick from Spanish-based midfielder Javad Nekounam looked like it had secured Iran victory over the South Koreans in February 2009, but Park Ji-Sung rescued a point with another late strike.

Three points against Korea DPR were then secured courtesy of a late goal from Kim Chi-Woo, leaving South Korea on the brink of qualification. A victory over United Arab Emirates in Dubai would send them to their seventh consecutive finals.

They wrapped up the game—and qualification—in the first half with goals from Park Chu-Young and Ki Sung-Yueng. The team played out two draws in their final fixtures against Saudi Arabia and Iran.

The team with the best World Cup qualifying record were back, having failed to suffer a single defeat in qualifying.

ROAD TO WORLD CUP 2010

South Korea	4-0	Turkmenistan
Korea DPR	0-0	South Korea
South Korea	2-2	Jordan
Jordan	0-1	South Korea
Turkmenistan	1-3	South Korea
South Korea	0-0	Korea DPR
Korea DPR	1-1	South Korea
South Korea	4-1	United Arab Emirates
Saudi Arabia	0-2	South Korea
Iran	1-1	South Korea
South Korea	1-0	Korea DPR
United Arab Emirates	0-2	South Korea
South Korea	0-0	Saudi Arabia
South Korea	1-1	Iran

LEFT South Korea's Kwak Tae-Hwi (right) heads a goal against United Arab Emirates in October 2008.

WORLD CUP 2010, TEAMS
SWITZERLAND

Switzerland enlisted the best to ensure they reached South Africa. Seasoned manager Ottmar Hitzfeld arrived, having left Bayern Munich for a second time.

Hitzfeld's track record was formidable, winning the European Cup with both Bayern and Borussia Dortmund. But it was his early coaching success in Switzerland that convinced the FA he was right for the job.

The Swiss were hoping to avenge their last World Cup finals appearance when they were eliminated without conceding a goal after defeat to Ukraine on penalties. Switzerland nearly kicked off with a win in Tel Aviv, but let a 2-0 lead slip.

Switzerland found themselves with just one point after two games when Luxembourg struck late to win in Zurich four days later. Victory over Latvia was their first, goals from Sebastian Frei and Blaise Nkufo—his third in three games—sealing the win.

The two strikers struck again to beat group favorites Greece in October 2008. Successive 2-0 victories over Moldova re-established the Swiss as a force and qualification was a real possibility. They went some way to realizing that dream by defeating Greece a second time, in Basel, to top the group.

After rescuing a point against Latvia, the Swiss defeated Luxembourg 3-0, Philippe Senderos firing two in two minutes before Basel's Benjamin Huggel added a third. It meant only one point was needed in the final match against Israel to qualify. While uninspiring, the drab 0-0 draw in front of their home support secured the necessary point. Switzerland had qualified for their eighth World Cup finals.

It was a deserved achievement. Johan Djourou and Philippe Senderos had been schooled at Arsenal, while Wolfsburg's Bundesliga-winning Diego Benaglio was consistent between the posts.

With relative veterans Alexander Frei and Hakan Yakin, and new players Gelson Fernandes and Johan Vonlan, this blend of youth and experience gave high hopes in Zurich.

ABOVE Midfielder Hakan Yakin (right) chases a loose ball with a Luxembourg defender.

BELOW Stephane Grichting hit his first international goal against Greece.

ROAD TO WORLD CUP 2010

Israel	2-2	Switzerland
Switzerland	1-2	Luxembourg
Switzerland	2-1	Latvia
Greece	1-2	Switzerland
Moldova	0-2	Switzerland
Switzerland	2-0	Moldova
Switzerland	2-0	Greece
Latvia	2-2	Switzerland
Luxembourg	0-3	Switzerland
Switzerland	0-0	Israel

WORLD CUP 2010, TEAMS
URUGUAY

Uruguay's passage to the World Cup finals was a 20-match marathon that began three years before the tournament.

The country credited with being the first-ever World Cup hosts and winners were hoping to put recent barren years behind them and recapture the trophy.

Head coach Oscar Tabárez had been brought back in after leading Uruguay to the World Cup in 1990, where they progressed to the last 16. Uruguay had only qualified once since—in 2002.

There had been a number of successful Uruguayan exports in Europe, none more than striker Diego Forlan. He was charged with delivering the goals alongside young Ajax man Luis Suárez. At the back, defensive duo Diego Lugano and Maxi Pereira were key players for Fenerbahçe and Benfica, respectively.

Uruguay's campaign got off to a great start with a 5-0 victory over Bolivia before a single-goal reverse against Paraguay. November 2007 saw Uruguay pick up just one point from two games as they drew with Chile and lost 2-1 to Brazil in Sao Paulo.

A 1-1 draw with Venezuela was followed by a 6-0 thrashing of Peru, with Forlan bagging a hat trick. Victory over Colombia and a frustrating 0-0 draw with Ecuador did little to move Uruguay ahead of the pack.

A loss to Argentina preceded a scrappy draw with Bolivia, meaning Uruguay ended 2008 with much to do. The following year started with a 2-0 win over Paraguay, then came a 0-0 draw against Chile. The team's inability to string wins together was threatening to cost Uruguay dearly.

Uruguay were thumped 4-0 by Brazil at the Estadio Centenario. It looked like they had recovered, leading Venezuela 2-1 days later, only to be held at the final whistle.

Two wins from their final three games secured a playoff place for Uruguay, despite losing to Argentina in their final match. Uruguay were then set to face Costa Rica, who finished fourth in their CONCACAF qualifying group.

Uruguay journeyed to San Jose first, where defender Lugano grabbed his fourth and most important goal of the qualifying fixtures. Uruguay headed back to Montevideo with a crucial away goal.

A 1-1 draw followed days later, confirming Uruguay's progression to the finals.

LEFT Sebastian Abreu heads the goal against Costa Rica that sent Uruguay to South Africa.

ROAD TO WORLD CUP 2010

Uruguay	5-0	Bolivia
Paraguay	1-0	Uruguay
Uruguay	2-2	Chile
Brazil	2-1	Uruguay
Uruguay	1-1	Venezuela
Uruguay	6-0	Peru
Colombia	0-1	Uruguay
Uruguay	0-0	Ecuador
Argentina	2-1	Uruguay
Bolivia	2-2	Uruguay
Uruguay	2-0	Paraguay
Chile	0-0	Uruguay
Uruguay	0-4	Brazil
Venezuela	2-2	Uruguay
Uruguay	3-1	Colombia
Ecuador	1-2	Uruguay
Uruguay	0-1	Argentina
Costa Rica	0-1	Uruguay
Uruguay	1-1	Costa Rica

EUROPE

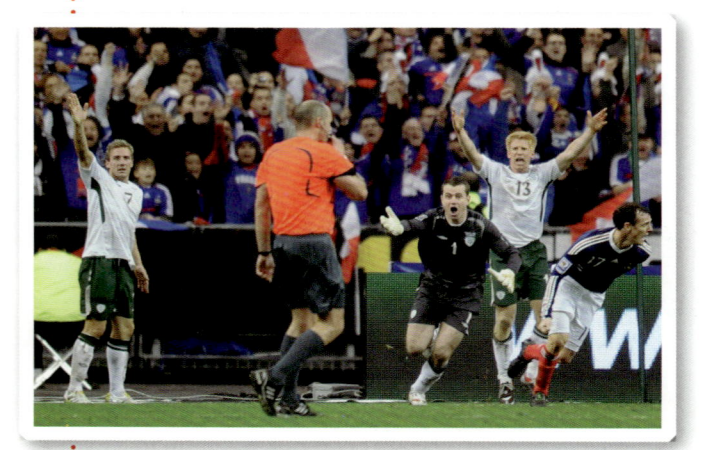

CONMEBOL

WORLD CUP MOMENTS 2010

ABOVE Republic of Ireland players protest the controversial France winner that sent them to South Africa.

RIGHT Spain celebrate victory over Belgium, qualifying with a perfect record.

ABOVE England secure qualification with a 5-1 drubbing of Croatia, Frank Lampard a scorer.

ABOVE Diego Maradona cuts a lonely figure as his Argentina side are humbled 6-1 by Bolivia.

BELOW Luis Fabiano celebrates scoring against Argentina. Only six points separated group winners Brazil from fourth place.

80 THE WORLD CUP 2010

CONCACAF   CAF   ASIA

BELOW Algeria's Khaled Lemmouchia (right) challenges Egypt's Ahmed Hassan (2nd right) during the second leg of the qualification playoffs.

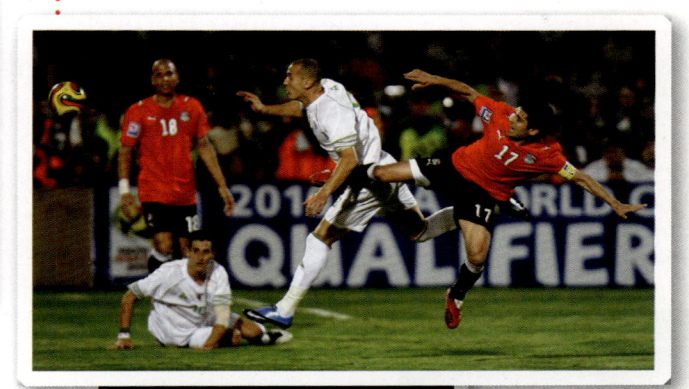

ABOVE A nation rejoices as Honduras reach only their second World Cup finals.

LEFT Lucas Neill salutes fans as Australia become the third team to earn qualification.

BELOW Political issues forced rivals South Korea and Korea DPR to play their qualifier in neutral China.

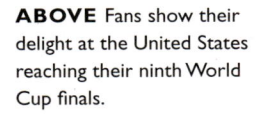

ABOVE Fans show their delight at the United States reaching their ninth World Cup finals.

RIGHT Ivory Coast made it through both stages of CAF qualification without losing a match.

MOMENTS 81

WORLD CUP 2010, STAR PLAYERS
CRISTIANO RONALDO

Cristiano Ronaldo burst onto the football scene in 2001. Now renowned as one of the planet's best player, there appears to be no stopping him.

RIGHT Cristiano Ronaldo (right) shields the ball from Sweden's Daniel Majstorovic (left) during an October 2008 match.

After signing with Sporting Lisbon at the age of 12, Ronaldo soared through the ranks and quickly made it to the first team, scoring a brace on his debut. It was a dazzling performance against Manchester United that inspired United manager Alex Ferguson to pay more than $US 20 million (£12 million) for him in 2003.

Less than a week after his United debut Ronaldo made his first appearance for Portugal. He was later included in their squad for Euro 2004. He scored in their opening match, a shock 2-1 defeat by eventual winners Greece, and again in the semi-final success against the Netherlands, but Portugal went on to lose in the final.

Despite this disappointment, Ronaldo went on to fire seven goals in Portugal's qualifying campaign for the 2006 World Cup. He scored once at the finals, as his country finished in fourth place, but major footballing honors were yet to come. In 2007 he won his first Premier League title, and was named Portugal's player of the year.

The following year, Ronaldo picked up another Premier League winner's medal, as well as scoring eight goals to help Manchester United lift the European Cup. He was crowned the world's greatest player by picking up the treble of FIFPro World Player of the Year, the Ballon d'Or, and the European Golden Shoe.

These awards made Ronaldo one of the most feared players in the game. Despite scoring eight goals in qualification, Ronaldo and Portugal could not progress past the quarter-finals of Euro 2008, losing 3-2 to Germany.

After a second successive Champions League final and third Premier League title in a row, Ronaldo became the most expensive player in the world when he signed for Spanish giants Real Madrid in 2009. He endured an indifferent World Cup qualifying campaign, however, Portugal scraping through the playoffs against Bosnia and Herzegovina.

ABOVE Portugal's prodigiously talented Cristiano Ronaldo.

FACTFILE

Full Name: Cristiano Ronaldo dos Santos Aveiro
Date of Birth: February 5 1985
Place of Birth: Funchal, Madeira, Portugal
Height: 6 ft 1 in (1.86 m)
Playing Position: Forward
National Team: Portugal
1st Appearance: 2003

WORLD CUP 2010, STAR PLAYERS
DIDIER DROGBA

Didier Drogba is the danger man of the Ivory Coast team. The striker's instincts in front of goal have made him a success both domestically and on the international stage, and he fired his teammates to their second successive World Cup finals in 2010.

Born in March 1978, Drogba started at French club Le Mans in Ligue 2, signing his first professional contract aged 21. Though starting his career somewhat late, he managed to score seven goals in his first full season with the team.

In 2002, Drogba moved to Guingamp. It was during his stint there, that he made his debut for the Ivory Coast, against South Africa in September. He scored his first goal for the national side in January 2003, beginning a phenomenal run that would see him score more than 40 goals by the time he received his 60th cap.

Domestically, Drogba left Guingamp for a season at French giants Marseille before his exploits attracted interest from cash-rich Chelsea. He signed for the London team for $US 40 million (£24 million) in 2004 and captured the Premier League championship with his new team in his first season.

It was no coincidence that Drogba's free scoring coincided with the Ivory Coast's most successful period. They finished second in the 2006 African Cup of Nations, the powerful striker hitting three goals including the winner in the semi-final.

Either side of that tournament, Drogba scored the goals to send his national side to their first-ever World Cup finals in Germany. He hit nine goals in qualifying as they topped their group. However, Drogba only scored one at the tournament as Ivory Coast were swiftly eliminated, finishing third behind Argentina and Netherlands in what was known as the "group of death."

This disappointment didn't stop Drogba, however, as he netted three more times in the 2008 African Cup of Nations. He also provided the firepower to secure a second World Cup appearance for the Ivory Coast. Drogba's six goals included the equalizer against Malawi that confirmed qualification.

FACTFILE

Full Name: Didier Yves Drogba Tébily
Date of Birth: March 11 1978
Place of Birth: Abidjan, Côte d'Ivoire
Height: 6 ft 2 in (1.88 m)
Playing Position: Striker
National Team: Ivory Coast
1st Appearance: 2002

LEFT Didier Drogba is the Ivory Coast's all-time leading goal-scorer.

WORLD CUP 2010, STAR PLAYERS
DIEGO FORLÁN

Diego Forlán is a player with a strong football pedigree. His father and grandfather were both professional footballers and Diego set out to be the most successful of the trio.

Winning the European Golden Shoe on two separate occasions has certainly confirmed that.

He made his professional debut at Argentinean side Independiente at the age of 19, and impressed after maintaining a ratio of nearly a goal every two games. He was rewarded with a transfer to English giants Manchester United.

It was while with United in 2002 that Forlán made his debut for his country; he grabbed his first goal after just four minutes in a 3-2 defeat to Saudi Arabia to announce his arrival on the international stage. Forlán was included in Uruguay's squad for the 2002 World Cup, and scored against Senegal in his only appearance of the tournament.

His goal tally at Manchester United was not as high as many had expected, despite helping the club win the Premier League and FA Cup double and, in 2004, Forlán moved to Villarreal. It was in Spain that his career began to take off both domestically and internationally.

Forlán helped Uruguay reach third place at the 2004 Copa America, and scored six times in their qualification campaign for the 2006 World Cup. However, Uruguay lost to Australia on penalties in the CONMEBOL versus OFC playoff.

In 2005 Forlán won his first European Golden Shoe after hitting 25 league goals for Villarreal. His three goals for Uruguay in the 2007 Copa America were not enough to help them to a 15th title, as they had to settle for fourth place.

Forlán's best campaign for Uruguay came during qualification for the 2010 World Cup, where he hit seven goals en route to their playoff victory over Costa Rica. In 2009 he won the Golden Shoe for the second time.

Diego Forlán has proved himself vital to both his clubs and his country during his career.

FACTFILE

Full Name:
Diego Martín Forlán Corazo
Date of Birth: May 19 1979
Place of Birth:
Montevideo, Uruguay
Height: 5 ft 10 ½ in (1.79 m)
Playing Position: Striker
National Team: Uruguay
1st Appearance: 2002

RIGHT Diego Forlan's seven goals fired Uruguay to their 11th World Cup.

WORLD CUP 2010, STAR PLAYERS
FERNANDO TORRES

Already an important player for his club and country before he had reached his 20th birthday, the responsibility didn't seem to faze Fernando Torres, who has thrived on pressure throughout his career.

The Spanish player signed his first professional contract with Atletico Madrid in 1999 at age 15, and made his club debut two years later. Once promoted to La Liga, Torres was noticed by national manager Iñaki Sáez, who gave him his first cap in 2003 against Portugal.

It was not Torres' first appearance in a Spain jersey, however, having come up through the youth ranks. His later teenage years were spent scoring for club and country at the top level.

An appearance at Euro 2004 yielded no goals, but Torres hit six to help Spain qualify for the World Cup in 2006. Five of his haul came in Spain's last two matches, keeping them in second qualifying spot ahead of Bosnia and Herzegovina. Torres scored a further three in the finals, but Spain could not progress beyond the second round.

Torres left Atletico in 2007 for five-time European champions, Liverpool, where he continued his goal-scoring, hitting more than 20 in his first season for the Reds.

Both Torres' and Spain's finest hour came at Euro 2008 as Spain captured the crown. Torres only scored two during the tournament, the first against Sweden in a group match. But his winner in the final against Germany gave Spain only the second trophy in their international history.

Torres went on to score three times at the 2009 Confederations Cup, courtesy of a hat trick against New Zealand, before Spain suffered a shock defeat to the United States. An injury-ravaged qualifying campaign for the World Cup left Torres without any goals, though his country still reached South Africa.

In 2009 Fernando Torres became the youngest Spanish international to reach 60 caps.

FACTFILE

Full Name: Fernando José Torres Sanz
Date of Birth: March 20 1984
Place of Birth: Madrid, Spain
Height: 6 ft 1 in (1.85 m)
Playing Position: Striker
National Team: Spain
1st Appearance: 2003

LEFT Fernando Torres was named man of the match in the Euro 2008 final when he helped Spain capture the trophy.

WORLD CUP 2010, STAR PLAYERS
FRANCK RIBÉRY

Franck Ribéry is a rising star in French football, despite only emerging in the national side at the relatively late age of 23.

FACTFILE

Full Name: Franck Bilal Ribéry
Date of Birth: April 7 1983
Place of Birth: Boulogne-sur-Mer, France
Height: 5 ft 7 in (1.70 m)
Playing Position: Winger
National Team: France
1st Appearance: 2006

RIGHT Franck Ribéry has become a key part of France's team in just three years.

Ribéry's attacking instinct and eye for a killer pass has made him an integral part of France's mission to regain international silverware.

He spent his early career plying his trade in the lower leagues in France before getting his break in Ligue 1 with FC Metz in 2004. He only stayed at each club for one season, however.

Ribéry arrived at Turkish giants Galatasaray in 2005 and, although it was to prove another brief stay, he captured the Türkiye Kupası—the equivalent of the FA Cup—scoring his only goal in the final.

From there, Ribéry moved to French club Olympique Marseille amid controversy, Galatasaray having allegedly not paid him for an extended period. He immediately won the Intertoto Cup and his performances, both domestically and in Europe, finally brought Ribéry to the attention of France manager Raymond Domenech.

Ribéry made his national debut in May 2006 and he was quickly included in France's squad for the World Cup in Germany a month later. His first international goal came against Spain in the last 16. He played from the start in the final but could not help his country overcome Italy.

Ribéry quickly became a mainstay in the national team, with recently retired legend Zinedine Zidane naming him "the jewel of French football." Bayern Munich clearly agreed, and paid US$ 40 million (25 million euros) for Ribéry's services in 2007, testament to his rising stock after languishing in France's lower leagues just a few years before.

Ribéry was selected for Euro 2008 where, after reaching the World Cup final, expectations were again high. After a disastrous group stage, the misery was compounded for Ribéry as he ruptured his ankle ligaments, leaving him sidelined.

He returned to score some crucial goals as France eventually qualified for the 2010 World Cup. His two in two games against Lithuania secured a vital six points for "Les Bleus," though injury forced Ribéry out of the playoff victory over the Republic of Ireland.

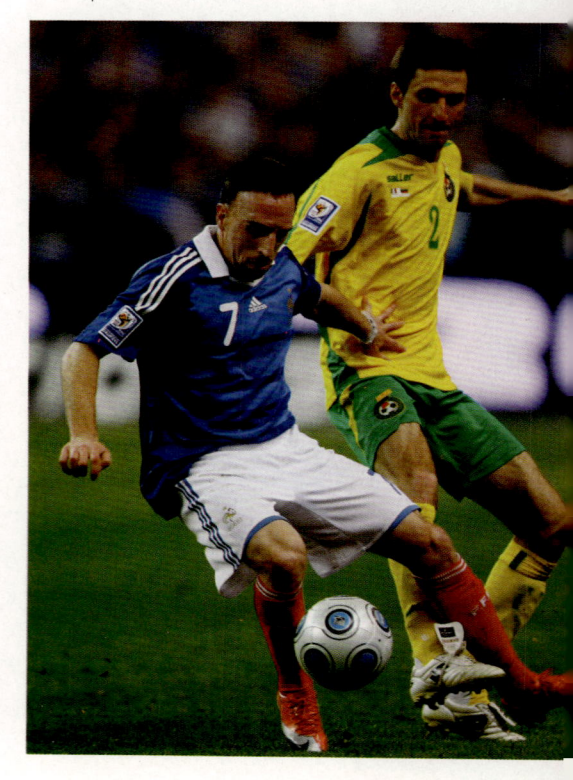

WORLD CUP 2010, STAR PLAYERS
GIANLUIGI BUFFON

Gianluigi Buffon made his professional debut at just 17. Since then, he has established himself as one of the great goalkeepers of his generation.

Two years after his first appearance for Serie A side Parma, he was picked for his country during a World Cup qualifier in Russia. Buffon acquitted himself well and made the squad for the 1998 tournament in France at just 20 years of age.

He was part of a Parma team including Hernan Crespo and Fabio Cannavaro that won the UEFA Cup and the Copa Italia in 1999, but he missed out on a spot at Euro 2000 due to a broken finger. Buffon had to watch established number one Francesco Toldo help Italy to second place.

In 2001 Buffon signed for Italian giants Juventus for a world record fee (for a goalkeeper) of more than US$ 80 million (50 million euros). It was here that his career would reach new levels; multiple Scudetto wins saw him recognized as the best goalkeeper in the world and helped him succeed Toldo as Italy's number one.

Buffon traveled to the World Cup in 2002 as Italy's first-choice goalkeeper, but the team could not progress beyond the second round, losing to hosts South Korea.

Buffon would go on to experience some troubled years, but still maintained his world-class standards. Italy exited Euro 2004 at the group stage despite not losing a game, and in 2006 Juventus were found guilty of match-fixing and relegated to Serie B. Buffon pledged allegiance to his club, claiming he had not yet won that league and wished to do so, testament to his loyalty and competitive nature.

That summer Buffon helped his country capture their fourth World Cup, keeping an incredible five clean sheets, and he was named in the team of the tournament. It was Buffon's finest hour—the world's best keeper helped Italy win the world's biggest prize.

Another inclusion for team of the tournament at Euro 2008 underlined Buffon's dominance as he passed 30.

LEFT Gianluigi Buffon has earned more than 100 caps for Italy in a career that has already seen him lift the World Cup.

FACTFILE

Full Name: Gianluigi Buffon
Date of Birth: January 2 1978
Place of Birth: Carrara, Italy
Height: 6 ft 3 in (1.91 m)
Playing Position: Goalkeeper
National Team: Italy
1st Appearance: 1997

WORLD CUP 2010, STAR PLAYERS
IKER CASILLAS

Iker Casillas is captain of his country with more than 100 international caps.

ABOVE Iker Casillas leads from the back as Spain's captain.

With goalkeepers usually playing until their mid-30s, Casillas has many years ahead of him and is already considered one of the greatest goalkeepers in the world.

He began his career aged just nine at Real Madrid, playing in the youth system before moving through their "C" and "B" teams. Casillas made his professional debut for the senior side in 1999 and quickly established himself as first choice. Success followed almost immediately, with Madrid capturing the Champions League in 2000. At just 19 years old, Casillas had already won the biggest prize in European club football, keeping a clean sheet in the final.

It was also in 2000 that Casillas debuted for Spain, after playing at almost every youth level in previous years. It took him longer to dislodge Santiago Cañizares from the first team, however; Casillas was included in the Euro 2000 squad, but failed to make an appearance.

By the 2002 World Cup, he had earned a second Champions League medal and was first choice for his country. Despite Casillas saving two penalties against the Republic of Ireland in the round of 16, Spain still exited the competition at the quarter-final stage to South Korea.

A two-time La Liga winner by Euro 2004, Casillas played in all of Spain's matches, conceding just two goals, though these were crucial enough to see his country eliminated at the group stage.

A quarter-final exit to France in the 2006 World Cup did not hint at the success to come for both Casillas and Spain. He entered Euro 2008 wearing the captain's armband, and kept clean sheets throughout the knockout stages as Spain stormed to the championship.

Casillas helped his country last nearly three years without losing an international match from November 2006 to June 2009. During this period, he and his deputy, Liverpool's Pepe Reina, played more than seven games without conceding a goal.

Spain went through their entire 2010 World Cup qualifying campaign without losing a game. Casillas played in all but one match, and conceded just four times.

By the time he reached his century of international caps, more than half of those appearances had resulted in clean sheets, proof of his skill and consistency.

FACTFILE

Full Name: Iker Casillas Fernández
Date of Birth: May 20 1981
Place of Birth: Mostoles, Madrid, Spain
Height: 5 ft 11 ½ in (1.82 m)
Playing Position: Goalkeeper
National Team: Spain
1st Appearance: 2000

WORLD CUP 2010, STAR PLAYERS
KAKÁ

Brazilian Kaká is regarded around the world as a footballing superstar. His goals and flair have seen him win nearly every trophy on the world and European stage with club and country.

Kaká began his career in the youth ranks at Sao Paulo and, on making his debut in the senior side, was noticed by national coach Luiz Felipe Scolari.

Despite only having two caps to his name, Kaká was included in the 2002 World Cup squad. Aged 20, he was the youngest player, and only appeared once in a 5-2 romp over Costa Rica, replacing Rivaldo. But Kaká still picked up a winner's medal as Brazil triumphed in Japan and South Korea.

Kaká was soon signed by Serie A giants AC Milan in 2003. He made a good start, scoring 10 goals in his first season and capturing the Scudetto, the first of many domestic trophies.

In 2005, Kaká triumphed again with the national team, this time at the Confederations Cup. He was much more influential than in 2002, scoring in the final against archrivals Argentina. However, Kaká scored only once at the 2006 World Cup, where Brazil could not get past the quarter-final stage.

He returned to Milan and 2007 proved to be a phenomenal year at club level. Kaká scooped the Champions League, UEFA Super Cup, and FIFA World Club Cup and, in the process, he was named European and World player of the year. Kaká was the hottest property in football, and continued to perform consistently.

2009 was a season of transition. After six years, Kaká left Milan for Real Madrid for a reported fee of $US 92 million (£56 million), a new world record. There was to be no rest, however, as he went straight into the 2009 Confederations Cup, scoring a brace in Brazil's opening fixture against Egypt, before going on to win the tournament for a second time.

Kaká fired five goals in Brazil's World Cup qualifying campaign. This gave him the opportunity to secure his second World Cup before his 30th birthday, and cement his position as one of the world's best players.

FACTFILE

Full Name: Ricardo Izecson dos Santos Leite
Date of Birth: April 22 1982
Place of Birth: Brasilia, Brazil
Height: 6 ft 1 in (1.86 m)
Playing Position: Attacking Midfielder
National Team: Brazil
1st Appearance: 2002

BELOW Kaká is considered one of the best players in the world, with a transfer value to match.

WORLD CUP 2010, STAR PLAYERS
LANDON DONOVAN

Landon Donovan is the crown jewel of modern American soccer. In a nation where football is trying to establish itself as a popular sport, Donovan's success for both club and country has gone some way to achieving that aim.

After coming through soccer academy, Donovan was noticed in Germany after a strike rate of nearly a goal a game for the US Under-17 side. He became the youngest American player to go abroad when he was signed by Bundesliga club Bayer Leverkusen in 1999.

Donovan made his senior debut for the national side in 2000 against Mexico and scored on his debut. It was the perfect start to a career that would see him become his country's all-time leading goal-scorer.

Unhappy with his opportunities in Germany, Donovan was loaned to San Jose Earthquakes in 2001 in a deal that would last three years and establish him as a force in the US league.

Donovan traveled with the national squad to Japan and South Korea for the 2002 World Cup, and immediately hit the headlines. He scored twice en route to the quarter-finals, being named FIFA's best young player in the process.

The United States reached the finals for the eighth time in 2006, thanks in no small part to Donovan's seven goals in qualification. It was during this period that he arrived at LA Galaxy, following a brief return to Leverkusen.

Donovan had a poor World Cup in Germany, where the US failed to win a single game. They recovered quickly, storming to the 2007 CONCACAF Gold Cup, with four goals from Donovan, including the first in the final.

He briefly returned to Germany for a loan spell at Bayern Munich in January 2009 during the MLS close season. Donovan was handed the US captain's armband for the first time competitively that summer in the group stages of the Confederations Cup. The States made it to the final, losing to Brazil, despite a Donovan goal that put them 2-0 up in the first half.

Donovan's five goals in qualifying brought the US a ninth World Cup appearance, including the goal against Honduras that confirmed their place. It was yet another achievement for Donovan, the most successful player in US football history.

FACTFILE

Full Name: Landon Timothy Donovan
Date of Birth: March 4 1982
Place of Birth: Ontario, California
Height: 5 ft 8 in (1.73 m)
Playing Position: Attacking Midfielder
National Team: United States
1st Appearance: 2000

ABOVE Landon Donovan holds the record for goals and caps for the United States.

WORLD CUP 2010, STAR PLAYERS
LIONEL MESSI

Announced by Diego Maradona as his "successor," Lionel Messi has been making headlines on the pitch ever since his breakthrough in 2004.

Messi became the youngest player to appear for Barcelona upon his debut, and added "youngest scorer in La Liga" to his accolades with his first career goal in 2005.

He gained further recognition that same year as the Argentina Under-20 side stormed the FIFA World Youth Championship, Messi picking up best player and top scorer accolades with six goals.

The following month he was called up to the senior side, but was sent off on his debut for an alleged elbow. Messi did enough to earn a spot at the 2006 World Cup finals, scoring in a 6-0 rout of Serbia and Montenegro and having a strike ruled offside against Mexico.

Messi nearly didn't make the tournament, however. An injury sustained for Barcelona against Chelsea in the Champions League threatened to sideline him. He watched his side pick up the European Cup while he was nursed back to health.

Messi's fine form continued as he scored two goals to help Argentina to the final of the 2007 Copa America, before they lost 3-0 to Brazil. At the end of the year, Messi came third in the voting for European Footballer of the Year.

His finest international moment so far came in China at the 2008 Olympic Games. Once Barcelona relented after initially refusing to let him go, he helped his country to football gold with the winner in the final against Nigeria—his third goal of the tournament.

Messi enjoyed a successful year in 2009 when he captured the Champions League with Barcelona, playing and scoring in the final. His goal was the second of the game and sealed a 2-0 triumph over Manchester United.

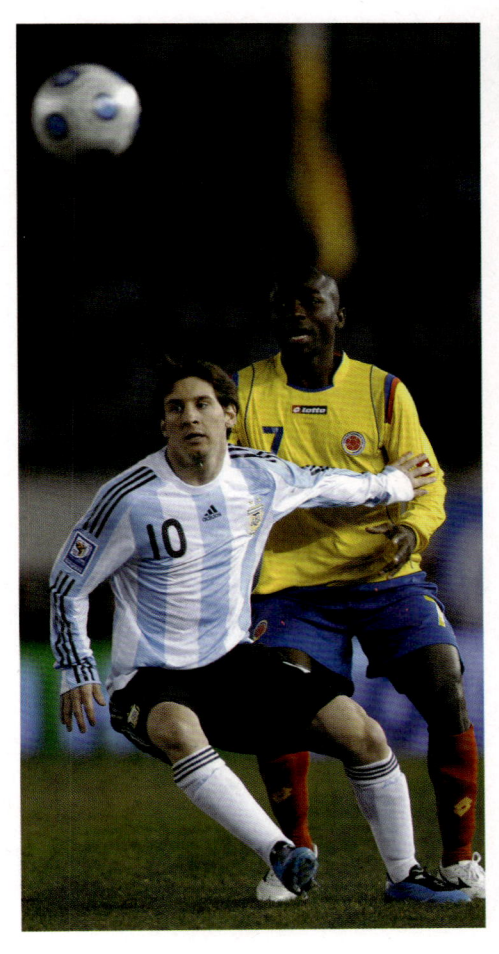

FACTFILE

Full Name: Lionel Andrés Messi
Date of Birth: June 24 1987
Place of Birth: Rosario, Argentina
Height: 5 ft 7 in (1.69 m)
Playing Position: Winger
National Team: Argentina
1st Appearance: 2005

LEFT Lionel Messi (left) vies for the ball with Colombian defender Pablo Armero (right) during a June 2009 World Cup qualification match.

WORLD CUP 2010, STAR PLAYERS
MICHAEL BALLACK

Despite winning a number of domestic trophies, the goal-scoring midfielder has yet to taste glory with the country he captains.

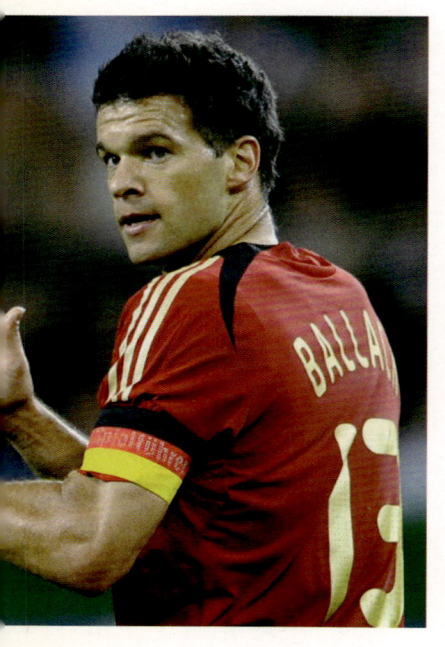

After solid performances in the lower leagues for local side Chemnitzer FC, Ballack was transferred to FC Kaiserslautern in 1997, immediately capturing the Bundesliga in his first season. It was here he got his break for the German national side; coach Berti Vogts noticed the qualities of the player known as "Little Kaiser" for his Beckenbauer-esque qualities.

Ballack debuted in April 1999 against Scotland and soon forced his way into the Euro 2000 squad. Though he only played one match at the tournament, he went on to help Germany reach the 2002 World Cup finals.

Ballack's first three goals for his country were not enough to help them qualify automatically, but he was instrumental in the playoff success over Ukraine, hitting three more in two games for a 5-2 aggregate victory.

2002 was a year of disappointment for Ballack, who narrowly missed out on the Champions League and Bundesliga with Bayer Leverkusen. And it got worse at the World Cup where, though he scored three times including the only goal of the semi-final victory over South Korea, a yellow card forced him out of the final. Germany compounded Ballack's misery by losing to Brazil.

Despite these setbacks, Ballack—by now at Bayern Munich—hit four goals in qualifying to send Germany to Euro 2004. However, they failed to progress from their group. It was after the tournament that new manager Jürgen Klinsmann awarded Ballack the national captaincy.

Ballack led his team to third place in the 2005 Confederations Cup with a four-goal haul, before leading them to another third-place finish in the following year's World Cup. More pain followed in Euro 2008 as Germany lost to Spain in the final.

Despite the upturn in German fortunes since Ballack's appointment as captain, he has yet to experience glory with his country.

ABOVE Ballack has captained his country since 2004.

ABOVE Michael Ballack has scored more than 40 goals from midfield in a 10-year career with Germany.

FACTFILE

Full Name: Michael Ballack
Date of Birth: September 26 1976
Place of Birth: Görlitz, Germany
Height: 6 ft 2 ½ in (1.89 m)
Playing Position: Midfielder
National Team: Germany
1st Appearance: 1999

WORLD CUP 2010, STAR PLAYERS
MICHAEL ESSIEN

Michael Essien has emerged as one of Africa's best players of recent years. He consistently turns in powerful performances in midfield, proving himself a key player for both Chelsea and Ghana.

Essien signed his first professional contract at French side Bastia at 18 years old, and was originally a defender. However, after impressing in midfield while covering an injury, it was quickly agreed it was his best position.

Essien made his debut for Ghana in January 2002 in a warm-up match for the African Cup of Nations. He also played in the tournament, where Ghana lost to Nigeria in the quarter-finals.

In 2003, French giants Olympique Lyonnais recognized Essien's talents and signed him for more than US$ 11.5 million (7 million euros). Here, he quickly established himself in a defensive midfield role, winning the Ligue 1 championship two years in a row.

This brought him to the attention of Premier League champions Chelsea, who signed him for US$ 40 million (£24.4 million) in 2005. Essien promptly helped them to their second successive title, his third in three seasons. His commitment and classy style of play made him a lynchpin for both club and country.

Essien was selected in Ghana's 2006 World Cup squad, and played in all three of their group matches. He was suspended for the round of 16 against Brazil, however, when his country were eliminated.

Essien assisted Ghana to third place at the 2008 African Cup of Nations, scoring twice, including a strike against Nigeria in the quarter-finals.

Injury during World Cup qualification sidelined Essien for nearly the entire 2008/09 season for Chelsea. However, due to the break in play between the second and third rounds of CAF qualification, he only missed one match, helping his country reach the 2010 finals.

Chelsea manager Carlo Ancelotti summed up Essien's versatility and importance: "I think Essien is one of the most important players in midfield in the world. He can play everywhere in midfield with the same result."

Essien leads the new crop of Ghanaian footballers that helped Ghana to their highest FIFA ranking in 2008.

FACTFILE

Full Name: Michael Kojo Essien
Date of Birth: December 2 1982
Place of Birth: Accra, Ghana
Height: 5 ft 10 in (1.78 m)
Playing Position: Midfielder
National Team: Ghana
1st Appearance: 2002

LEFT Michael Essien is widely regarded as one of the best midfield players in world football.

WORLD CUP 2010, STAR PLAYERS
MIROSLAV KLOSE

Miroslav Klose was born in Poland, but he qualified for the German national team through his grandfather.

Since his debut, Klose has become one of his adopted country's most successful strikers.

Klose made his professional debut at the late age of 19, at FC Kaiserslautern. After playing for the reserve side, he broke into the first team and impressed Germany coach Rudi Völler. Klose made his debut for Germany in March 2001.

His choice paid off when, in his first World Cup in 2002, Germany topped their group. Klose became Germany's top scorer in the competition with five goals, including a hat trick against Saudi Arabia; Germany made it to the final but lost to Brazil.

A poor Euro 2004 preceded a move from Kaiserslautern to Werder Bremen, where Klose was valued as much for his assists to other players as for his goals.

He made Germany's 2006 World Cup squad, and again scored five as Germany attempted to regain the trophy on home soil.. Though he finished as the tournament's top marksman, and was voted best player, Germany lost to eventual winners Italy in the semi-final.

In 2007, Klose moved to German champions Bayern Munich, and he helped them win the Bundesliga and DFB-Pokal double in his first season.

Klose scored five times while helping Germany qualify for Euro 2008, going on to score in both the quarter-finals and semi-finals of the tournament. Unfortunately for Klose, his wait for an international trophy continued as Germany failed to overcome Spain in the final.

Germany finished top of their qualifying group for the 2010 World Cup and Klose netted an impressive seven goals on the way, the most important condemning Russia to the playoffs and ensuring Germany's passage to South Africa.

ABOVE Miroslav Klose is head over heels after scoring the goal that sent Germany to South Africa.

FACTFILE

Full Name: Miroslav Marian Klose
Date of Birth: June 9 1978
Place of Birth: Opole, Poland
Height: 5 ft 11 ½ in (1.82 m)
Playing Position: Striker
National Team: Germany
1st Appearance: 2001

LEFT Klose finds the net against Azerbaijan, one of his seven goals during World Cup qualifying.

WORLD CUP 2010, STAR PLAYERS
ROBIN VAN PERSIE

Robin Van Persie is a striker of both amazing talent and volatile temperament.

While Van Persie's potential is unquestionable, off-field incidents have threatened to curtail the development one of the most promising young players in world football.

Van Persie began his club career, aged 14, with Erste Divisie side SBV Excelsior. His pace and natural eye for goal soon got him noticed by other clubs. But disagreements with coaching staff led to a move to Feyenoord, the two clubs having an agreement allowing the fast transfer of players.

It was the beginning of a turbulent period at the Rotterdam club, where more arguments—this time with coach Bert Van Marwijk—reduced his playing time. He eventually moved to Arsenal for less than £4 million in 2004.

A year later, Van Persie finally got the call from his country, debuting in a World Cup qualifier in 2005. He scored in only his second game and played his way into manager Marco Van Basten's squad for the finals.

Van Persie started every match at the tournament. He scored against Ivory Coast as the Netherlands progressed past the group stage, but they lost to Portugal in the last 16.

Van Persie was instrumental in Netherlands reaching Euro 2008, topping his country's scoring charts with four goals, only for them to lose to Russia in the quarter-finals.

Many onlookers may have believed Van Persie's international career was in doubt after the tournament, because old adversary Van Marwijk was appointed national manager. But the two showed there were no hard feelings and the forward found himself in his new coach's squads.

It appeared Van Persie was coming into his own for the Netherlands, as well as making good progress at Arsenal, but he suffered a bad ankle injury in November 2009.

LEFT Van Persie has the potential to make a big impact on the 2010 World Cup.

FACTFILE

Full Name: Robin Van Persie
Date of Birth: August 6 1983
Place of Birth: Rotterdam, Netherlands
Height: 6 ft 2 in (1.88 m)
Playing Position: Striker
National Team: Netherlands
1st Appearance: 2005

WORLD CUP 2010, STAR PLAYERS
SAMUEL ETO'O

Samuel Eto'o is one of the most successful African footballers in history. His speed, skill, and eye for goal have made him a deadly force both in Europe and internationally over the last decade.

FACTFILE

Full Name: Samuel Eto'o Fils
Date of Birth: March 10 1981
Place of Birth: Douala, Cameroon
Height: 5 ft 11 in (1.80 m)
Playing Position: Striker
National Team: Cameroon
1st Appearance: 1996

RIGHT Samuel Eto'o proudly captains Cameroon to their sixth World Cup finals appearance.

Though his early career in European football was characterized by uncertainty, Eto'o's country recognized his skill immediately; he won his first international cap at 16 in 1996. He was included in Cameroon's 1998 World Cup squad, but only made one appearance, a 3-0 group-stage loss to Italy.

Meanwhile, Eto'o was successively loaned out to Spanish trio Leganés, Espanyol, and Mallorca by Real Madrid before settling on a permanent move to Mallorca in 2000.

His successful spell on the Spanish island coincided with many international triumphs. At just 19, Eto'o won a gold medal at the 2000 Olympic Games in Sydney; he hit the equalizer for Cameroon against Spain to take the final to extra time and, eventually, penalties.

Five goals in Cameroon's two successive African Cup of Nations wins in 2000 and 2002 sent Eto'o on his way to becoming both the tournament's, and his country's, top scorer. He netted his first World Cup goal in 2002, the winner against Saudi Arabia in the group stages. But Cameroon failed to qualify for the finals in 2006, despite Eto'o's four goals.

By this point, Eto'o had signed for Barcelona and had already picked up his first La Liga title. Despite missing out on Germany in 2006, he made up for it by helping his club win the Champions League, scoring in the final against Arsenal. Three years later, he became only the second player to score in two Champions League finals when he struck after just 10 minutes against Manchester United to help secure a second European Cup in 2009.

Eto'o scored nine goals to help Cameroon reach the 2010 World Cup, including the winner in their final match against Morocco.

With an international strike rate of nearly one goal every two games, Eto'o is every part as important to Cameroon as Roger Milla was in the nation's 1990 journey to the quarter-finals.

96 SAMUEL ETO'O

WORLD CUP 2010, STAR PLAYERS
THIERRY HENRY

In a career spanning nearly two decades, Thierry Henry has become one of the most decorated players in the game.

ABOVE Thierry Henry's pace is too much for Serbia goalkeeper Vladimir Stojkovic.

His instinct in the penalty area has seen Henry register more than 300 goals, and pick up every major honor in world football.

Henry graduated from the prestigious French football academy at Clairefontaine and made his first professional appearance for Monaco under Arsène Wenger. Success came in the form of the Ligue 1 championship and an appearance in a Champions League semi-final.

This brought Henry to the attention of France manager Aimé Jacquet, who gave him his debut in October 1997. He was a surprise inclusion in the 1998 World Cup squad, but ended the tournament with three goals and a winner's medal.

A brief spell at Juventus preceded a move to Arsenal, where Henry would establish himself as one of the world's deadliest strikers. He picked up another international trophy in 2000, when France won the European Championship, three more goals making him his country's top scorer in successive tournaments.

After missing out on France's 2001 Confederations Cup win, Henry had a disastrous 2002 World Cup, being red-carded against Uruguay; his country crashed out without him contributing a goal. The pain was eased slightly by Arsenal picking up the Premier League and FA Cup double, Henry scoring 32 goals in all competitions.

He hit four goals, including the winner, in the final as France retained the Confederations Cup in 2003, completing a treble of international victories. A surprise exit in Euro 2004 to Greece soured Henry's enjoyment of a second Premier League title, though he scored two goals at the tournament.

Losses to Barcelona and Italy in the Champions League and World Cup finals, respectively, were low points in an otherwise successful 2006 for Henry. He became Arsenal's all-time leading goal-scorer that year and achieved the same milestone for France in 2007.

Following a move to Barcelona from Arsenal, he was France's only scorer in another below-par performance at Euro 2008, but in 2009 he would finally capture the Champions League.

Henry scored four times as France qualified for the 2010 World Cup finals, though he attracted rare criticism by controversially handling the ball while creating France's winner in the playoffs against the Republic of Ireland.

RIGHT It took Henry just 10 years to surpass Michel Platini as France's all-time top scorer.

FACTFILE

Full Name: Thierry Daniel Henry
Date of Birth: August 17 1977
Place of Birth: Les Ulis, Essonne, France
Height: 6 ft 2 in (1.88 m)
Playing Position: Striker
National Team: France
1st Appearance: 1997

THIERRY HENRY 97

WORLD CUP 2010, STAR PLAYERS
TIM CAHILL

Tim Cahill has become perhaps the most recognizable face in Australian football, but it could have been so different.

FACTFILE

Full Name: Timothy Joel Cahill
Date of Birth: December 6 1979
Place of Birth: Sydney, Australia
Height: 5 ft 10 in (1.78 m)
Playing Position: Midfielder
National Team: Australia
1st Appearance: 2004

Two substitute appearances for Western Samoa in an Under-20 tournament when he was just 14 threatened to derail Cahill's international ambitions.

FIFA would initially not let him play for another country but, since the ruling was overturned, Cahill has never looked back, becoming an integral cog in the Australian national team. His career skyrocketed after one goal in particular brought him to the attention of the football world.

Cahill arrived in England in 1997 after Millwall snapped him up from Sydney United. He made his debut the following year, but it wasn't until he scored the only goal in an FA Cup semi-final against Premier League Sunderland that his career took off. Though Millwall lost the final to Manchester United, interest in Cahill was high and he signed for Everton two months later.

He finally made his debut for Australia in March 2004, while still at Millwall, four years after the Australian FA originally called him up for the 2000 Olympic Games. Cahill participated in the 2004 Games, but Australia finished second to eventual winners Argentina in the group stage.

Cahill scored seven goals in qualification for the 2006 World Cup, helping Australia reach the finals for only the second time in their history. And it was in Germany that he had his proudest moment to date for the national team.

Australia were trailing 1-0 to Japan in their opening group match when Cahill was brought on. He scored twice in the last six minutes to turn the game on its head, before John Aloisi hit a third in injury time. These heroics counted for little, however, as the Australians were knocked out by Italy via a controversial 95th-minute penalty.

Cahill struck four goals as Australia reached their second consecutive finals in South Africa.

LEFT Tim Cahill displays his trademark goal celebration against Qatar.

WORLD CUP 2010, STAR PLAYERS
WAYNE ROONEY

Wayne Rooney has often been hailed as the great hope of English football, and has already proven vital to the national team's success.

Rooney's burst onto the scene at just 16 years of age, and his pace and power soon made him one of the world's best strikers.

He came off Everton's bench to score the winner against then League champions Arsenal in 2002, and was immediately hailed as Britain's best young player. The hype did not faze him and he made his debut for England a year later, aged just 17.

Rooney's debut against Australia made him the team's youngest-ever player. He added youngest scorer to his list of personal accolades when he netted against Macedonia in September 2003. Rooney had his breakthrough tournament for England at Euro 2004, scoring twice against Switzerland and again against Croatia.

The weight of the nation was on his shoulders as fans hoped for their first trophy since 1966. However, disaster struck against Portugal in the quarter-finals when Rooney was injured, and his team went on to lose on penalties.

Rooney gained interest from a host of other clubs and signed for Manchester United in August 2004 for a fee of more than US$ 40 million (£25 million)—a record figure for a player less than 20.

Panic struck when Rooney was injured in the run-up to the World Cup in 2006. He made the tournament after intense rehabilitation, but it was a case of history repeating against the Portuguese in the quarter-final stage as he again exited the game early, this time sent off for a foul on Ricardo Carvalho.

The quick-tempered forward returned to competitive action after suspension, scoring twice in a disappointing Euro 2008 qualifying campaign, where England failed to qualify.

England's path to South Africa saw Rooney hit an incredible nine goals, including braces against Andorra, Belarus, and Kazakhstan, on the way to them finishing top of their group.

His goal tally cemented his importance to the team and his country's hopes, a fact recognized when he was made captain for a friendly against Brazil in late 2009.

LEFT Rooney scores his ninth qualifying goal in a 5-1 win over Croatia at Wembley Stadium.

ABOVE Despite being only 24 years old, Wayne Rooney has already scored more than 100 career goals.

FACTFILE

Full Name: Wayne Mark Rooney
Date of Birth: October 24 1985
Place of Birth: Croxteth, Liverpool, England
Height: 5 ft 10 in (1.78 m)
Playing Position: Striker
National Team: England
1st Appearance: 2003

EUROPEAN CHAMPIONSHIP

The creation of the European Championship and UEFA, the governing body of football in Europe, went hand in hand. FIFA had existed since 1904 and it ruled the world, but half a century later the European countries opted to register their own identity. By the end of the 1950s, not only was the European Championship a reality but the European Champion Clubs' Cup had sparked a revolution.

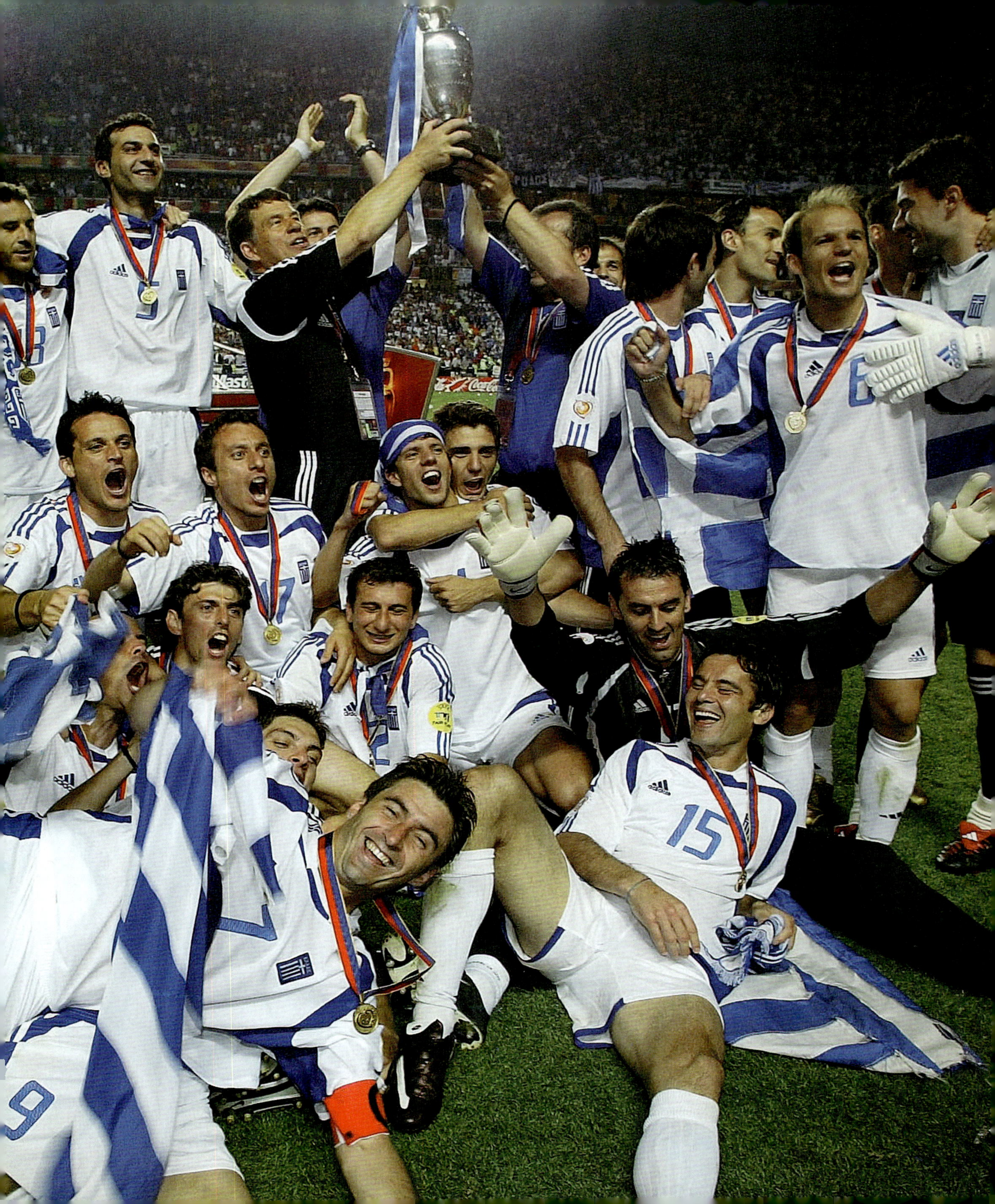

EUROPEAN CHAMPIONSHIP
FOUNDATION & 1960s

The idea of a rival competition to the World Cup was nothing new. Frenchman Henri Delaunay, who lent his name to the tournament, discussed the concept before World War II but never saw his dream become reality.

PAGE 36 Miroslav Klose scores for Germany against Turkey, 2008

PAGE 37 Euro 2004 winners Greece celebrate

THE RESULT 1960
Location: Paris
Final: Soviet Union 2 Yugoslavia 1 (after extra time)
Shirts: Soviets red, Yugoslavia blue
Scorers: Metreveli, Ponedelnik; Galic

SOVIET UNION

Yashin
Tchekeli   Maslenkin   Kroutikov
Voinov   Netto
Metreveli   Ivanov   Ponedelnik   Bubukin   Meskhi
Kostic   Galic   Jerkovic   Matus   Sekularac
Perusic   Zanetic
Jusufi   Miladinovic   Durkovic
Vidinic

YUGOSLAVIA

FIFA feared such a tournament for the elite might undermine the status of its own World Cup but finally, in 1958, the European Championship took shape under its original name of the European Nations Cup. Sadly, Delaunay, Secretary General of the French Football Federation, died in 1954 and was unable to witness the creation of his dream. So his colleagues ensured that his name lived on by giving the tournament the alternative title of Coupe Henri Delaunay.

The inaugural competition comprised 17 countries playing on a two-leg knockout basis followed by the semi-finals, a third place play-off and then the final in one host country—appropriately enough in France.

Spain withdrew from their quarter-final against the Soviet Union because of political pressure by dictator Francisco Franco while England, Italy and West Germany failed to enter for fear of fixture congestion. The Soviets, inspired by legendary goalkeeper Lev Yashin, went on to become the first winners. They recovered from a one-goal deficit to overcome Yugoslavia 2-1 in a tense final in the old Parc des Princes in Paris.

The next competition, in 1964, was also marred by political interference. This time, Greece withdrew, after being told to face Albania in an early round though the nations were officially at war.

At least by now Cold War tension between the Soviet Union and Spain had eased, which was fortunate because the Soviets qualified for the finals that were hosted by Spain. In the semi-finals, the Soviet Union defeated Denmark 3-0 in Barcelona, while Spain scrambled past Hungary, courtesy of a 2-1 in extra time win in Madrid.

Spain soon went a goal behind in the final at Real Madrid's Santiago Bernabéu Stadium, much to the distress of most of the 79,115 spectators. Fortunately for the hosts, Barcelona's Jesus María Pereda equalized and Zaragoza's Marcelino Martínez wrote himself into Spanish sporting history by heading in a late winner. England had entered for the first time, but had not progressed beyond the first round. New manager Alf Ramsey saw his men held 1-1 by France at Sheffield Wednesday's Hillsborough stadium, to then collapse 5-2 four months later in Paris.

CHALLENGE OF COMPETITION CHANGES

The tournament's name was now altered to the European Championship for the 1968 event and along with it came a change of format. For this event, eight groups of teams faced each other twice, with the top nation from each group progressing to two-legged quarter finals. Italy were hosts and for the first and only time a match was decided on the toss of a coin.

England, as the reigning World Champions, qualified for the inaugural European Championship finals with largely the same squad that had won the 1966 World Cup. So hopes were high that the Three Lions could roar to a second successive major championship. But England fell 1-0 to a late goal by Yugoslavia in a match littered with fouls and marred by Alan Müllery's sending-off one minute from the final whistle with Dragan Dzajic scoring the decisive strike.

Italy beat the Soviets in the other semi-final on an infamous coin toss after a scoreless stalemate and no time to organize a replay.

Yugoslavia dominated in the final at Rome, but were punished for not being able to beat Dino Zoff more than once. Italy equalized nine minutes from time, made five changes for the replay and strolled past the exhausted Yugoslavs 2-0.

RIGHT The Henri Delaunay Cup

BELOW Spain vs USSR in the 1964 final, Madrid

THE RESULT 1964
Location: Madrid
Final: Spain 2 Soviet Union 1
Shirts: Spain blue; Soviets red
Scorers: Pereda, Martínez; Khusainov

SPAIN
Iribar
Rivilla Zoco Olivella Calleja
Pereda Fusté Suárez
Amaro Martínez Lapetra
Khusainov Ponedelnik Chislenko
Korneev Ivanov Voronin
Mudrik Anichkine Shesternev Chustikov
Yashin
SOVIET UNION

THE RESULT 1968
Location: Rome
Final: Italy 1 Yugoslavia 1 (after extra time)
Shirts: Italy blue, Yugoslavia white
Scorers: Domenghini; Dzajic

ITALY
Zoff
Burgnich Castano Guarneri Facchetti
Domenghini Ferrini Juliano Lodetti
Anastasi Prati
Dzajic Musemic Petkovic
Holcer Acimovic Trivic
Damjanovic Paunovic Pavlovic Fazlagic
Pantelic
YUGOSLAVIA

FOUNDATION & 1960s 103

EUROPEAN CHAMPIONSHIP 1970s

"I don't think we could have played any better."
— HELMUT SCHÖB

West Germany produced the finest football yet seen in the competition en route to a 1972 victory in Belgium, seeing off the Soviet Union at the Heysel Stadium. But both Italy and England failed to reach the finals.

1972

Belgium had delighted their fans by sending home holders Italy along the way, while England were ousted by the in-form West Germans in the two-leg knock-out quarter-finals.

West German manager Helmut Schön rebuilt his team after reaching the 1970 World Cup semi-finals in Mexico. Veteran striker Uwe Seeler had retired, so Schön looked to fast-rising Bayern Munich for the foundation of his new team.

The key man was Franz Beckenbauer, already a World Cup hero in 1966 and 1970, who was moved back from midfield to his personally favored role of attacking sweeper.

Striker Gerd Müller was another of the 1970 heroes alongside the new stars from Bayern Munich, namely attacking left back Paul Breitner and striker Uli Hoeness. Furthermore, Schön replaced Wolfgang Overath in midfield with the Borussia Mönchengladbach playmaker general Gunter Netzer.

Beckenbauer and Netzer commanded the first leg of the quarter-final at England's Wembley Stadium guiding the Germans to their inaugural victory with a 3-1 success. They had little difficulty securing a scoreless draw in the return leg against Sir Alf Ramsey's surprisingly unadventurous England side in West Berlin.

Belgium hosted the four-team finals but faced favorites West Germany at the semi-final stage.

The Germans edged through 2-1 with two goals from the prolific Müller. In the other semi-final, the Soviet Union maintained their record of reaching the last four of every final since the tournament's inception and overcame Hungary—which missed a late penalty—via Anatoli Konkov's deflected shot.

In the final, West Germany were in control, with the Soviets psychologically beaten by their recent 4-1 thrashing at the hands of West Germany. Müller, who had scored all four in the recent friendly, was on fire in the final and notched a goal in each half in the 3-0 triumph. Midfielder Herbert Wimmer added the third to claim Germany's first European Championship in front of 50,000 fans.

THE RESULT 1972
Location: Brussels
Final: West Germany 3 Soviet Union 0
Shirts: Germany white, Soviets red
Scorers: Müller 2, Wimmer

WEST GERMANY
Maier
Höttges Beckenbauer Schwarzenbeck Breitner
Hoeness Wimmer Netzer Heynckes
Müller Kremers

Kozinkevich Banischevsky Baidachny
(Onishenko)
Konkov Kolotov Troshkine
(Dolmatov)
Kaplichny Istomine Khurtsilava Dzodzuaschvili
Rudakov
SOVIET UNION

RIGHT Captains Bobby Moore of England and Franz Beckenbauer of West Germany, 1972

1976

The tournament, in Yugoslavia, was the last in which the hosts were chosen at a late stage after the qualifying rounds. The finals went on to be expanded to eight nations, with the hosts granted automatic exemption for the qualifying rounds.

Czechoslovakia emerged as surprise winners—launching their outsiders' campaign in the semifinals by stunning Holland. Two years earlier, the Dutch had come close to being crowned world champions and, with many of their outstanding players peaking, had been expected to reach the final at the very least.

It was a sad occasion for Johan Cruyff because it was to be his last shot at glory as an international player. This became his final major tournament in a Dutch national team shirt.

West Germany, as World Cup holders, had good reason to assume that they were well-placed to win, but that complacency meant they found themselves trailing 2-0 at halftime against hosts Yugoslavia. Gerd Müller had retired from national team football but another Müller, Köln center forward Dieter, (no relation), came to the Germans' rescue on his international debut. He scored twice in the second half with his 82nd-minute equalizer forcing extra-time. Müller went on to complete a hat-trick in a famous 4-2 victory.

The final offered yet more drama, with Czechoslovakia taking an early two-goal lead against the West Germans. Manager Helmut Schön was kept waiting until the last minute of normal time before he could celebrate an equalizer from Bernd Holzenbein. Extra time failed to produce a winner, so penalties were necessary to decide the title for the first time in the history of the championship. West Germany's Uli Hoeness was the first to crack when he kicked the ball over keeper Ivo Viktor's bar and Czechoslovakia took the title after their midfield general Antonin Panenka kept his cool and scored with a chip past the West German keeper Sepp Maier.

THE RESULT 1976

Location: Belgrade
Final: Czechoslovakia 2 West Germany 2 (Czechoslovakia 5-3 on penalties after extra time)
Shirts: Czechs red, Germany white
Scorers: Svehlík, Dobiás; Müller, Hölzenbein

CZECHOSLOVAKIA

Viktor
Pivarnik Ondrus Capkovic Gögh
Dobiás (Vesely) Móder Panenka Masny
Svehlík (Jurkemik) Neboda
Hölzenbein Müller
Hoeness Beer (Bongartz) Bonhof Wimmer (Flohe)
Vogts Schwarzenbeck Beckenbauer Dietz
Maier

WEST GERMANY

LEFT Herbert Wimmer scores West Germany's second goal in the 1972 final against the Soviet Union

EUROPEAN CHAMPIONSHIP
1980s

UEFA responded to the fast-increasing popularity of the European Championship in 1980 by opting to widen out the qualifying potential and make the finals tournament itself more of a spectacle.

THE RESULT 1980
Location: Rome
Final: West Germany 2 Belgium 1
Shirts: Germany white, Belgium red
Scorers: Hruebsch 2; Vandereycken

WEST GERMANY

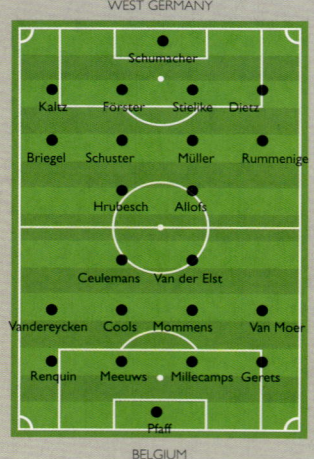

Schumacher
Kaltz Forster Stielike Dietz
Briegel Schuster Müller Rummenige
Hrubesch Allofs
Ceulemans Van der Elst
Vandereycken Cools Mommens Van Moer
Renquin Meeuws Millecamps Gerets
Pfaff

BELGIUM

1980

This time, seven countries progressed out of a solely group-based qualifying system to contest the title in Italy along with the host nation, staging the event for the second time in four tournaments. Two groups of four were contested, the winners of each progressing directly to the final in the Stadio Olimpico in Rome.

Hosts Italy had fully expected to be there for the climax after being drawn in the easier of the two groups. The formidable West Germans, holders Czechoslovakia, and two-times World Cup runners-up Holland had all wound up in the other pool. Instead Italy scored a single goal and missed out on top spot, underdogs Belgium taking their place instead. England failed to progress beyond the group, their concentration disturbed by hooligan violence at their tie against hosts Italy in Turin.

RIGHT West Germany's Horst Hrubesch hails his last-minute winning goal

TOP RIGHT Holland's captain Ruud Gullit in triumph in 1988

106 EUROPEAN CHAMPIONSHIP

1984

Michel Platini dominated the finals from start to finish, scoring a record nine goals and captaining hosts France to their first major international trophy. On his way to winning the European Player of the Year three times, Platini scored the lone winning goal against Denmark in the opening match, hat-tricks against Belgium and Yugoslavia, one against Portugal in the semis and the opener against Spain in the final.

Manager Michel Hidalgo used Platini in a free attacking role at the apex of a superbly balanced midfield featuring Luis Fernandez, Jean Tigana, and Alain Giresse. They topped their group with three wins in three games, nine goals scored and only two conceded by keeper Joel Bats.

Holders West Germany failed to progress even beyond the group stage. They finished third behind Spain and Portugal and ahead of only Romania, and sacked manager Jupp Derwall, their winning boss in 1980, on their return home.

THE RESULT 1984
Location: Paris
Final: France 2 Spain 0
Shirts: France blue, Spain red
Scorers: Platini, Bellone

FRANCE
Bats
Domergue (Amoros) — Battiston — Le Roux — Bossis
Tigana — Fernandez — Platini — Giresse
Lacombe (Genghini) — Bellone
Carrasco — Santillana
Casas (Sarabia) — Manrique — Gomez — Javier
Urquiaga — Puig (Bonillo) — Redondo — Camacho
Echarri
SPAIN

The decisive match in the other group was played out in Naples between West Germany and Holland. Playing their best football since the 1974 World Cup, West Germany seized the initiative and carved out a 3-0 lead with a hat-trick by Klaus Allofs before a Johnny Rep penalty and Rene Van de Kerkhof's long-distance effort gave Holland late but vain hope. Man of the match for the Germans was young blond midfielder Bernd Schuster.

West Germany were clear favorites to beat Belgium in the final and snatched an early lead through giant center forward Horst Hrubesch. Belgium came out fighting at the start of the second half, however, and equalized through a penalty converted by Rene Vandereycken, though the Germans claimed that sweeper Uli Stielike's foul had been committed just outside the box. In the final minutes, Hrubesch scored again, heading home a corner from another outstanding newcomer in Karl-Heinz Rummenigge.

1988

Holland landed their one and only major prize in the 1988 finals in West Germany to complete a continental double, PSV Eindhoven having carried off the European Champions' Cup only weeks earlier. As ever, the Dutch had internal problems to resolve along the way. Striker Marco Van Basten had to be persuaded to play by friend and mentor Johan Cruyff. Manager Rinus Michels left Van Basten out of the line-up for the Dutch players opening group defeat by the Soviet Union, but Van Basten started next time out against England and hit a hat-trick. England, already beaten by the Irish Republic, then lost 3-1 to the Soviets and finished bottom of the group.

Confident hosts West Germany topped the other group ahead of Italy, Spain, and Denmark, but were knocked out in the semi-finals proved the end of their road. Holland hit back from one-down to beat their hosts 2-1 in extra time and followed this up by beating an injury and suspension-weakened Soviet Union in the final. Van Basten's volleyed second goal was hailed as one of the finest of all time.

THE RESULT 1988
Location: Munich
Final: Holland 2 Soviet Union 0
Shirts: Holland orange, Soviet white
Scorers: Gullit, Van Basten

HOLLAND
Van Breukelen
Van Aerle — Rijkaard — R Koeman — Van Tiggelen
Vanenburg — E Koeman — Wouters — Muhren
Gullit — Van Basten
Protasov (Pasulko) — Belanov
Mikhailichenko — Zavarov — Litovchenko — Aleinikov
Rats — Demanyenko — Khidiyatulline — Gotsmanov (Baltacha)
Dassaev
SOVIET UNION

1980s 107

EUROPEAN CHAMPIONSHIP MOMENTS

1960s

LEFT Slav goal keeper Blagoje Vidinic halts a Soviet attack

RIGHT Eusébio's Portugal crashed out early in the 1964 event

BELOW Spain celebrate their 1964 success

1980s

BELOW England fall to hosts Italy in Turin in the first round

BELOW Michel Platini was France's nine-goal top scorer in 1986

108 EUROPEAN CHAMPIONSHIP

1980s

BELOW Kevin Keegan is sent crashing by a Spanish defender

RIGHT Denmark's Kim Vilfort holds the 1992 trophy

ABOVE Iain Giresse of France controls the ball during the 1984 European Championship final

RIGHT England celebrate their second goal against Holland in 1996

1990s

2000s

BELOW Spanish reserve goalkeeper Pepe Reina (right) and teammate David Villa celebrate victory in 2008

ABOVE England prepare to take the three Lions to the 2000 finals

MOMENTS 109

EUROPEAN CHAMPIONSHIP
1990s

The dynamic Danish team surprised Europe in Sweden in 1992. This was also the first time a unified Germany took part in international competition and the first time that players' names were printed on their backs.

FAR RIGHT Paul Gascoigne volleys England's second goal against Scotland at Euro 96

1992

Denmark's remarkable feat was as unexpected as their very participation. The Danes joined the tournament only after Yugoslavia were barred for security reasons on the eve of the finals—and when the Yugoslav squad was already in Sweden—after political instability in the Balkans had erupted into armed conflict.

Richard Moller Nielsen, the Danish team's manager, was at home redecorating his kitchen when he took the call instructing him to recall his players from their family holidays in the sun.

Not surprisingly, the Danes failed initially to impress before managing to finally string their game together for the last group match against France. The French, managed by Michel Platini, disappointed despite having been unbeaten in the qualifiers and fielding an attack that featured Jean-Pierre Papin and Eric Cantona.

UEFA had changed the tournament format once more, inserting knock-out semi-finals between the group stage and the final.

Denmark, defying numerous injuries, took the lead twice in their semi-final against a complacent Holland, both goals scored by Henrik Larsen. In the resultant penalty shoot-out, Marco Van Basten—Holland's match-winner from the 1988 final—saw his penalty saved by Peter Schmeichel.

In the other semi-final, holders Germany never needed to get out of second gear on their way to a 3-2 victory over hosts Sweden. The unified German side included the likes of Karlheinz Riedle, Thomas Hässler, and Jürgen Klinsmann, and few believed Denmark could test them in the final in the Ullevi stadium in Gothenburg.

Instead, they showed skill, cunning, and determination in abundance. Schmeichel laid claim to being the best goalkeeper in the world, while Lars Olsen was a rock in the center of defense and Brian Laudrup—young brother of Michael—proved a danger on the counterattack.

Against the Germans, midfielder John Jensen put Denmark ahead and Kim Vilfort capped a fairytale fortnight with a second goal 12 minutes from the end of the game.

1996

In 1966, the number of finalists doubled to 16 for the first major tournament staged in England since the World Cup 30 years earlier. Germany clinched their third crown when Oliver Bierhoff scored the first ever "golden goal" in the competition's history.

The golden goal was a short-lived attempt to find a better solution to deciding drawn matches. Instead of using penalties, a match was halted the moment a breakthrough goal was scored during extra time.

England, who had lost in the semi-finals, at least had the satisfaction of seeing Germany, their competition, re-establish their position on the footballing map after their failure to qualify for the previous World Cup and a decade of disaster.

THE RESULT 1992
Location: Gothenburg, Germany
Final: Denmark 2 Germany 0
Shirts: Denmark red, Germany white
Scorers: Jensen, Vilfort

DENMARK
Schmeichel
Sivebaek Nielsen Olsen Piechnik
(Christiansen)
Christofte Jensen Vilfort Larsen
Povlsen Laudrup
Riedle Klinsmann
Brehme Hässler Sammer Effenberg
(Doll) (Thom)
Helmer Reuter Kohler Buchwald
Illgner
GERMANY

Granting hosting rights to England had been an important signal from UEFA that it considered the English game had at last got on top of the problem of hooliganism. England boasted the finest stadia in Europe because of the massive rebuilding necessitated by the imposition of all-seater requirements.

Paul Gascoigne's wonder goal against Scotland set the tournament alight, but even better was to come when England swept Holland aside 4-1 at Wembley with a display rarely matched in their modern footballing history.

In the semi-finals, however, Germany broke English hearts by holding their nerve in a penalty shoot-out. Gareth Southgate saw his penalty saved by German keeper Andy Köpke, and midfielder Andreas Möller made no mistake with his subsequent penalty shot. The Germans thus progressed to a final back at Wembley against the technically adroit Czechs, who had ousted Aimé Jacquet's France in yet another shoot-out in the other semi-final.

The Germans, under the management of former title-winner Berti Vogts, were typically well-organized, with Matthias Sammer an excellent sweeper. But they failed initially to break down a counterattacking Czech side, who took the lead though a penalty from Patrik Berger.

The Czechs were 30 minutes from victory at that point. But then German manager Vogts sent on center forward Bierhoff as a substitute. First he equalized and then, five minutes into extra time, wrote himself into the record books with the first-ever golden goal in a major tournament.

THE RESULT 1996

Location: Wembley, London
Final: Germany 2 Czech Republic 1 (Germany on golden goal in extra time)
Shirts: Germany white, Czechs red
Scorers: Bierhoff 2; Berger

GERMANY

Köpke

Babbel Helmer Sammer Ziege

Hässler Strunz Eilts Scholl
(Bode) (Bierhoff)

Klinsmann Kuntz

Kuka

Berger Bejbl Nedved Poborsky
(Smicer)
Nemec Suchoparek Kadlec Rada Hornak

Kouba

CZECH REPUBLIC

1990s

EUROPEAN CHAMPIONSHIP 2000s

> "At last we have proved Spain can be winners."
>
> MANAGER LUIS ARAGONES

France, the reigning world champions, beat Dino Zoff's Italy at the first European Championship final to be co-hosted—by Belgium and Holland—in 2000. Greece won the 2004 contest and resurgent Spain the 2008 finals.

FAR RIGHT Cristiano Ronaldo of Portugal in action during the 2004 quarter-final match between Portugal and England

BOTTOM France enjoy their second title win in Rotterdam in 2000

2000

France squeezed past bitter rivals Italy in the final of the 2000 European Championship. Sylvain Wiltord equalized in the final seconds of the 90 minutes, allowing David Trezeguet to score 13 minutes into extra time with a thunderous volley. France thus became the first reigning World Cup Champions to add the European crown to their list of achievements.

Italy had come so close to winning the title, but manager Dino Zoff resigned in anger after the defeat, upset by the public criticism of his tactics and team selection by Prime Minister Silvio Berlusconi.

For England, the event proved a huge disappointment. Under the management of former player Kevin Keegan, they failed to progress beyond the group stage.

THE RESULT 2000
Location: Rotterdam
Final: France 2 Italy 1
(France on golden goal in extra time)
Shirts: France blue, Italy white
Scorers: Wiltord, Trezeguet; Delvecchio

FRANCE
- Barthez
- Thuram, Desailly, Blanc (Pires), Lizarazu
- Djorkaeff (Trezeguet), Deschamps, Vieira, Zidane
- Henry, Dugarry (Wiltord)

ITALY
- Toldo
- Maldini, Cannavaro, Nesta, Pessotto
- Fiore, Iuliano (Del Piero), Di Biagio (Ambrosini), Albertini
- Delvecchio, Totti (Montella)

112 EUROPEAN CHAMPIONSHIP

2004

The 2004 finals produced an upset few had predicted. Greece, who had qualified previously for only one World Cup (1994) and one European championship (1980), shocked hosts Portugal 1-0 by beating them in a dramatic final.

The Greeks, who had begun the tournament as 150-1 outsiders, also eliminated holders France as well as the Czech Republic, in this case with a silver goal, a rule that replaced the previous golden goal in 2003 before being abolished shortly afterwards. The silver goal meant that teams played on to the next formal stoppage (half-time or full-time) in extra time after a goal had been scored.

Greece's victory over Portugal in the final in Lisbon came courtesy of a solid defense, great goalkeeping, and an opportunist goal by Angelos Charisteas. The result stunned European football. However, it was not the only surprise of the tounament—Germany, Italy, and Spain had all been knocked out in the group stage.

Portugal's defeat in the final in Lisbon—in front of their own fans, denied manager Luiz Felipe Scolari a unique feat. Scolari would have become the first non-European manager to have won the continental crown.

2008

Spain ended a 44-year losing spell by winning the finals in Austria and Switzerland. Neither of the co-hosts made it through the opening group stage, but that did not affect the party atmosphere in Vienna after Spain, winners in 1964 and runners-up in 1984, defeated Germany 1-0 in the final. Liverpool's Fernando Torres scored the winning goal after 33 minutes.

Veteran manager Luis Aragones, a reserve to the winners of 1964, said afterwards: "At last we have proved that Spain can win the big prizes." After years of underachievement in major tournaments. Spain won all six of their matches, albeit they needed two fine saves from goalkeeper-captain Iker Casillas to defeat World Cup-holders Italy on penalties in the quarter-finals. Xavi Hernandez, the Barcelona midfielder who laid on Torres's goal in the final, was hailed as UEFA's official player of the tournament.

Portugal, Croatia, Holland, and Spain were decisive winners of the groups. All were certain of qualifying after two of their three matches and rested key players in their concluding matches. That break in competitive momentum proved fatal for all but Spain, however, since the other three all lost in the quarter-finals.

Portugal blamed their quarter-final exit to Germany partly on the distractions raised by manager Luiz Felipe Scolari's imminent move to Chelsea, and partly on a media frenzy over the uncertain future of Cristiano Ronaldo.

Germany struggled to get the better of Austria in their concluding group match before defeating Portugal and then Turkey 3-2 in a dramatic semi-final. Major disappointments were World Cup runners-up France, who were first-round failures.

THE RESULT 2004
Location: Lisbon, Portugal
Final: Greece 1 Portugal 0
Shirts: Greece white, Portugal red
Scorers: Charisteas

PORTUGAL

Ricardo
Miguel Andrade Ricardo Carvalho Nuno
(Paulo Ferreira)   Valente
Ronaldo Maniche Costinha Deco
         (Rui Costa)
         Figo   Pauleta
                 (Nuno Gomes)
        Charisteas   Vryzas
                     (Papadopoulos)
Giannakopoulos Basinas Katsouranis Zagorakis
                (Venetidis)
Fyssas   Dellas   Kapsis   Seitaridis
              Nikopolidis

GREECE

THE RESULT 2008
Location: Vienna, Austria
Final: Spain 1 Germany 0
Shirts: Spain red, Germany white
Scorers: Torres

SPAIN

            Casillas
Ramos   Puyol Marchena   Capdevila
            Senna
Iniesta Xavi   Fabregas   Silva
                (Alonso)   (Cazorla)
            Torres
            Klose
           (Gomez)
     Podolski   Ballack Schweinsteiger
  Hitzlsperger (Kuranyi) Frings
Lahm   Metzelder Mertesacker Friedrich
(Jansen)
            Lehmann

GERMANY

REGIONAL CUPS

The speed with which football encircled the globe as well as the rapid-fire popularity of the World Cup inspired players, officials, and fans from Chile to China. Each region soon created its own governing body, which ultimately launched its own "copycat" competitions for national teams. The Copa America was the first, launched in 1916, and this was eventually copied in Africa, Asia, Europe, and Oceania, plus Central and North America.

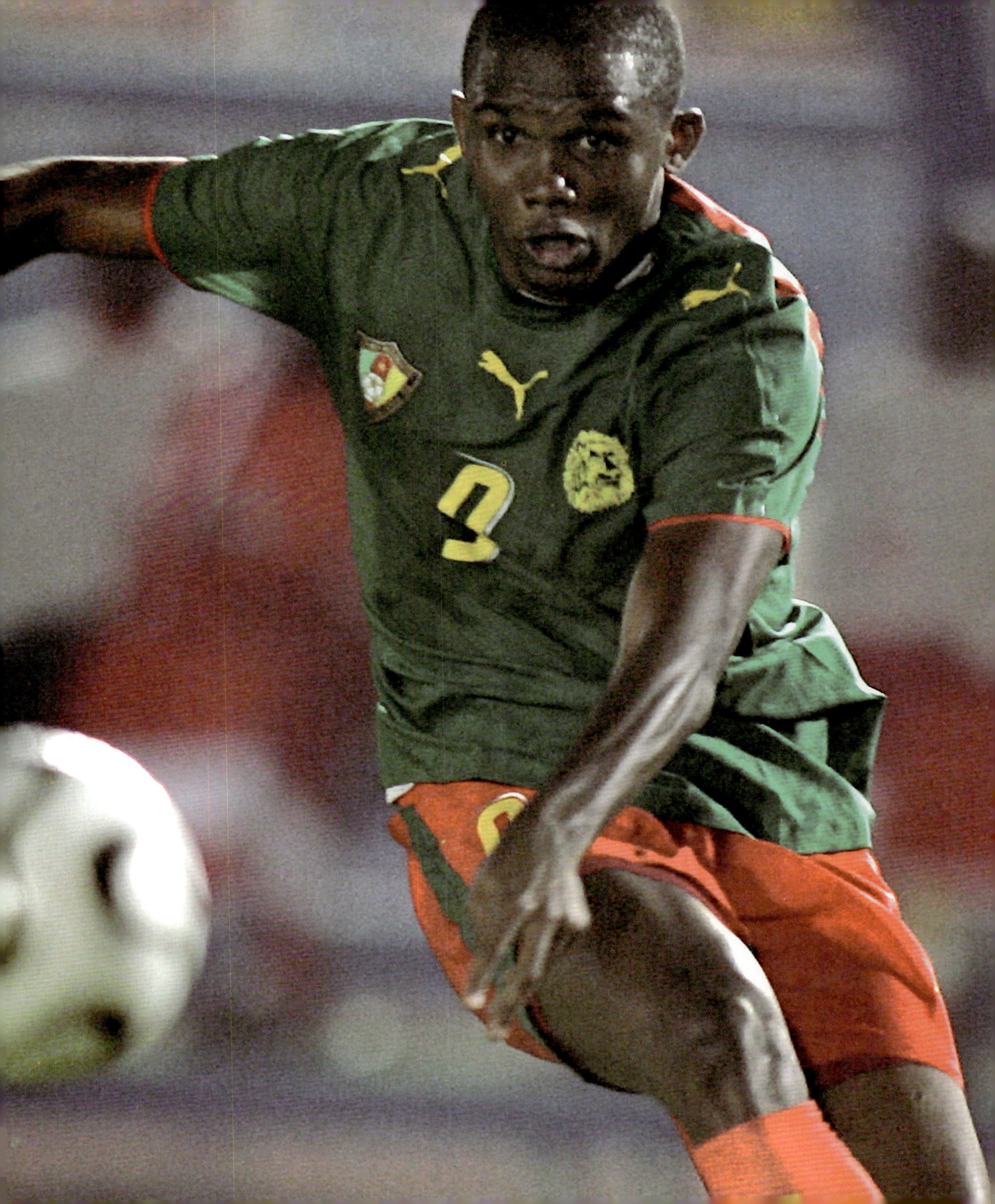

REGIONAL CUPS
COPA AMERICA

The Copa America boasts the unique distinction of being the world's longest-running international football tournament. It began in July 1916 as part of Argentina's centenary independence celebrations.

ABOVE Argentina's midfielder Juan Roman Riquelme takes on Coloia in 2007

PAGE 50 The Uruguay team which won the 1917 Copa America

PAGE 51 Samuel Eto'o scores against Angola in the 2006 African Nations Cup

The competition was originally called the Campeonato Sudamericano de Selecciones (South American Championship of National Teams). Participation was limited initially to member nations of CONMEBOL, the South American football confederation. However, because the organization comprises only ten nations, the competition was expanded in 1993 to include invited participants from the Caribbean and North and Central America.

Usually two or three teams receive such an invitation, invariably one of them being Mexico, partly because of the geographical proximity and partly because of the lucrative television rights.

The United States have also been invited regularly since 1997, but have turned down the offer several times because of scheduling conflicts with Major League Soccer. However, they did accept an invitation for the 2007 tournament, ending a 12-year absence.

Until recently, the tournament used to take place every two years, but in 2007, CONMEBOL decided that it should be held every four years but in an odd-numbered year so that it did not clash with the World Cup and European Championship. The 2007 event took place in Venezuela, so a second rotation will begin in 2011, starting with Argentina. Uruguay and Argentina have each won the championship 14 times, followed by Brazil with eight. These totals exclude unofficial, early 20th-century competitions.

SOUTH AMERICAN CHAMPIONSHIP

In its early years, when it was known as the South American Championship, the tournament did much to popularize the game and raise standards of play across the continent.

The 1940s are regarded as its heyday, but a generation later it fell into neglect, because South America's military governments looked disparagingly at their neighbors. The national federations of major countries such as Brazil, Argentina, and Uruguay also began to question the wisdom of competing after scouts from Italy and Spain began to converge on the event and, almost before the final whistle had been blown, lured their star players away to Europe.

Most painfully hit were Argentina. They won the 1957 tournament on the inspiration of an outstanding inside-forward trio of Humberto Maschio, Antonio Valentin Angelillo, and Omar Enrique Sivori. The manner of their triumph prompted predictions of World Cup glory the following year. However, within months, all three had been spirited away to Italy; all three were even playing for Italy within three years.

The gradual return of democracy in the mid-1980s—coupled with the growing power of television—sparked a resurgence of interest in the competition, with the event played in a single country, rather than on a home-and-away basis.

Problems remain for South American administrators to resolve. The most important is the fact that the Copa is staged in the middle of the South American winter—which is also the close-season in Europe, where all the most glamorous players operate. Not only are European clubs reluctant to release their players, but the stars themselves are wary of the risk of burn-out. Thus Barcelona's Ronaldinho and Milan's Kaka both withdrew from the Brazilian squad heading for the 2007 event in Venezuela. As it happened, even without them, Brazil won the trophy. In the final they defeated Argentina for the second time in a row.

EXPLOSIVE FINAL

In 2004, in Lima, Brazil won on penalties after Argentina had twice taken the lead, the second time through substitute Cesar Delgado, with three minutes of normal time remaining. Adriano equalized in the third minute of stoppage-time with his seventh goal of the competition.

That goal sparked a brawl as Brazil's players celebrated in front of the Argentina bench. Argentina responded by squirting water at their opponents and referee Carlos Amarilla summoned riot-police to stop the trouble. Adriano was booked for removing his shirt.

Argentina seemed more unsettled by the incident and missed their first two penalties: Andres D'Alessandro fired his effort at goalkeeper Julio Cesar and Gabriel Heinze fired wildly over the bar. Brazil converted all their penalties, just as they had in their semi-final win over Uruguay.

In 2007, Brazil found it much easier. Argentina were favorites but never justified their status and subsided to one early spectacular goal from Julio Baptista, an unfortunate own goal by their own captain Roberto Ayala, and then a superb counterattacking strike from Dani Alves.

FOOTBALL FACTS

RECENT WINNERS
1987 Host: Argentina. Winners: Uruguay
1989 Host: Brazil. Winners: Brazil
1991 Host: Chile. Winners: Argentina
1993 Host: Ecuador. Winners: Argentina
1995 Host: Uruguay. Winners: Uruguay
1997 Host: Bolivia. Winners: Brazil
1999 Host: Paraguay. Winner: Brazil
2001 Host: Colombia. Winners: Colombia
2004 Host: Peru. Winners: Brazil
2007 Host: Venezuela. Winners: Brazil

ALL-TIME WINNERS
Argentina, Uruguay 14 each; Brazil 8; Paraguay, Peru 2 each; Bolivia, Colombia 1 each.

LEFT Brazilian players celebrate their victory against Argentina in 2007

COPA AMÉRICA

REGIONAL CUPS
AFRICAN NATIONS CUP

Africa has become a magnet for cash-rich European clubs who are seeking an apparently unending source of talents. The biennial tournament has been played since 1957.

Players such as Didier Drogba, Samuel Eto'o, Michael Essien, and Jay-Jay Okocha have moved into superstardom within the European club system, using their experience and talents to inspire youngsters back home to follow in their footsteps. But it was not always the case. In the colonial era of much of the last century, European national teams brought African players such as Just Fontaine and Eusébio onboard for their own use.

Fontaine, born and brought up in Morocco, set a World Cup record of 13 goals in 1958 while representing France. Eusébio, born and brought up in Mozambique, finished as top scorer with nine goals for Portugal in the 1966 World Cup finals. But a move for change was already underway. Ten years earlier, in 1956, the Confederation of African Football had been organized in Lisbon and plotted a first Cup of Nations the following year in Khartoum, the capital city of Sudan. It has since been staged virtually every two years, which makes it international football's African regional championship.

RIGHT Jay-Jay Okocha on the attack for Nigeria in the 2004 finals

BELOW South Africa's "Bafana Bafana" line up before their 2002 clash with Burkina Faso

EGYPT CROWNED AS SIX OF THE BEST
Only three nations competed that first time. There should have been four but South Africa were barred because its own government, wedded to the segregationist apartheid system, refused to approve the selection of a multi-racial team.

Ironically, 39 years later—after the downfall of apartheid—South Africa returned to rescue the Confederation by staging the event after Kenya's late withdrawal as hosts.

118 REGIONAL CUPS

Egypt, Ethiopia, and Sudan became the pioneer nations of a tournament that grew steadily down the years to encompass four, six, eight, 12, and eventually 16 finalists. In the early days, north African countries were the sides to beat, a trend that has also been the case half a century later, judging by the last three competitions.

Holders Egypt, the very first African champions, have a poor World Cup record. However, they have won the African title a record six times, most recently in Ghana in 2008.

A team inspired by the goalkeeping of Essam El-Hadary, the creative talent of Hosny Abd Rabou, and the penetration of Amr Zaky opened up with a 4-2 win over Cameroon. Egypt beat Sudan 3-0 and drew 1-1 with Zambia when they were already assured of topping their group. Egypt went on to beat Angola 2-1 in the quarter-finals, Ivory Coast 4-1 in the semis, and Cameroon 1-0 in the final at the Ohene Djan Stadium, Accra.

Mohamed Aboutrika became the individual hero after grabbing the winning strike in the 77th minute, his fourth goal of the finals. Cameroon's consolation was that Barcelona's Eto'o pipped Aboutrika as top scorer with five goals.

THE EARLY YEARS

Eto'o and Aboutrika follow in a tournament tradition for showcasing gifted individuals including heroes of yesteryear, such as the Ghanaian dribbling wizard Osei Kofi, Ethiopian captain Luciano Vassallo, and Egypt's captain Rafaat Ateya. In that inaugural tournament he scored the very first goal in a 2-1 win over Sudan then scored all four in Egypt's 4-0 thrashing of Ethiopia in the final.

The organization of the second tournament was granted to Egypt with the same three nations. A last-minute goal saw Egypt retain the trophy with a breathtaking 2-1 win over Sudan.

Four teams met in Addis Ababa for the third edition, with hosts Ethiopia seeing off the challenge of Egypt 4-2 in an exciting final. Ethopia's last Emperor, Haile Selassie, handed over the Cup to skipper Vassallo. Eight nations took part in Ghana in 1963, with a new format of an elimination round, semi-finals, and final. This format remained until 1976, when a second round league system was introduced.

Morocco took advantage, although the new formula proved unpopular and, in 1978, knockout semi-finals and a final were restored, along with penalty shoot-outs. Further alterations were made for the 1992 event in Senegal, when a dozen sites competed. By now the qualifying rounds were organized into mini-leagues rather than a straightforward knockout system.

A more recent expansion raised the number of entrants in the finals to 16, which proved popular with Africa's own nations but unpopular in Western Europe, where clubs resented being forced to relinquish their key players in the middle of their own league campaigns.

The most notable trend over the last two generations has been a significant shift of power. Ethiopia versus Sudan (both former champions) would have been a classic in the 1960s, whereas Cameroon against Nigeria brings excitement now.

FOOTBALL FACTS

RECENT WINNERS
1990 Host and Winner: Algeria
1992 Host: Senegal, Winner: Ivory Coast
1994 Host: Tunisia, Winner: Nigeria
1996 Host and Winner: South Africa
1998 Host: Burkina Faso, Winner: Egypt
2000 Co-hosts: Nigeria/Ghana, Winner: Cameroon
2002 Host: Mali, Winner: Cameroon
2004 Host and Winner: Tunisia
2006 Host and Winner: Egypt
2008 Host: Ghana, Winner: Egypt

ALL-TIME CHAMPIONS
Egypt (6); Cameroon, Ghana (4 each); Nigeria, Zaire/Congo Kinshasa (2 each); Algeria, Congo, Ethiopia, Ivory Coast, Morocco, South Africa, Sudan, Tunisia (1 each).

BELOW Didier Drogba enjoys Ivory Coast's progress to the 2006 semi-finals

REGIONAL CUPS
OTHER NATIONAL TEAM COMPETITIONS

"To play for your country is the greatest possible honor."
FIFA PRESIDENT SEPP BLATTER

The history of national team competitions and their status as the ultimate peak of football achievement goes all the way back to the first official Scotland v England match on November 30, 1872. That goalless draw at Hamilton Crescent in Partick led to the creation of the British Home Championship.

RIGHT Ante Milicic strikes for Australia against the Solomon Islands in 2004

BELOW Harry Kewell leads the "Socceroos" to an easy win

Association football's first national team competition was staged annually until 1984, when it was killed off by dwindling crowds and the fixture congestion engendered by qualifying matches for the World Cup and European Championship.

At one stage, the British Home Championship also served as the World Cup qualifying section.

That was after the World War II, when the British associations—England, Scotland, Wales, and Northern Ireland—had rejoined FIFA after a gap of more than 25 years. FIFA designated two seasons of the British championship as the qualifying group. England finished top and went to Brazil. The runners-up were also granted a place in the finals, but the Scottish association said it would only send a team if they finished top of the group. They finished runners-up to England and duly stayed at home.

The British championship was put to the same use before the 1954 World Cup, but for the last time. Other nations objected that this gave the British a guaranteed place at the finals and the smaller British nations—Wales and Northern Ireland—objected that they were always going to be at a qualifying disadvantage against England and Scotland. Ironically, for the next World Cup, "open" qualifying saw all four home nations go on to the finals, for the first and last time.

The awkward nature of international travel in football's early years was a significant factor in the creation of regional competitions.

Small, impoverished federations in days long before the advent of television and sponsorship could barely afford—or manage—to send a squad of players and handful of officials to a neighboring country for a tournament. Criss-crossing the world's oceans in an era when passenger flights were merely the stuff of science fiction would have been virtually impossible. Thus the South Americans set up their own tournament in the early 1900s, but it was not until the late 1950s that Europe and Africa dared go fully international.

THE GROWTH OF COMPETITIONS

A European nation teams' competition had been organized in the 1920s and 1930s. This was the brainchild of Austrian and Hungarian football administrators, among them the Austrian Hugo Meisl, who also dreamed up the Mitropa Cup for the clubs of central Europe. The Gerö Cup was organized under the auspices of the world federation, FIFA, since a formal European federation was not brought into existence until the mid-1950s.

Elsewhere around the world, the desire for national team competition saw the fledgling central American confederation launch its own event in 1941; the first winners were Costa Rica. Further championships were staged only irregularly, even after the formal creation in 1963 of CONCACAF, which finally bonded into one organization the various nations, large but mainly small, who made up the football world of central America (including some northern South American countries), the Caribbean and, of course, North America (which meant the United States and Canada).

The regional competition was eventually reorganized and stabilized, in 1991, as the Gold Cup. It takes place in spring, every two years. Mexico and the United States, the two major powers of the region, have dominated the modern era with four wins apiece. Canada have won once, while none of the central American nations have won it at all.

Oceania remains the world game's poor relation in all senses, including competitive status. The region is FIFA's smallest, with only 11 members, and its standing within the world game was further reduced by Australia's departure in 2006 to join the Asian confederation.

An Oceania Nations Cup was begun in 1973 but its diminished entry has placed its long-term future in doubt.

ASIAN CUP

RECENT WINNERS
1972 Iran
1976 Iran
1980 Kuwait
1984 Saudi Arabia
1988 Saudi Arabia
1992 Japan
1996 Saudi Arabia
2000 Japan
2004 Japan

ALL-TIME WINNERS:
Iran, Japan, Saudi Arabia 3 each; South Korea 2; Iraq, Israel, Kuwait 1 each

CONCACAF GOLD CUP
(North, Central American, and Caribbean Nations)

RECENT WINNERS
1991 United States
1993 Mexico
1996 Mexico
1998 Mexico
2000 Canada
2002 United States
2003 Mexico
2005 United States
2007 United States

ALL-TIME WINNERS
Mexico, United States 4 each; Canada 1

OCEANIA NATIONS CUP

RECENT WINNERS
1973 New Zealand
1980 Australia
1996 Australia
1998 New Zealand
2000 Australia
2002 New Zealand
2004 Australia

ALL-TIME WINNERS
Australia 4; New Zealand 3

OTHER NATIONAL TEAM COMPETITIONS

REGIONAL CUPS
CLUB WORLD CHAMPIONSHIPS

AC Milan have been crowned champions four times in the event's various guises. The competitions are now reformed after early years were marred by scandal and violence.

WORLD CLUB CUP

RECENT WINNERS
1998 Real Madrid (Spa) 2
Vasco da Gama (Brz) 1
1999 Manchester United (Eng) 1
Palmeiras (Brz) 0
2000 Boca Juniors (Arg) 2
Real Madrid 1 [World Club Cup]
Corinthians (Brz) 0
Vasco da Gama (Brz) 0
(Corinthians 4-3 on on pens)
[Club World Championship]
2001 Bayern Munich 1 (Ger)
Boca Juniors (Arg) 0
2002 Real Madrid (Spa) 2
Olimpia Asuncion (Par) 0

ALL-TIME CHAMPIONS
Milan (Ita) 4;
Boca Juniors (Arg), Nacional (Uru), Penarol (Uru), Real Madrid (Spa), São Paulo (Brz) 3 each;
Ajax (Hol), Bayern Munich (Ger), Independiente (Arg), Internazionale (Ita), Juventus (Ita), Porto (Por), Santos (Brz) 2 each;
Atletico Madrid (Spa), Borussia Dortmund (Ger), Corinthians (Brz), Estudiantes (Arg), Feyenoord (Hol), Gremio (Brz), Internacional (Brz), Manchester Utd (Eng), Olimpia (Par), Racing (Arg), Red Star Belgrade (Ser), River Plate (Arg), Velez Sarsfield (Arg) 1 each

The Intercontinental Cup kicked off in 1960 as a home and away meeting between the champions of Europe and South America. The idea had sprung from South American officials, who had launched their own Copa Libertadores for the purpose of challenging Europe at club level.

Real Madrid were crowned the first winners. Their legendary team, inspired by the greats of Alfredo Di Stefano and Ferenc Puskás, drew 0-0 with Peñarol of Uruguay in the torrential rain at Montevideo, then stormed to a 5-1 victory back in their Santiago Bernabéu fortress in Spain. Within a matter of a few years, the competition almost ground to a halt, following a string of brutal matches involving Argentinian sides. Celtic were furious at their treatment by Racing Club in 1967. A year later, Manchester United's maverick George Best lost his temper after incessant provocation by his marker José Hugo Medina of Estudiantes de La Plata and both were sent off.

Estudiantes, under coach Osvaldo Zubeldia, were notorious for their cynical tactics. In 1969, the Estudiantes players bombarded their Milan opponents with practice balls as they tried to warm up before the game in Argentina. Milan won 4-2 on aggregate, but three Estudiantes players—goalkeeper

RIGHT Milan's Pippo Inzaghi (Number 9) scores for Milan against Boca Juniors in 2007

Alberto José Poletti, plus defenders Ramón Alberto Aguirre Suárez and Raúl Horacio Madero—received lengthy bans for their bad behavior.

Several European champions, such as Bayern Munich, Liverpool, and Nottingham Forest, declined to compete. The teams usually cited fixture congestion, because they feared losing key players to tough South American tackling. The 1975 and 1978 contests were not held.

EIGHTIES REVIVAL

The competition was rescued in 1980, when the Japanese Football Federation, keen to promote the sport in the Far East, found sponsorship support from car manufacturer Toyota to host the final as a one-off game. The inaugural showpiece was played in Tokyo until 2001, with neighboring Yokohama hosting the 2002 and 2004 finals.

The competition always mattered more to the South Americans than the Europeans. Even the wealthiest South American clubs could not match their European rivals in financial terms, so the Intercontinental Cup gave them a chance to underline a belief in their superior skill and talent.

The last final in Tokyo's National Stadium saw Bayern Munich edge past Boca Juniors 1-0 in extra time. The final moved to Yokohama's new National Stadium the following year.

CLUB WORLD CHAMPIONSHIP

Meanwhile, FIFA had become directly involved in football at international club level. FIFA staged a Club World Championship in 2000 at Brazil's Maracanã Stadium. Noisily impatient clubs from outside Europe and South America were invited. European champions Manchester United even withdrew from the FA Cup in England to play at the urging of the FA, who were bidding in vain to host the 2006 World Cup. Corinthians beat Vasco da Gama 4-3 on penalties after the goalless all-Brazilian affair.

FIFA set a precedent and, in 2004, it swallowed up the original match into its expanded mini-tournament. Japan remained, initially at least, as host nation. But no longer was the competition the preserve of the Europeans and South Americans.

In 2005, FIFA followed up its 2000 experiment. The competition would still be played in Japan, but now it was global. The top teams from all over the world would play off. Brazil's São Paulo won the first of the revised events, beating European champions Liverpool 1-0 in the final.

They now had rivals in hosting, which included Al-Ahly (Egypt), Al-Ittihad (Saudi Arabia), Deportivo Saprissa (Costa Rica), and Sydney (Australia). Internacional of Porto Alegre maintained Brazilian domination in 2006, beating Barcelona 1-0. Coach Abel Braga said: "Our club's history will now come under two headings, before and after Japan 2006. We're world champions!"

Al-Ahly were there again in 2006, along with some new challengers: Auckland (New Zealand), Club America (Mexico), and Jeonbuk Hyundai (South Korea).

AC Milan's 4-2 victory over Boca Juniors in 2007 was Europe's first triumph since Porto's in 2004. Perhaps more significantly for the future, Japan's Urawa Reds took third place and African champions Etoile du Sahel were fourth.

ABOVE Skipper Paolo Maldini and his Milan team-mates celebrate world domination

REGIONAL CUPS MOMENTS

1960s

1970s

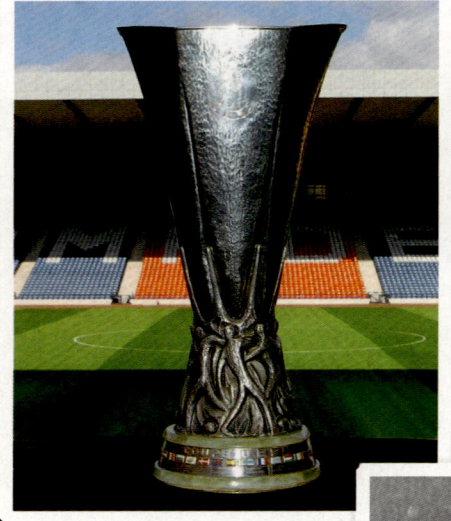

ABOVE The UEFA Cup is second in status to the Champions League

RIGHT Archie Gemmell scores Celtic's second goal during the 1970 European Cup final

ABOVE Liverpool's Steve Heighway on target against Servette

ABOVE Colin Bell scores for Manchester City against Lierse

ABOVE Tottenham knock Milan out of the UEFA Cup in 1972

124 REGIONAL CUPS

1970s

ABOVE Fans cheer Liverpool on to final victory over Borussia Mönchengladbach

ABOVE A consolation goal for Wolves against Porto in 1974

2000s

ABOVE Corinthians celebrate their Club World Cup triumph in 2000

LEFT Liverpool in triumph after their golden goal win over Alaves in 2001

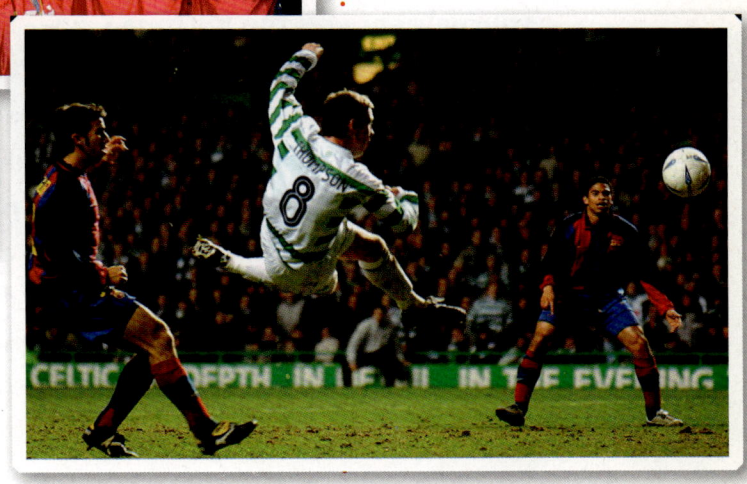

RIGHT Alan Thompson's goal for Celtic knocks out Barcelona

MOMENTS 125

INTERNATIONAL CLUB COMPETITIONS

The **UEFA Champions League** is the most lucrative international club competition ever to be played. It has evolved over the last 80 years, and there are further exciting changes planned for the future that will make matches more entertaining for fans. The original tournament was the **Mitropa Cup**—also known as the La Coupe de l'Europe Centrale. This was held among the leading clubs of central Europe during the late 1920s and 1930s. The European Champions' Club Cup was launched in the mid-1950s, along with the now renamed **UEFA** Cup and the defunct **UEFA** Cup Winners' Cup. Each contest has provided a flood of memorable goals, unforgettable moments, and great drama.

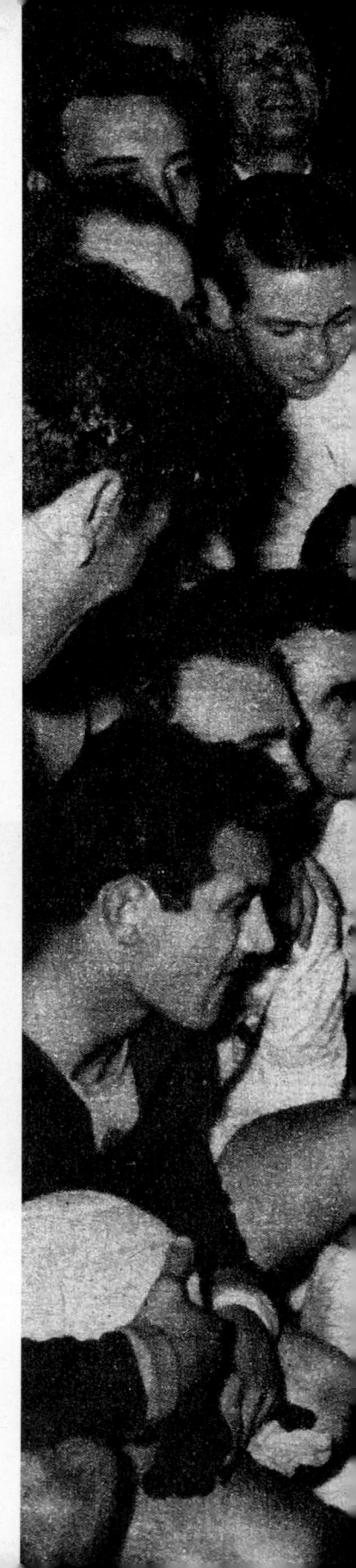

COUPE
CHAMPIONS
EUROPÉENS
Finale
1956

INTERNATIONAL CLUB COMPETITIONS
FOUNDATION & 1950s

"The Champions League is where every player wants to be."
KAKA OF MILAN

UEFA has come a long way since it was founded in Basel on 15 June 1954. It currently stands as the richest and most important of the six continental confederations of world governing body FIFA. UEFA oversees the numerous competitions from its headquarters in Nyon, a town on the shores of Lake Geneva in Switzerland.

EUROPEAN CUP
1950s FINALS
1956 Real Madrid 4 Reims 3
1957 Real Madrid 2 Fiorentina 0
1958 Real Madrid 3 Milan 2 (after extra time)
1959 Real Madrid 2 Reims 0

All the world's greatest players—from South America to southern Africa to south-east Asia—have a strong desire to play for European clubs, tempted by both the lucrative contracts and the chance of winning high-profile titles and medals.

UEFA was formed as a result of talks between the respective Football Federations of Belgium France and Italy. It was set up during the 1954 World Cup.

France's Henri Delaunay was the driving force. and immediately tackled the role of general secretary; Denmark's Ebbe Schwartz was voted in as the inaugural president.

UEFA grew hand in hand with the European Champions' Club Cup. This tournament was dreamed up by the then editor of the French sports daily newspaper *L'Equipe*, Gabriel Hanot, who became irritated by the claims of a

ABOVE The FIFA president, Sir Stanley Rous

RIGHT Red Star goalkeeper Beara foils a Manchester United attack

PAGE 62 Arie Haan is carried off the pitch by Ajax fans in 1971

PAGE 63 The victorious 1956 Real Madrid team celebrates

national English newspaper that Wolverhampton Wanderers—after beating Hungary's Kispest Honvéd in a friendly—were the champions of the world. Hungary had recently humiliated England 6-3 and 7-1.

So Hanot proposed a formal annual competition, but the concept proved so popular with the top clubs that the organisational work exceeded the newspaper's organising capacity.

In April 1955, UEFA agreed to take over the running of the European Champions' Club Cup. That decision laid the foundation for its power base, just in time. Later that month, three leading officials—Ernst Thommen (Switzerland), Dr Ottorino Barassi (Italy) and Sir Stanley Rous (England)—conceived the idea of the International Inter-Cities' Industrial Fairs Cup, the forerunner to today's UEFA Cup.

Three years later, UEFA introduced the European Nations' Cup and in 1960 the UEFA Cup Winners' Cup became a reality, running parallel with the European Champions' Clubs Cup.

The Champions' Club Cup, based on a two-leg knock-out system, grew from strength to strength despite severe problems with hooliganism, political turmoil, and stadium disasters. Lennart Johansson, the UEFA president between 1990 and 2007, was the man responsible for converting the Champions' Club Cup into the Champions League.

UEFA became a political player too, clashing with the European Union over television rights. Then came the Bosman Judgement, which established the primacy of EU labor law over football's own regulations and sparked the mass migration of leading players to Western Europe. In January 2008 Johansson was replaced as president by Michel Platini, the former France star who had won the Champions' Cup.

Real Madrid dominated the early European Champions' Club Cup, crowned winners at the first five successive wins. Santiago Bernabéu was the president who oversaw their phenomenal rise. He had the vision to raise Madrid's 20,000 capacity Chamartín ground and create a giant stadium that would house a great team. Bernabeu and his secretary Raimundo Saporta built that team. Their best signing was the Argentinian forward Alfredo Di Stefano. Madrid beat Barcelona to sign him from Colombian club Millonarios, aided by some help from the Spanish sports ministry.

Di Stefano was the pivotal figure in Madrid's success. He was the team's leader and finished league top scorer every season between 1955 and 1959. Madrid scaled the heights with a 7-3 victory over Eintracht Frankfurt in the 1960 final at Hampden Park, Glasgow. Di Stefano netted three, Puskas four.

BELOW Joseito, one of Real Madrid's home-grown Spanish heroes

INTERNATIONAL CLUB COMPETITIONS
EUROPE 1960s

Real Madrid launched a new European competitive decade in glory. Their 7-3 thrashing of Eintracht Frankfurt—West Germany's first finalists—in Glasgow in 1960 was hailed by experts as the greatest match of all time.

FOOTBALL FACTS

THE FINALS
1960 Real Madrid 7 Eintracht Frankfurt 3
1961 Benfica 3 Barcelona 2
1962 Benfica 5 Real Madrid 3
1963 Milan 2 Benfica 1
1964 Internazionale 3 Real Madrid 1
1965 Internazionale 1 Benfica 0
1966 Real Madrid 2 Partizan Belgrade 1
1967 Celtic 2 Internazionale 1
1968 Manchester Utd 4 Benfica 1, after extra time
1969 Milan 4 Ajax Amsterdam 1

The inspirational Alfredo Di Stefano hit a hat-trick but was out-scored by Hungarian Ferenc Puskas who scored four goals. Madrid's five-year reign ended the next season, when they were beaten by Spanish rivals Barcelona. The Catalans had long envied Madrid their headline status in Europe; their success had been limited to a couple of victories in the lesser Inter-Cities' Fairs Cup.

They signed some of the world's finest players and coaches and believed their hour had come when, with the help of refereeing errors, they defeated Madrid in the opening rounds of the 1960–61 Champions' Cup.

Barcelona were then clear favorites to win the final but they were surprisingly beaten by Benfica from Lisbon. Two of Barcelona's stars, the Hungarian forwards Sandor Kocsis and Zoltan Czibor, had finished on the favorites' losing side at the same stadium in Bern, Switzerland, seven years earlier in the World Cup final against West Germany. Then, as now, the score was 3-2.

Benfica, unlike cosmopolitan Barcelona, relied solely on Portuguese players but this gave them the option of plucking many outstanding players from Portugal's African colonies. The most important was Eusebio da Silva Ferreira, from Mozambique, who scored two goals the following year when Benfica thrashed the aging maestros of Real Madrid 5-3 in Amsterdam. The Hungarian veteran Puskas ended up on the losing side despite scoring another Champions' final hat-trick.

A hat-trick of titles proved beyond Benfica, however, as the balance of power in Europe swung towards Italy and the city of Milan.

AC Milan overthrew Benfica in 1963, in the first European final at Wembley. Eusebio struck early for Benfica but was then played out of the game by Milan winghalf Giovanni Trapattoni as the Italians hit back twice through their Brazilian center-forward Jose Altafini. He thus finished with 14 goals in the campaign, then a record. Milan's creative inspiration came from their "Golden Boy" inside forward Gianni Rivera, supported by other Italian internationals such as captain and sweeper Cesare Maldini and winger Bruno Mora.

Milan's reign lasted only one season, however. They fell in the quarter-finals the next term to Real Madrid, who were, in turn, beaten 3-1 in the final in Vienna by Internazionale, Milan's city neighbors.

Inter were managed by master coach Helenio Herrera. In the spring of 1960 Herrera had been sacked by Barcelona after a European defeat at Madrid's hands. Now he enjoyed taking his belated revenge. Herrera was born in Morocco but brought up in Argentina. He became a professional footballer in France and had worked hard on the tactics, science, and psychology of football. At Inter he imposed

130 INTERNATIONAL CLUB COMPETITIONS

ABOVE George Best celebrates United's second goal against Benfica

RIGHT Celtic's Billy McNeill takes delivery of the European Cup

a ruthless tactical system based on a rugged sweeper in Armando Picchi, man-marking defenders such as Tarcisio Burgnich and Giacinto Facchetti, a perceptive playmaker in Luis Suarez and lightning counterattackers such as Sandro Mazzola and Jair da Costa.

Inter secured two cups—against Real Madrid in 1964 and Benfica in 1965—before Celtic and Manchester United struck the first blows for British football. In 1967 Scotland's Celtic, under the shrewd management of Jock Stein, carried all before them at home and abroad. Their brand of thrilling football swept aside even iron-clad Inter in the final in Lisbon. Not surprisingly, Celtic's team earned the nickname of the "Lisbon Lions."

One year later Manchester United marked the tenth anniversary of the Munich air disaster by seizing the trophy for the first time themselves. Matt Busby had built a remarkable new team, built around the inspiration of another Munich survivor Bobby Charlton. Charlton was partnered in attack by George Best and Denis Law. Injury meant Law missed the final in which United beat Benfica 4-1 in extra time at Wembley, thanks to two goals from Charlton, now United's captain.

Their reign, however, lasted only one year. United were dethroned in the 1969 semi-finals by Milan—still led by Rivera—who then beat Holland's emerging Ajax Amsterdam in the final in Madrid's Estadio Bernabeu. Ajax were the first Dutch club to have reached the Champions' final. Their coach Rinus Michels was building a team and a style which would earn worldwide admiration. But their day had yet to dawn.

INTERNATIONAL CLUB COMPETITIONS
EUROPE 1970s

The 1970s was a European Cup decade which could be split into three reigns—those of Ajax Amsterdam, Bayern Munich, then the English. First though, in 1970, came Feyenoord of Rotterdam, Ajax's long-time rivals.

ABOVE Ajax Amsterdam, hat-trick winners in the early 1970s

Feyenoord, managed by the former Austrian international defender Ernst Happel, became the first Dutch team to win the trophy, beating 1967 winners Celtic 2-1. Sweden striker Ove Kindvall scored the winner four minutes from the end of extra time.

Ajax followed, with a vengeance. Their center forward Johan Cruyff was one of the all-time greats. His touch and vision inspired Ajax to three European titles and Holland to reach the 1974 World Cup Final.

Johan Neeskens was a tough-tackling, driving midfielder, Gerrit Muhren added craft, while Ruud Krol was a marauding leftback. In addition, coach Rinus Michels's players could switch positions in bewildering style in the formation known as "total football." They won three finals, all comfortably. They defeated Panathinaikos of Greece 2-0 at Wembley put together their best performance of the three to defeat Internazionale 2-0 in Rotterdam, and then finished off with a 1-0 win over Juventus in Belgrade. Cruyff scored both goals against Internazionale.

It had been clear, however, that he would be lured away at some stage to Spanish football and that ultimately occurred in the summer of 1973 when Ajax reluctantly sold him to Barcelona for a then world record £922,000.

The departure of Cruyff left Ajax vulnerable to a challenge from German champions Bayern Munich, led by Franz Beckenbauer, a great creative midfielder who had perfected the role of attacking sweeper. Sepp Maier was a brilliant goalkeeper and Gerd Muller the greatest striker of his age. Muller scored 365 times in 427 Bundesliga appearances and 68 times in 62 games for West Germany.

Georg Schwarzenbeck was a defensive rock beside Beckenbauer, Paul Breitner was a gifted attacking full back, and Uli Hoeness was a clever forward. But Bayern had to battle for their three successive final wins. First opponents were Atletico Madrid in Brussels in 1974. Only a last-minute goal by Schwarzenbeck at the end of extra time earned a replay—the only one in the

132 INTERNATIONAL CLUB COMPETITIONS

history of the competition—which Bayern won easily by 4-0. Leeds had a seemingly good goal disallowed before Franz Roth and Muller netted in the 1975 final; then Dominque Rocheteau hit the woodwork for Saint-Etienne ahead of Roth's winner a year later at Hampden Park, Glasgow.

Bayern grew old together—and the English succeeded them. The quiet, thoughtful Bob Paisley at Liverpool and the charismatic, and outspoken, Brian Clough at Nottingham Forest both built winning teams.

Liverpool's revival had been masterminded by Scottish manager Bill Shankly and Paisley, his assistant, was comparatively unknown when he took over in the summer of 1975. Very soon, however, it became clear that Paisley was a managerial giant. It was under his guidance that Liverpool won their first European Champions' Cup by defeating Borussia Monchengladbach 3-1 in the 1977 final in Rome.

At the time, Borussia were one of Europe's outstanding football teams under the guidance of meticulous coach Hennes Weisweiler and with an attack inspired by Denmark's first European Footballer of the Year, Allan Simonsen.

In Rome, however, Weisweiler's planning and Simonsen's energy proved no match for a Liverpool side, who had found a style pitched midway between the demands of frenetic English league football and the more thoughtful version demanded by European competition.

The match was a personal triumph for Liverpool's England right-winger Kevin Keegan, who memorably outwitted the Germans' terrier-like defender Berti Vogts.

It was Keegan's last game for Liverpool. Within weeks he had been sold to Hamburg and Liverpool used the fee to replace him with an even more outstanding player in Scotland forward Kenny Dalglish, bought from Celtic.

Dalglish emulated Keegan's success when, a year later, he scored the lone winning goal for Liverpool in their second Champions' final victory over Brugge of Belgium. Liverpool's reign ended early the next season with the success of the English team Nottingham Forest. Under the idiosyncratic management of the controversial Brian Clough, Forest went all the way to defeat Sweden's Malmo in the 1979 final. The decisive goal was scored by the England forward Trevor Francis.

Months earlier Francis had become Britain's first $2 million (£1 million) footballer when Clough bought him from Birmingham City. The Malmo game was his Champions' Cup debut.

LEFT John Robertson flies the flag for Nottingham Forest

FOOTBALL FACTS

THE FINALS
1970 Feyenoord 2 Celtic 1
(after extra time)
1971 Ajax Amsterdam 2 Panathinaikos 0
1972 Ajax 2 Internazionale 0
1973 Ajax 1 Juventus 0
1974 Bayern Munich 4 Atletico Madrid 0
(replay after 1-1 extra time draw)
1975 Bayern Munich 2 Leeds United 0
1976 Bayern Munich 1 Saint-Etienne 0
1977 Liverpool 3 Borussia Monchengladbach 1
1978 Liverpool 1 Club Brugge 0
1979 Nottingham Forest 1 Malmo 0

INTERNATIONAL CLUB COMPETITIONS
EUROPE 1980s

"Heysel is a wound that cannot be healed."
— MICHEL PLATINI

One event overshadowed the European Cup in the 1980s: the Heysel disaster of 1985. Thirty-nine fans, Italian and Belgian, were crushed to death as Liverpool fans attacked Juventus fans before a European Cup final in Brussels.

ABOVE The wrecked terracing at Heysel in 1985

It was Juventus' first Champions' Cup victory but that went almost unnoticed amid the carnage. Michel Platini, now UEFA president, and their star forward, said: "I'm physically and emotionally incapable of going back to Heysel. It's a wound that cannot be healed."

UEFA blamed Liverpool and their supporters. English fans had long been associated with hooliganism. UEFA banned all English teams indefinitely. That was later reduced to a five-year ban with an extra year for Liverpool. UEFA and other officials were also punished by the Belgian legal system for a series of blunders, which extended from choosing an inadequate venue in the first place, to failure to ensure sufficient security controls. For instance, the wire fence which separated Liverpool and Juventus fans at the Heysel stadium was little more than chicken wire and easily breached.

In due course the Heysel—which had hosted previous Champions' Cup finals in 1958, 1966, and 1974—was razed. The King Baudouin Stadium was built in its place, in the shadow of the Atomium (this had been constructed for the world exhibition of 1958, which had been hosted by Brussels).

The tragedy was all the more shocking for English football since it took place only 18 days after 56 people had died in a fire at the Bradford City stadium. Not until after the 1989 Hillsborough disaster, however, were draconian measures finally put in place to improve security and safety at sports stadia. These were adopted across English sport and were just in time to avert the threatened introduction of a restrictive and potentially ruinous membership-card system.

English clubs had extended their domination of the European Champions' Cup throughout the early 1980s, in a series of low-key finals. First Nottingham Forest extended their successful run to two years by defeating Kevin Keegan's

Hamburg on a lone goal from Scotland winger Jimmy Robertson in 1980. Then Liverpool were equally cautious in beating Real Madrid the following year on a late goal from fullback Alan Kennedy. In 1982, Aston Villa pipped Bayern Munich also by 1-0, despite losing their keeper, Jimmy Rimmer, to injury early in the match. Center-forward Peter Withe scored the goal from close range, almost falling over the ball as he did so.

The only interruption to English command came from Hamburg who, inspired now by midfielder Felix Magath, beat Juventus 1-0 in 1983. It was a second win with a different club for Hamburg's Austrian coach, Ernst Happel. He had previously guided Feyenoord to victory in 1970.

Hamburg's reign did not last long however. In 2004, Liverpool returned to lift the trophy again; this time with a penalty shoot-out win over Roma on the Italians' home ground. The game marked the end of the love affair between Roma's fans and their Brazilian midfielder Paulo Roberto Falcao after his apparent reluctance to take one of the spot kicks.

The expulsion of English clubs from European competition in the second half of the 1980s left a gap which no one other European club could fill. Romania's Steaua Bucharest became the first eastern European winners on penalties against favorites Barcelona—coached by Englishman Terry Venables—in 1986. Porto beat Bayern 2-1 the following season; a result Uli Hoeness described as among the worst in Bayern's history. Holland's PSV Eindhoven shaded Benfica on penalties again in 1988.

Soon afterwards, real champions soon emerged in Italy's revived club Milan. The club had been refinanced in the mid-1980s by media magnate and future prime minister Silvo Berlusconi. He paid off the club's debts, invested heavily in Dutch stars such as Ruud Gullit, Frank Rijkaard,

ABOVE Marco Van Basten raises the reward for his two goals against Steaua

and Marco Van Basten. All three men had been instrumental in their country's 1988 European Championship victory.

Milan won the Italian league in 1988, then thrashed Steaua Bucharest in the following season's Champions' Cup final. The final was staged in Barcelona amid a TV blackout after local technicians went on strike. Berlusconi flew in staff from his own Italian TV channels to ensure that no-one in Europe should miss his team's achievement.

Already, however, the talismanic Van Basten was starting to become more vulnerable to a series of ever-more damaging injuries which would ultimately force him into premature retirement—he played his last game in 1993.

FOOTBALL FACTS

THE FINALS
1980 Nottingham Forest 1 Hamburg 0
1981 Liverpool 1 Real Madrid 0
1982 Aston Villa 1 Bayern Munich 0
1983 Hamburg 1 Juventus 0
1984 Liverpool 1 Roma 1 (Liverpool 4-2 on penalties after extra time)
1985 Juventus 1 Liverpool 0
1986 Steaua Bucharest 0 Barcelona 0 (Steaua 3-0 on penalties after extra time)
1987 FC Porto 2 Bayern Munich 1
1988 PSV Elindhoven 0 Benfica 0 (PSV 6-5 on penalties after extra time)
1989 Milan 4 Steaua Bucharest 0

INTERNATIONAL CLUB COMPETITIONS MOMENTS

1950s   1960s   1970s

ABOVE A derby goal for Alfredo Di Stefano (left) of Real Madrid against Atletico

BELOW Ferenc Puskas scores Real Madrid's first goal in the 1962 Champions' final against Benfica

RIGHT George Best takes on the Benfica defence single-handed in 1968

ABOVE Ray Kennedy strikes for Arsenal in the 1979 Fairs Cup final

ABOVE Chelsea's David Webb heads past Brugge keeper Luc Sanders

136 INTERNATIONAL CLUB COMPETITIONS

1980s

ABOVE Liverpool manager Joe Fagan relaxes with the European Cup

ABOVE Arsenal easily see off FK Austria in 1991

1990s

RIGHT Celtic's Lubomir Moravcik outwits the Juventus defense

BELOW Sol Campbell heads Arsenal in front against Barcelona in the 2006 Champions League final

BOTTOM Pippo Inzaghi grabs Milan's second against Liverpool in 2007

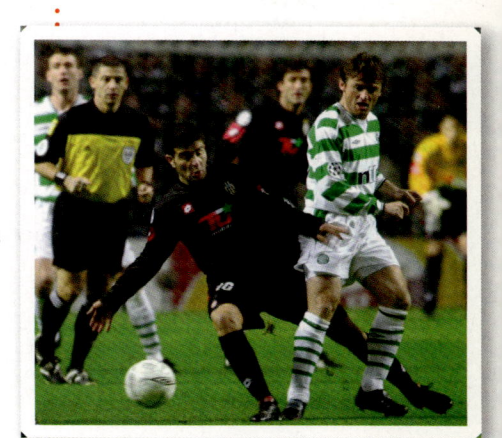

RIGHT Paolo Maldini in triumph after Milan's thrashing of Barcelona in 1994

2000s

MOMENTS 137

INTERNATIONAL CLUB COMPETITIONS
EUROPE 1990s

The late 1990s marked the biggest change in the format of the European Cup since the competition was established more than 40 years earlier. No longer would it be a knockout competition for league champions.

From 1956 onward, the structure had been simple. The holders and the champions of each European county had met in a series of two-leg ties, leading to a one-match final. The team who scored most goals in the matches, home and away, progressed. It was a copy of the formula devised for the Mitropa Cup, which had proved hugely popular in central Europe in the 1930s.

Initially, if scores were level after two matches a replay on neutral territory was organized. When it became more difficult to find neutral zones the clubs tossed to decide who would stage the replay. Eventually, however, the pressures of time led to the play-offs being scrapped—with the second leg of a balanced tie being extended into 30 minutes of extra time and then, if necessary, to a penalty shoot-out.

In 1991–92 this format was radically altered under pressure from wealthy clubs, including Real Madrid, Barcelona, Milan, Internazionale, Manchester United, Liverpool, and Bayern Munich. Extra clubs were admitted from the major nations and experiments began with a mini-league formula, until the present system—eight groups, then three knockout rounds before the final—was perfected.

These changes, which also raised the clubs' income through TV and sponsorship, were matched by another crucial development—the Bosman Judgement which, in December 1995, ruled that restrictions on the number of foreign players in any team and playing squad were illegal. The world's best players inevitably gravitated to a handful of rich European clubs, largely in England, Italy, and Spain.

These changes were presided over by a Swedish president of UEFA, Lennart Johansson, who managed efficiently the difficult jobs of maintaining

BELOW Ole Gunnar Solskjaer wins the 1999 final for Manchester United

UEFA's control over the European competitions, while simultaneously keeping the big clubs happy, largely thanks to the share of the revenue generated by the European competitions.

The drama of the European finals continued. One of the most dramatic moments came in 1999, when Teddy Sheringham and Ole Gunnar Solskjaer scored in the last seconds of stoppage time to lead Manchester United to an astonishing victory over Bayern Munich in Barcelona. Bayern had led by a single goal from Mario Basler for most of the match. United's victory secured them a historic treble of European Cup plus domestic league and FA Cup success, a unique achievement by an English club.

Johan Cruyff's "Dream Team" earned Barcelona's first Champions' Cup in 1992, when Ronald Koeman's rocket settled the contest against Sampdoria in extra time at Wembley. Fabio Capello's Milan then produced the finest performance of the 1990 finals when they unexpectedly came out in attack to rout Cruyff's Barcelona in 1994.

Surprisingly, Milan were beaten themselves a year later by a revived Ajax Amsterdam. Coincidentally, Ajax were guided to victory out on the pitch by the experienced string-pulling in midfield of Frank Rijkaard, a European Cup-winning hero with the Italian club in 1989 and 1990.

Ottmar Hitzfeld, a winning coach with Borussia Dortmund and Bayern, oversaw Dortmund's 3-1 success against Juventus in 1997 when Karlheinz Riedle scored twice, then fellow German Jupp. Heynckes guided Real Madrid to victory in 1998. Pedja Mijatovic scored Madrid's winner to secure their seventh Champions' Cup at the expense of favorites Juventus and their French midfield star, Zinedine Zidane.

Surprisingly, Heynckes was sacked by Madrid's impatient president Lorenzo Sanz on the grounds that the team had not, in addition, won the Spanish league. Sanz's unpredictable direction of the club backfired when impatient fans voted him out of a job and voted in millionaire builder Florentino Perez.

The decade was not without its scandal. Olympique de Marseille became the first French champions of Europe in 1993. They beat Milan 1-0 in what would prove the last final in Munich's Olympic stadium. But their victory was tarnished by revelations that they had fixed matches to help secure their domestic dominance in France.

In particular, several Marseille players had been approached to fix a match the previous weekend, because a draw would secure the French league title for Marseille while also keeping their opponents, Valenciennes, within sight of safety at the other end of the table. Jacques Glassmann, one of the Valenciennes players who had been approached, informed his club's directors. A process was launched, which ended in a jail term for, among others, the Marseille president Bernard Tapie. Glassman, booed by French crowds in the aftermath, was awarded a FIFA Fair Play award in 1995 in recognition of his actions.

ABOVE Red Star Belgrade, first and last Yugoslav winners, in 1991

FOOTBALL FACTS

THE FINALS
1990 Milan 1 Benfica 0
1991 Red Star Belgrade 0 Marseille 0 (Red Star 5-3 on penalties after extra time)
1992 Barcelona 1 Sampdoria Genoa 0 (after extra time)
1993 Marseille 1 Milan 0
1994 Milan 4 Barcelona 0
1995 Ajax Amsterdam 1 Milan 0
1996 Juventus 1 Ajax 1 (Juventus 4-2 on penalties after extra time)
1997 Borussia Dortmund 3 Juventus 1
1998 Real Madrid 1 Juventus 0
1999 Manchester United 2 Bayern Munich 1

INTERNATIONAL CLUB COMPETITIONS
EUROPE 2000s

By 2000, the European Cup had become the Champions League, though not a league of champions. The format had been swayed heavily in favor of the elite clubs that made up the G-14 group from the major western leagues.

FOOTBALL FACTS

THE FINALS
2000 Real Madrid 3 Valencia 0
2001 Bayern Munich 1 Valencia 1 (Bayern 5-4 on penalties after extra time)
2002 Real Madrid 2 Bayer Leverkusen 1
2003 Milan 0 Juventus 0 (Milan 3-2 on penalties after extra time)
2004 Porto 3 Monaco 0
2005 Liverpool 3 Milan 2 (Liverpool 3-2 on penalties after extra time)
2006 Barcelona 2 Arsenal 1
2007 Milan 2 Liverpool 1
2008 Manchester United 1 Chelsea 1 (Manchester United 6-5 on penalties after extra time)

The G-14 group could enter three or four teams each season and dominated the competition. But it was not the teams which towered over their domestic leagues who lifted the Champions' Cup. Only three winners—Bayern Munich in 2001, Barcelona in 2006, and Manchester United in 2008—also won their domestic championships in the same season.

It was as if chasing a domestic championship and the Champions League was a task too far. But a few clubs adapted ideally to the last 16 knock-out system. Liverpool, under Rafa Benitez, were the prime example. They won the Champions' Cup in 2005, despite finishing 37 points behind Chelsea in the Premiership.

In 2007, when they lost to Milan, they ended up 21 points behind Manchester United. English critics claimed that Benitez knew Liverpool could not match the consistency of Chelsea or Manchester United; his season's strategy revolved around the latter stages of the Champions League.

Chelsea twice fell to Liverpool in Champions League semi-finals, much to coach Jose Mourinho's disgust. Revenge was sweet in 2008 after the high-profile Portuguese "Special One" had been replaced by Israeli Avram Grant who subsequently

RIGHT Delight for Milan's Kaka means despair for Liverpool

led Chelsea to victory in the semi-final.

Milan, meanwhile, also put all their eggs in the Champions League basket. The 2007 winners finished 36 points behind Serie A champions and local rivals Internazionale. Both Liverpool and Milan rested and rotated players with the European Cup in mind, a pragmatic possibility often denied to their championship-chasing rivals.

Only once was the cycle of big clubs winning broken, when the favorites all went down in the 2004 quarter-finals. That left Mourinho to guide Porto to an easy victory over Monaco.

The most dramatic final of the decade was staged in 2005 in Istanbul. Milan led Liverpool 3-0 at half time through Paolo Maldini's early goal and two strikes by Hernan Crespo. Steven Gerrard inspired Liverpool's fight back as he, Vladimir Smicer, and Xavi Alonso scored within seven minutes of each other to force extra time. The tie was settled on penalties. Andriy Shevchenko, Milan's winning penalty taker in 2003 against Juventus, had his shot saved by Jerzy Dudek.

Madrid, playing with pace and power, had swarmed over Valencia in the all-Spanish final of 2000. Fernando Morientes, Steve McManaman, and Raul swept aside Hector Cuper's team. Caretaker boss Vicente Del Bosque had quelled the competing egos in the Madrid dressing room. He guided them to victory again in 2002, when Zinedine Zidane volleyed a magical winner against Bayer Leverkusen at Hampden Park, Glasgow. Leverkusen thus finished the season as runners-up not only in the Champions League but also in the German league and cup.

Barcelona won again for Spain in 2006 in the Stade de France after teetering on the verge of defeat against Arsenal who went ahead through center-back Sol Campbell and held out until an unlucky 13 minutes from time. Arsenal, ultimately, suffered for having to play much of the game with ten men after the early expulsion of their German goalkeeper, Jens Lehmann.

One factor in this decade had been a demonstration of the power of the big leagues. After an all-Spanish final in 2000 (Real Madrid beating Valencia) came an all-Italian final in 2003 (Milan beating Juventus) and then an all-English final in 2008.

The latter saw Manchester United win the crown for the third time after defeating Chelsea, also runners-up to United in the Premier League, on penalties. It was the first Champions final to have been staged in Moscow and the prospect of an invasion of English fans prompted the Russian authorities to make the unique concession of converting match tickets into visas.

Just to prove that football is no respecter of personalities, the three failures in the shoot-out were committed by United's Cristiano Ronaldo and by Chelsea's John Terry and Nicolas Anelka. Ronaldo's miss was particularly surprising—he had scored a career-best 42 goals for United over the course of the season and he would go on to lead Portugal into the quarter-finals of the European Championship.

United's success was perfectly timed in the year which marked the 50th anniversary of the Munich air disaster.

ABOVE Zinedine Zidane strikes his magnificent volleyed goal for Real Madrid in the 2002 final

INTERNATIONAL CLUB COMPETITIONS
UEFA CUP & CUP WINNERS' CUP

The UEFA Cup and the now-defunct Cup Winners' Cup have always been poor relations of the Champions League.

ABOVE Tottenham's John White, Bill Brown, Cliff Jones, Ron Henry, and Terry Dyson enjoy a happy homecoming to the UK in 1963

These were competitions for the "nearly" clubs who had fallen short of winning the major domestic trophy. Originally, the UEFA Cup was known as the Fairs Cup. It was founded in 1955—a fortnight after the Champions' Cup—by future FIFA president Sir Stanley Rous and vice-presidents Ottorino Barrasi of Italy and Ernst Thommen of Switzerland.

With one eye on post-war rapprochement between Europe's former enemy nations, it was originally confined to representative teams whose cities staged trade fairs. Since the games were organized to coincide with the trade fairs, the first tournament lasted three years. The final was held in 1958, when a team made up entirely of FC Barcelona players beat a London representative side 8-2 on aggregate over two legs.

Club teams were admitted to the next competition, and Barcelona beat Birmingham City 2-0 on aggregate in the 1960 final. Barcelona's heroes were the Hungarian Ladislav Kubala and Spain's own Luis Suarez. The competition was played annually after that. Initially, southern European clubs dominated, but Leeds' win in 1968 heralded a change. English teams (Newcastle, Arsenal, Leeds, Tottenham, and Liverpool) won the trophy for the next five years.

In 1971, the tournament was re-named after the European federation took formal control. The Fairs label was scrapped and the competition was called the UEFA Cup. Initially it continued as a two-leg knockout competition and the closing stages sometimes boasted a more glamorous mixture of clubs than the Champions' Cup. Winners down succeeding years included the likes of Real Madrid, Internazionale, Juventus, and Roma.

Everything changed, however, with the development of the Champions League. The quality threshold dropped significantly with the departure from the UEFA Cup of the bigger second, third, and fourth-placed clubs and the massive influx of clubs from the newly independent nations thrown up by the fragmentation of the Soviet Union and Yugoslavia.

UEFA also bowed to pressure from the clubs to produce a group stage which guaranteed three home matches for each club, while then allowing some teams that were knocked out of the Champions League entry into the UEFA Cup at the halfway stage for the knockout rounds. However, the system of five-team groups was unsatisfactory for fans and fixture patterns and is being reorganized again from 2009.

Sevilla, under coach Juande Ramos, proved masters of the competition in 2006 and 2007, though they had to thank a spectacular shoot-out performance from goalkeeper Andres Palop for the second of their two victories, over fellow Spanish opposition in Espanyol.

An intriguing factor in the UEFA Cup has been evidence of the revival of Russian club football after the chaos that followed the collapse of the Soviet Union. CSKA Moscow won the UEFA Cup in 2005, beating Sporting of Libson in front of their own fans, and then Zenit St Petersburg beat Rangers in 2008. Zenit also provided the nucleus of the Russian national side which proved outstanding six weeks later in reaching the semi-finals of the European Championship.

From 1999 onward, entrance into the UEFA Cup was also the formal reward for clubs who had won their national cups. This followed UEFA's decision to scrap the Cup Winners' Cup which had been running since 1960. The Cup Winners' Cup was always a poor relation because, while popular in Britain, the domestic knockout event had barely caught on in many other countries.

Italy's Fiorentina won the first final, beating Rangers of Scotland. Tottenham became the first British winners of a European competition when they defeated Atletico Madrid 5-1 in the final in 1963. The last final, in 1999, saw Italy's Lazio, coached by Sven-Goran Eriksson, beat Mallorca at Villa Park, Birmingham.

ABOVE Andres Palop wins the 2007 UEFA Cup for Sevilla by saving Marc Torrejon's penalty

UEFA CUP
RECENT FINALS
1999 Parma 3 Marseille 0
2000 Galatasaray 0 Arsenal 0 (Galatasaray 4-1 on penalties after extra time)
2001 Liverpool 4 Alaves 4 (golden goal after extra time)
2002 Feyenoord 3 Borussia Dortmund 2
2003 Porto 3 Celtic 2 (silver goal after extra time)
2004 Valencia 2 Marseille 0
2005 CSKA Moscow 3 Sporting Lisbon 1
2006 Sevilla 4 Middlesbrough 0
2007 Sevilla 2 Espanyol 2 (Sevilla 3-1 on penalties after extra time)
2008 Zenit St Petersburg 2, Rangers 0

ALL-TIME WINNERS
(UEFA Cup and Fairs Cup) Internazionale, Juventus, Liverpool, Valencia 3 each; Barcelona, Borussia Mg, Feyenoord, IFK Gothenburg, Leeds United, Parma, Real Madrid, Sevilla, Tottenham Hotspur 2 each; Ajax Amsterdam, Anderlecht, Arsenal, Bayer Leverkusen, Bayern Munich, CSKA Moscow, Dinamo Zagreb, Eintracht Frankfurt, Galatayasaray, Ipswich Town, Napoli, Newcastle United, Porto, PSV Eindhoven, Roma, Schalke, Zaragoza, Zenit St Petersburg 1 each.

CUP WINNERS CUP
ALL-TIME WINNERS (1961–99)
Barcelona 4; Anderlecht, Chelsea, Kiev Dynamo, Milan 2 each; Aberdeen, Ajax Amsterdam, Arsenal, Atletico de Madrid, Bayern Munich, Borussia Dortmund, Everton, Fiorentina, Hamburg, Juventus, Lazio, Magdeburg, Manchester City, Manchester United, Mechelen, Paris S-G, Parma, Rangers, Sampdoria, Slovan Bratislava, Sporting Clube, Tbilisi Dynamo, Tottenham Hotspur, Valencia, Werder Bremen, West Ham United, Zaragoza 1 each.

INTERNATIONAL CLUB COMPETITIONS MOMENTS

1963

2000s

ABOVE Eusébio thunders Benfica ahead against Milan in the 1963 Champions' final

ABOVE Real Madrid stars enjoy their 2000 Champions League triumph over Valencia

LEFT Oliver Kahn hails his own vital penalty stop against Valencia in 2001

ABOVE Jimmy Greaves takes Atletico Madrid apart to make history in 1963 Champions' final against Benfica

RIGHT Juan Riquelme (right) leads Boca Juniors to Libertadores glory against Cruz Azul

144 INTERNATIONAL CLUB COMPETITIONS

2000s

ABOVE Boca coach Carlos Bianchi leads the celebrations after victory over Santos

ABOVE Pepe Reina of Liverpool celebrates beating Chelsea in the 2007 semi-final

ABOVE Ever Alfaro of Deportivo Saprissa takes Mexico's Pachuca by surprise

BELOW Liverpool players hail their victory over Milan in 2005

RIGHT Ronaldo heads Manchester United ahead against Chelsea

BELOW David Beckham on MLS duty for Galaxy against Chivas

MOMENTS 145

INTERNATIONAL CLUB COMPETITIONS
SOUTH AMERICA

"For me, penalties are a lottery."
COACH RENATO GAUTO

The Copa Libertadores is the South American equivalent of the European Champions' Cup. The winners tackle their European counterparts for the prestigious honor of becoming the world's greatest club.

ABOVE Boca captain Diego Cagna strikes a cup-winning pose in 2003

The Copa Libertadores grew out of a tournament of seven south American champions, played in Santiago de Chile in 1948 and won by the Brazilian club Vasco da Gama—a side that were named after the great Portuguese explorer.

A dozen years later the Copa Libertadores was launched as an annual tournament. The reasoning was that South American club directors, notably those of Peñarol from Uruguay, had seen the success of the European Champions' Cup and wanted a version of their own.

Once the Copa Libertadores was established, then the vision was to eventually introduce an annual series matching the champions from Europe and South America to tackle each other for the coveted world club crown.

The Copa Libertadores kicked off in 1960 with the participation of the champions from Argentina, Bolivia, Brazil, Chile, Colombia, Ecuador, Paraguay, Peru, and Uruguay.

Much to the delight of many South American club directors, Peñarol from Uruguay were crowned champions after defeating Paraguay's Olimpia 2-1 on aggregate.

Pedro Spencer, the free-scoring Ecuadorian striker, was Peñarol's inspiration and went on to become the most prolific marksman in the history of the Copa Libertadores.

Peñarol, happily fulfilling their original ambition, went on to arrange a world club showdown with their European counterparts Real Madrid. However, the Spanish side steamrolled past Peñarol to the tune of 5-0.

Peñarol bounced back to be crowned South American champions the following season, but then they were toppled by Brazilian outfit Santos. The legendary Pelé proved to be the inspiration for Santos, who also won two years in a row and saw off the first serious Argentinian challenge from Boca Juniors.

Although Peñarol and Montevideo rivals Nacional would both win the Copa Libertadores again, Uruguay's pre-eminence faded and the tournament is currently dominated by clubs from Argentina and Brazil. Their supremacy has been interrupted only by a trio of wins for Olimpia, two successes apiece from Colombia's Atlético Nacional and Once Caldas, and a single triumph by Chile's Colo Colo.

Over the years the Copa Libertadores has featured a string of dramas—from crowd pitch invasions to 20-plus penalty shoot-outs and some of the most cynical football imaginable. Culprits for the latter were the Argentinian club Estudiantes de La Plata in the late 1960s. Under influential coach Osvaldo Zubeldía, they took anti-football to a vicious new art and a new low for the sport.

Originally the competition involved only the champions from each country. Since the knock-out formula failed to grip the imagination of the fans,

LEFT Hugo Ibarra (left) sends Robinho flying in Boca's 2003 victory over Santos

COPA LIBERTADORES

**RECENT FINALS
(OVER TWO LEGS)**
1999 Palmerias (Brz) 2 Deportivo Cali (Col) 2 (on agg, Palmeiras 4-3 on penalties)
2000 Boca Juniors (Arg) 2 Palmerias (Brz) 2 (on agg, Boca 4-2 on penalties)
2001 Boca Juniors (Arg) 1 Cruz Azul (Mex) 1 (on agg, Boca 3-1 on penalties)
2002 Olimpia (Par) 2 Sao Caetano (Brz) 2 (on agg, Olimpia 4-2 on penalties)
2003 Boca Juniors (Arg) 5 Santos (Brz) 1 (on agg)
2004 Once Caldas (Col) 1 Boca Juniors (Arg) 1 (on agg, Once Caldas 2-0 on penalties)
2005 Sao Paulo (Brz) 5 Atletico Paranense (Brz) 1 (on agg)
2006 Internacional (Brz) 4 Sao Paulo (Brz) 3 (on agg)
2007 Boca Juniors (Arg) 5 Gremio (Brz) 0 (on agg)
2008 LDU Quito (Ec) 5 Fluminense (Brz) 5

ALL-TIME WINNERS
Independiente (Arg) 7; Boca Juniors (Arg) 6; Penarol (Uru) 5 each; Estudiantes de La Plata (Arg), Nacional (Uru), Olimpia (Par), Sao Paulo (Brz) 3 each; Cruzeiro (Brz), Gremio (Brz), River Plate (Arg), Santos (Brz) 2 each; Argentinos Juniors (Arg), Atletico Nacional (Col), Colo Colo (Chi), Flamengo (Brz), Internacional (Brz), LDU (Ec), Liga de Quito (Ec), Once Caldas (Col), Palmeiras (Brz), Racing (Arg), Vasco da Gama (Brz), Velez Sarsfield (Arg) 1 each

most countries stage two league championships in a single year. Opening up the Copa Libertadores to two teams proved a successful solution. The simultaneous introduction of a first-round group stage also assisted with travel costs, as the two clubs from whichever country would be drawn in the same group as the two clubs from another country. This meant teams could travel together and, for convenience, play their matches on successive days.

The tournament expanded in the 1970s, allowing Argentina and Brazil five clubs each along with three teams each from other countries—including new participants, Venezuela and Mexico.

Mexico does not belong to the South American confederation and are guests in the competition, their best ever showing was Cruz Azul losing to Boca Juniors in the 2001 final.

Boca Juniors, winners of the Copa Libertadores in 2000, 2001, 2003, and 2007, can lay claim to being the dominant club of South American soccer's new century. Brazilian clubs are their only real challenge, often led by three-time winners São Paulo. However, Liga de Quito pulled off a major surprise in the 2008 final after they became the first Ecuadorian winners and earned a place in FIFA's 2008 Club World Cup in Japan.

Opponents, Brazil's Fluminense were also in the final for the first time and were red-hot favorites. Liga de Quito won the first leg of the final with surprising ease, 4-2, at high altitude in Quito. Fluminense fought back to square the final on aggregate with a 3-1 success, winning the return match 3-1 in Rio de Janerio's Maracanã Stadium, but paid a literal penalty for complacency. The contest was decided by penalty kicks, which Liga de Quito won 3-1, courtesy of the heroics of three saves by veteran goalkeeper José Cevallos.

SOUTH AMERICA | 147

INTERNATIONAL CLUB COMPETITIONS
REST OF THE WORLD

The contest between national champions is not confined to Europe and South America. Central and North America started its own championship in 1962. Africa followed two years later. Asia began its continent-wide challenge in 1967.

AFRICAN CHAMPIONS LEAGUE

RECENT WINNERS
2003 Enyimba (Nigeria)
2004 Enyimba (Nigeria)
2005 Al-Ahly (Egypt)
2006 Al-Ahly (Egypt)
2007 Etoile Sahel (Tunisia)

LEADING ALL-TIME WINNERS
Al-Ahly (Eg), Zamalek (Eg) 5 each; Canon (Cameroon), Hafia Conakry (Guinea), Raja Casablanca (Morocco) 3 each

ASIAN CLUB CUP

RECENT WINNERS
2003 Al-Ain (United Arab Emirates)
2004 Al-Ittihad (S Arabia)
2005 Al-Ittihad (S Arabia)
2006 Jeonbuk Motors (S Korea)
2007 Urawa Red Diamonds (Japan)

LEADING ALL-TIME WINNERS
Esteghlal (Iran), Al-Hilal (S Arabia), Al-Ittihad (S Arabia), Maccabi Tel-Aviv (Israel), Pohang Steelers (S Korea), Thai Farmers Bank (Thailand) 2 each

Only the Oceania confederation held back, until 2004–05. But the defection of Australia to the Asian confederation has robbed the tournament of its strongest teams.

The central American competition has long been dominated by Mexican clubs. Teams from North America have yet to make an impact, despite the emergence of the NASL and David Beckham's move to LA Galaxy. The biggest challenge to Mexican supremacy has come from Costa Rica. LD Alajualense and Deportivo Saprissa have both proved recent powers in the tournament.

Interest in the CONCACAF club competitions was enhanced by the creation first of the Copa Interamericana and then by the expansion of the Club World Championship. The Copa Interamericana pitched the winners of the CONCACAF Champions' Cup against the champions of South Americans, the winners of the Copa Libertadores.

Early in the 21st century FIFA scrapped the old World Club Cup, contested by the champions of "only" Europe and South America, and replaced it with the Club World Championship into which the winners of all the regional club competitions were guaranteed entry.

Clubs from the Arab north have historically dominated the African Club Championship. Egypt's Al-Ahly from Cairo have been the team to beat.

Their toughest opponents have been the Tunisian side Etoile du Sahel.

Other major rivals have come from west Africa, a prominent recent recruiting ground for Western European clubs. Perhaps this is one reason for the North African clubs' success: they do not lose as many players to Europe as their southern neighbors.

Southern Africa has yet to make its mark, despite boasting some of the richest and most passionately supported clubs on the continent, such as the Kaizer Chiefs and Orlando Pirates, South Africa's only winners in 1995. Ahead of the country's staging of the 2010 World Cup, a major disappointment for South African fans has been that its clubs have not made a greater impression at international competitive level.

Israeli teams dominated the opening days of the Asian competition. Maccabi Tel-Aviv won twice and Hapoel once, before the Israelis were forced out for political reasons. The Arab-dominated Asian confederation expelled Israel, whose clubs remained absent from international competition for almost 30 years. Israel joined UEFA in the 1990s after which its clubs entered the European competitions.

In the meantime, middle-eastern sides had taken command of the Asian club tournaments until the development of the ambitious, rich new leagues in both Japan and South Korea. The J.League side Urawa Red Diamonds underlined the power of the J.League when they became Asian champions in 2007 after beating Sepahan from Iran. They succeeded Jeonbuk Hyundai Motors, who ended the Arab supremacy in 2006.

The Japanese and Koreans gained in power thanks both their importing of European and South American coaches but also from the experience the best of their players had gained playing in Europe. The Middle East countries largely missed that international exchange, partly because their clubs could pay the players so well there was no financial incentive for them to seek a move to Europe.

Africa, Asia—now strengthened by Australia — and central/North American have already shown they can challenge the traditional powers. But Oceania seems destined to remain a backwater. The departure of Australia to join the Asian confederation was a serious blow to the status of Oceania and the champions of the region—always now the champions of New Zealand—are not certain to retain their place in the Club World Championship.

The FIFA president, Sepp Blatter, has said: "We want everyone to take their place in the greatest competitions but we also have to protect the status and value of those competitions."

LEFT Etoile de Sahel guard the African Super Cup

BELOW LEFT Pachuca players celebrate after beating Los Angeles Galaxy in a shoot-out in 2007

OCEANIA CLUB CHAMPIONSHIP

RECENT WINNERS
2005 Sydney FC (Australia)
2006 Auckland City (New Zealand)
2007 Waitakere United (New Zealand)

CENTRAL/NORTH AMERICAN CLUB CUP

RECENT WINNERS
2003 Toluca (Mexico)
2004 LD Alajuelense (Costa Rica)
2005 Deportivo Saprissa (Costa Rica)
2006 America (Mexico)
2007 Pachuca (Mexico)

LEADING ALL-TIME WINNERS
America (Mexico), Cruz Azul (Mexico) 5 each; Deportivo Saprissa (Costa Rica), UNAM (Mexico) 3 each

REST OF THE WORLD

GREAT NATIONS

International power in football is defined by a mixture of achievement and history. Success or failure at the World Cup finals is what counts to today's modern critic, followed by titles in the various regional championships. Brazil boast five World Cup victories, one more than mighty Italy. Germany have scored a hat-trick of successes on the world stage, with Argentina and Uruguay twice crowned as world champions, while England and France have each triumphed once. The role of the four British Home Nations is acknowledged worldwide, especially as England are major crowd pullers.

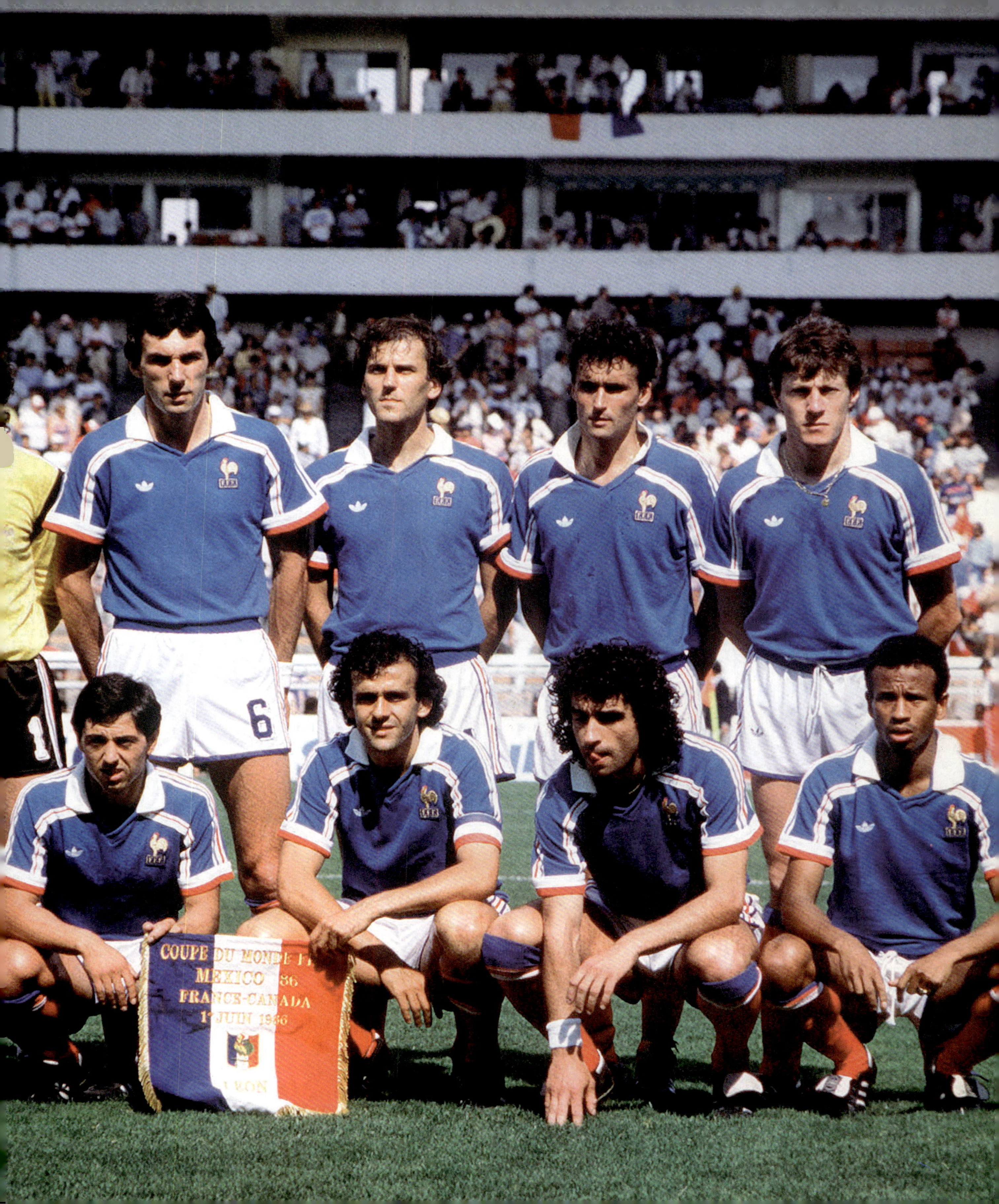
COUPE DU MONDE
MEXICO 86
FRANCE-CANADA

GREAT NATIONS
BRAZIL

England may have invented the modern game, but Brazil —and Edison Pelé in particular—have perfected it to such an extent that they can now boast a record-breaking five World Cup wins.

ABOVE Brazil team in 1970

PAGE 86 Brazil star Garrincha skips past Wales defender Terry Hennessey in 1962

PAGE 87 The 1986 France team before their match against Canada

Few dare argue with the Brazilian pre-eminence in modern football—especially after watching the timeless re-runs of Garrincha and Pelé swaggering their way to Brazil's first World Cup win in 1958 or, 12 years later, witnessing the color-soaked TV scenes from Brazil's third World Cup triumph in the Mexican sunshine.

Since then, successive new generations of Brazilians have consistently lived up to Pelé's romantic notion of "the beautiful game." But the original link was an English one. In 1894, Brazilian Charles Miller, whose father was originally from England, brought over the first footballs to be seen in Brazil, after a study trip in Southampton where he was taught the game. Miller envisaged a game for expatriates and their families, but its popularity swiftly spread and Brazil can now boast the proud achievement of being the only nation to have competed in every World Cup final.

The country's first footballing hero was Arthur Friedenreich, who, in the early part of the 20th century, was also popularly supposed to have been the first senior player to have scored over 1,000 goals. Emulating him was Leonidas, who spearheaded Brazil's attack at the 1938 World Cup finals in France. Unwisely, the team's directors decided to rest Leonidas from the semi-final against World Cup title holders Italy in order to be fresh for the final—which, of course, they never reached.

Brazil were awarded hosting rights to the next World Cup finals, but its realization had to wait until after World War II. It was originally due to be played in 1949, but a mixture of European uncertainty and slow preparation work put the staging back to 1950. Brazil reached the final only to suffer a shock 2-1 defeat to Uruguay in front of almost 200,000 disbelieving fans. As Brazil had lost the final while dressed in all-white, they superstitiously decided to make the switch to their current strip of yellow shirts and blue shorts—arguably today's most famous football uniform.

Brazil reached the quarter-final stage at the 1954 World Cup finals in Switzerland, returning to Europe to take the world title in Sweden four years later with almost an entirely new team. Coach Vicente Feola had brought in the mercurial outside right Garrincha and a 17-year-old inside left called Pelé.

As a teenage sensation, Pelé shared top billing for Brazil with wizard dribbler Garrincha, nicknamed "the Little Bird," and the midfield duo of Didi and Zito. In 1970, Pelé was complemented by the likes of Gerson, Roberto Rivelino, Tostao, and explosive Jairzinho—the last of whom was the only winner to score in every match per round at the World Cup finals. When Pelé retired in 1977, he boasted over 1,000 goals in a career with Brazil, Santos and New York Cosmos.

Brazil had to wait for 24 years to claim their fourth World Cup, edging past Italy on penalty kicks at the 1994 finals in the United States. Brazil's Bebeto and Romario were the deadliest strike pairing at the tournament going into the match against Italy, yet the match finished goalless.

Ronaldo was a member of the 1994 squad without playing and, in 1998, he was hampered by injury and illness as Brazil surrendered their crown to France. Yet Ronaldo was the two-goal hero in the 2002 final victory over Germany and in 2006 became the World Cup's all-time leading scorer.

Brazil's immense size long hindered the development of a national league until 1971, and the traditional old regional championships still generate fierce rivalry. Flamengo and Fluminense insist that they are the best-supported clubs, although São Paulo have a record five league titles.

The wealth of Brazilian football has always rested on the Rio-São Paulo axis, with the South American country now the world's greatest exporter of players. Most members of Brazil's recent World Cup squads have been European-based, a stark contrast to 1958 and 1962, when their entire squads played for Brazilian clubs.

Santos have been the most internationally acclaimed club in Brazilian football history. This is largely due to their perpetual global touring in the 1960s, when they cashed in on the fame and drawing power of Pelé. Despite the touring, Santos—even at their peak—were an extremely fine team that in 1962 and 1963 won both the Copa Libertadores and the World Club Cup.

Outstanding Brazilian coaches over the years have included World Cup-winning managers Feola, Aimoré Moreira, Mario Zagallo, Carlos Alberto Parreira, and Luiz Felipe Scolari, as well as Claudio Coutinho, Sebastião Lazaroni, and Tele Santana.

Heroes down the years have included Kaka, the 2007 World Player of the Year, and Cafu—the only player to have featured in the final of three consecutive World Cups (1994, 1998, and 2002).

ABOVE Pelé in action against Italy in the 1970 World Cup final

FOOTBALL FACTS

CHAMPIONS—LAST TEN YEARS
1998 Corinthians
1999 Corinthians
2000 Vasco da Gama
2001 Atlético Paranaense
2002 Santos
2003 Cruzeiro
2004 Santos
2005 Corinthians
2006 São Paulo
2007 São Paulo

GREAT NATIONS
ARGENTINA

Argentina took until 1978 to lift the World Cup despite producing legendary coaches, players, and teams. Their greatest player was the controversial Diego Maradona, who inspired them to a second world title in 1986.

Argentina has been producing great coaches, players, and teams for so long that it was remarkable that it took until 1978 before the talented men in the distinctive blue-and-white stripes won their first World Cup.

Argentina had come close to the title before, but finished as runner-up in the inaugural 1930 finals to hosts Uruguay. In 1978, it took home advantage, with brilliant goals from Mario Kempes, the midfield promptings of Ossie Ardiles, and shrewd managerial guidance by César Luis Menotti to fire them to victory.

They added a second crown at the 1986 World Cup finals in Mexico. This time they were inspired by Diego Maradona, who had failed to make the successful 1978 squad due to a lack of experience.

Argentina then finished as the runner-up to West Germany at the 1990 World Cup finals, despite Maradona's talents being restricted by his knee injury.

Maradona's slide from glory continued at the 1994 World Cup finals in the United States, when he failed a dope test and was immediately sent home in disgrace. In his absence, Argentina bowed out to Romania in the second round. They reached the quarter-final stage four years later, crashed out in the first round in 2002 and made it to the quarter-finals in 2006.

Despite a controversial career, Maradona remains an idol for his outrageous talent and the sheer nerve with which he scored a remarkable two goals against England in the 1986 World Cup finals. These goals are legendary. One was helped in with his hand, the other one after a solo run from the halfway line.

Argentina have played a major role in the history of the Copa Libertadores, the South American equivalent of Europe's Champions League, which has been dominated by six clubs —Argentinos Juniors, Boca Juniors, Estudiantes, Independiente, Racing Club, and River Plate.

BELOW Alfredo Di Stefano scores for Real Madrid

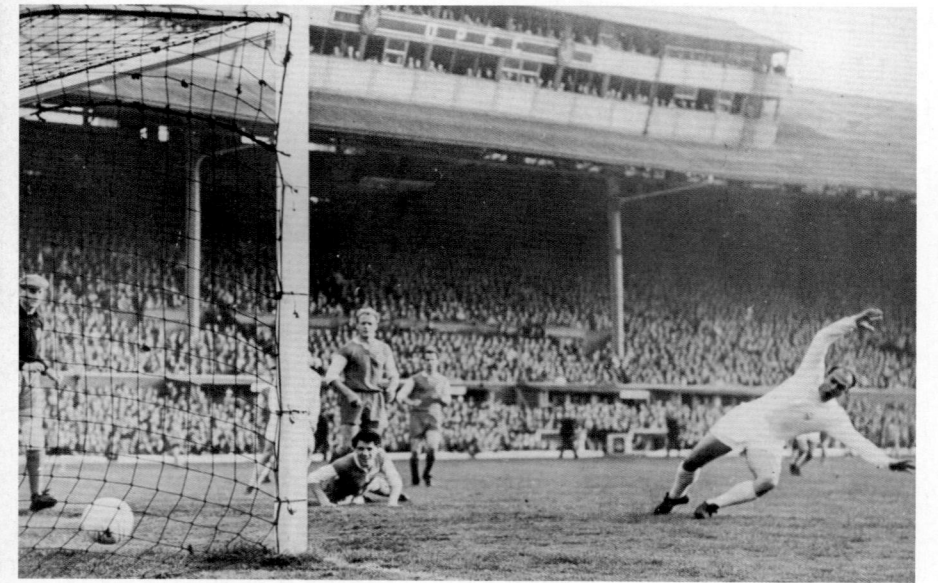

Argentina's Boca Juniors and River Plate are among the world's greatest clubs, with the majority of the country's finest players having used them as a springboard to lucrative careers in Europe. Boca Juniors' uniform is blue and yellow, River Plate famously play in white shirts with a red sash.

In the late 1940s, River carried all before them with a forward line nicknamed "The Machine" for its goal-scoring efficiency. They fielded two inside forwards, Juan Manuel Moreno and Angel Labruna, while in reserve was a young Alfredo Di Stefano. The side broke up in the early 1950s, when Argentinian league players went on strike in a demand for improved contracts and wages. Many players, including Di Stefano, were lured away to a "pirate" league in Colombia and never returned.

Boca became the first Argentinian club to reach a South American club final in 1962, but narrowly lost to Pelé's Santos in the Copa Libertadores. Independiente, from neighboring city Avellaneda, became Argentina's first Continental champions in 1964 and Racing Club were crowned as the country's first Intercontinental Cup champions in 1967.

Argentina have won the Copa America 11 times, most notably in 1957 when the inspirational performances of inside forward Humberto Maschio, Antonio Valentín Angelillo, and Omar Sivori established them as early favorites to win the following year's World Cup. By the 1958 World Cup finals, the trio had been sold to Italian clubs and Argentina's hopes went with them.

From then on there was a steady stream of Argentinian players heading for the riches on offer in Europe. By the mid-1990s, as most Western European countries eased their restrictions on foreign players, a minor industry grew up in "finding" European forebears—and European Union passports—for many Argentinian players.

The national game has been split down the years between a clash of styles. In the 1960s and 1970s, coaches such as Juan Carlos Lorenzo (Boca), Manuel Giudice (Independiente) and Osvaldo Zubeldía (Estudiantes de La Plata), ruthlessly put the achievement of results above the quality of play and entertainment. Yet the country's football federation deserved enormous credit for appointing the more positive Menotti as coach. Under Menotti, Argentina's triumph and style of play at the 1978 World Cup finals inspired a significant shift in opinion.

There has, however, been a failure to deal with hooligan violence in domestic Argentinian football. In fact, many club directors have preferred to provide complementary match tickets and transport for the more notorious hooligans, known as "Barras Bravas," to avoid major disruption in the stadiums and around the grounds.

FOOTBALL FACTS

CHAMPIONS—LAST TEN YEARS
1999 Boca Juniors / Boca Juniors
2000 River Plate / River Plate
2001 Boca Juniors / San Lorenzo
2002 Racing Club / River Plate
2003 Independiente / River Plate
2004 Boca Juniors / River Plate
2005 Newell's Old Boys / Velez Sarsfield
2006 Boca Juniors / Boca Juniors
2007 Estudiantes / San Lorenzo
2008 Lanus
Note: two league seasons per year

BELOW Maradona's "hand of God" goal against England in 1986

ARGENTINA 155

GREAT NATIONS
ITALY

"We play to win, otherwise what's the point?"
PAOLO ROSSI

Italy has tasted glory on the world stage with four World Cup crowns. A dramatic penalty shoot-out won them the final against France in 2006—12 years after they lost the World Cup to Brazil on penalties.

ABOVE Luigi Riva outpaces Brazil defender Brito in the 1970 World Cup final

Italy is second only to Brazil in terms of World Cup wins, having lifted the Jules Rimet trophy four times. Known as "the Azzurri," or "Blues," the national side also triumphed at the 1968 European Championship, but this has been their lone triumph at confederation level. They came close, however, in 2000. Under the management of former World Cup-winning goalkeeper Dino Zoff, they had a 2-1 defeat to France on the "golden goal" rule in Rotterdam, Holland.

A combination of English and Swiss students and teachers introduced the sport to Italy in the second half of the 19th century, with the English influence still evident in the anglicized style of club names such as AC Milan and Genoa (rather than Milano and Genova).

Their national league was founded in the late 1920s, and top Italian clubs took part with limited success in the Mitropa Cup—an inter-war predecessor of the modern-day competition known as the Champions League.

Turin-based Juventus proved to be the outstanding side of the 1930s, winning the league title five years in a row and providing the backbone of the national team that won the World Cup in 1934.

Italy had refused to play in the 1930 World Cup finals in Uruguay, but won the next two world crowns thanks to the managerial wisdom of Vittorio Pozzo and the genius of inside forward Giuseppe Meazza. Pozzo played three Argentinians in the team that beat Czechoslovakia in the 1934 final. Pozzo responded to criticism by pointing out their eligibility to national service, saying: "If they can die for Italy, then I'm sure they can play football for Italy!"

Torino also won five consecutive titles in the 1940s with an outstanding squad that was so strong the national team used ten of their players in one match. However, the Torino squad was destroyed by a 1949 plane crash returning from playing a testimonial match in Lisbon.

The Torino disaster wrecked the national team's prospects ahead of their World Cup defence in Brazil in 1950. Also, many clubs invested financial strength in foreign players, which did nothing to help rebuild the national team. In 1958, Italy failed for the first time to progress through the qualifying system and into the World Cup finals.

During the early 1960s, clubs such as AC Milan and their bitter rivals Inter Milan ruled the European scene, even though the national team were unable to follow suit. Italy's participation in the 1966 World Cup finals remains notorious for their 1-0 defeat at the hands of North Korea, one of football's biggest upsets.

Adversity turned to glory when Italy captured the 1968 European Nations Cup after a replay. And two years later, inspired by the legendary

ABOVE Dino Zoff defies Brazil's Roberto and Oscar

RIGHT Paolo Rossi hails Alessandro Altobelli's third goal in the 1982 World Cup Final

figures of Giacinto Faccheti, Sandro Mazzola, Gigi Riva, and Gianni Rivera, Italy took part in one of the greatest games ever played. They edged past West Germany 4-3 in extra time to secure a place in the final of the World Cup. But they were so exhausted after the victory in the altitude of Mexico that they surrendered 4-1 to Brazil.

Italy arrived at the 1982 World Cup finals in the wake of a match-fixing scandal. Coach Enzo Bearzot and veteran captain Dino Zoff imposed a press blackout. Paolo Rossi had just returned from a two-year ban for his alleged role in the scandal and proved to be their inspiration, with six goals—including a hat-trick against Brazil—guiding his nation to overall victory.

For the next 24 years, the leading league clubs kept the Italian flag flying at international level with a string of European trophies.

Pride was finally restored at national team level in 2006 when, after Zinedine Zidane's infamous head butt, Italy became world champions again by beating France in a penalty shoot-out in Berlin. Yet this triumph was partially overshadowed by another match-fixing scandal that saw a number of teams, including Juventus, relegated as punishment to Serie B. Juventus had been under investigation for the illegal administration of unspecified stimulants to their players when telephone-tap investigators uncovered a match manipulation system created by Juventus' "transfer king" Luciano Moggi.

Evidence produced at a variety of hearings suggested that Moggi had used his influence with referees to generate yellow and red cards and suspensions for opposing players before they were due to play against Juventus and that he had also put pressure on players and coaches over transfers and even national team selection.

FOOTBALL FACTS

CHAMPIONS—LAST TEN YEARS
1999 AC Milan
2000 Lazio
2001 Roma
2002 Juventus
2003 Juventus
2004 AC Milan
2005 (not awarded: Juventus title revoked)
2006 Internazionale
2007 Internazionale
2008 Internazionale

ITALY 157

GREAT NATIONS
NETHERLANDS

Dutch football is synonymous with "total football"—the all-action strategy pioneered by Ajax Amsterdam under the inspiration of center forward Johan Cruyff in the early 1970s.

FOOTBALL FACTS

CHAMPIONS—LAST TEN YEARS
1999 Feyenoord
2000 PSV Eindhoven
2001 PSV Eindhoven
2002 Ajax Amsterdam
2003 PSV Eindhoven
2004 Ajax Amsterdam
2005 PSV Eindhoven
2006 PSV Eindhoven
2007 PSV Eindhoven
2008 PSV Eindhoven

Yet while Cruyff provided the brains and leadership out on the pitch, it was Ajax Amsterdam's coach Rinus Michels who masterminded the strategy. With two fabulous feet and mesmeric ball skills, Cruyff was at the heart of the Holland team—all of their goals in the 1974 World Cup finals either started or ended with a contribution by their captain.

Cruyff was supported by Johan Neeskens out of midfield, Ruud Krol from full back, and the duo of Johnny Rep and Rob Rensenbrink in attack. At the peak of their success, the team were nicknamed "Clockwork Orange," after the color of their shirts as well as their precision passing. They again finished as runner-up at the World Cup finals, even without Cruyff at the helm in 1978.

Yet in terms of international status, Holland had been late developers. A crucial reason was the fact that it was not until the the mid-1950s that domestic clubs such as Feyenoord, Sparta and Excelsior—notably all from Rotterdam—forced the recognition of professionalism, even initially part-time. The amateur status that ruled the Dutch game previously meant that star players, such as Faas Wilkes, had been forced abroad to the likes of Italy and Spain to earn a living from their talent.

Feyenoord became the first Dutch club to reach the semi-final stage of the European Champions' Cup in 1963, when they lost narrowly to Benfica. This was the start of a remarkable era, during which Feyenoord won the domestic double—league and cup—in both 1965 and 1969.

They then became the first Dutch club to win a European crown in 1970, edging past Celtic in extra time with a team that included outside left Coen Moulijn—one of the finest of Dutch players before the Ajax era.

Later Feyenoord, while largely playing second fiddle to Amsterdam Ajax at home, won the UEFA Cup twice. In recent years, PSV Eindhoven have also been regular group stage contenders in the Champions League.

Holland's national team had not qualified for the World Cup finals since the inter-war period but this, and the entire international status of Dutch football, was about to change with the explosive eruption of Amsterdam Ajax, which had reached the 1969 Champions' Cup final and then won it in 1971, 1972, and 1973, before Cruyff was sold to Barcelona.

Cruyff stepped out of national team football at the end of 1977 but Dutch football continued to produce an apparently endless stream of talented players and coaches.

PSV Eindhoven won the 1988 European Champions' Cup under the wily management of Guus Hiddink, while Holland won the European Championship in West Germany six weeks later. The Dutch national hero at that time was AC

Milan—and former Amsterdam Ajax—striker Marco van Basten, who scored a group stage hat-trick against England, a semi-final winner against West Germany and a magnificent volleyed winning goal against the Soviet Union in the final at Munich's Olympic Stadium.

Controversy was never far away whenever the Dutch faced their German arch rivals. A spitting incident involving Holland midfielder Frank Rijkaard and German striker Rudi Völler marred a dramatic clash in the second round of the 1990 World Cup finals in Italy, which Holland lost 2-1.

Too often at major tournaments, Holland's potential has been undermined by squabbling between players and coaching staff over tactics and team selection. Inspirational forward Ruud Gullit, a former World and European Player of the Year, refused to put on the shirt and play for Holland at the 1990 World Cup finals. Manager Hiddink sent midfielder Edgar Davids home during Holland's continued involvement in the 1996 European Championship after internal squabbling among the squad.

The unpredictability of the Dutch game's biggest names was evident up to the spring of 2008. Van Basten, by now manager of Holland, agreed to return as coach to Amsterdam Ajax after the European Championship in Austria and Switzerland, with Cruyff as a senior consultant. However, Cruyff had barely been confirmed in the role before he withdrew in an apparent disagreement with Van Basten—his one-time protégé—over youth strategy.

This is a sector that has become more crucial than ever to the Dutch game. The Ajax youth set-up is famed worldwide, with its players coached in a style and tactical system imposed on all the teams right through to the senior professionals. The club raises significant income selling players to the big leagues in England, Italy, and Spain to supplement its income from regular annual participation in European competitions.

ABOVE Johan Cruyff, captain and center forward of Holland and Ajax Amsterdam in the early 1970s

GREAT NATIONS MOMENTS

1960s

ABOVE North Korea and Portugal emerge for their sensational 1966 World Cup tie

BELOW The Soviet Union greet their English host fans in 1966

1970s

RIGHT Pelé celebrates Brazil's first in the 1970 World Cup final victory

BELOW Fabio Capello (front, left) lines up for Italy against England in 1973

RIGHT Franz Beckenbauer betters rival captain Johan Cruyff in the 1974 World Cup final

160 GREAT NATIONS

1970s 1980s 1990s 2000s

ABOVE Argentina poised to win their first World Cup, in 1978

RIGHT England line up, optimistically, ahead of their 1982 World Cup assault

BELOW Holland in 1978 —about to finish World Cup runners-up once more

ABOVE Didier Six opens up for France against Czechoslovakia in 1982

ABOVE Mexico head for a 2-1 defeat by Portugal in Germany in 2006

LEFT Gary Lineker's penalty goal against West Germany in 1990 is not enough for England

MOMENTS 161

GREAT NATIONS
ENGLAND

England lays justifiable claim to be the home and birthplace of football—the game itself is thought to originate in the Middle Ages, but its rules weren't formalized until the mid-19th century.

The formation of the Football League in 1863, the first FA Cup Final in 1872, and the introduction of a revolutionary league system in 1888 were major events in the game's development in England.

But the country has only one World Cup triumph to date; the 1966 glory at London's Wembley Stadium. This victory was founded upon Alf Ramsey's coaching, Bobby Moore's captaincy, Bobby Charlton's long-range shooting, and Geoff Hurst's famous hat-trick. Bobby Robson's team, inspired by Paul Gascoigne and Gary Lineker, came close to tasting success by reaching the 1990 World Cup semi-final in Italy.

Despite international disappointment, England has some of the world's richest and most watched domestic teams. The national game's image was marred by hooliganism and tragedy in the 1980s and only booming television revenues and the lucrative FA Premier League's 1992 launch have helped tempt over some of the world's top talents. Manchester United, the world's best supported club, have dominated this in recent years, with big-spending Chelsea now wanting a slice of glory.

Manchester United claimed England's first European Champions' Cup by beating Lisbon's Benfica in 1968, some five years after Bill

FOOTBALL FACTS

CHAMPIONS—LAST TEN YEARS
1999 Manchester United
2000 Manchester United
2001 Manchester United
2002 Arsenal
2003 Manchester United
2004 Arsenal
2005 Chelsea
2006 Chelsea
2007 Manchester United
2008 Manchester United

RIGHT England Captain Bobby Moore plants a winning kiss on the World Cup in 1966

162 GREAT NATIONS

Nicholson's Tottenham had become the first English winners of a European trophy in the Cup Winners' Cup. Under the management of Sir Alex Ferguson, Manchester United won an unique hat-trick for an English club in 1999, with victory in the Premier League, FA Cup, and the Champions League to complete a unique hat-trick for an English club.

A third Champions League triumph followed in 2008, when United defeated Chelsea in a penalty shoot-out in Moscow in the first all-English final in the competition's history.

English clubs dominated Europe, with the European Cup won by an English side for five successive years in the late 1970s and early 1980s.

The dark side of the English passion for football has been a long history of hooliganism. Trouble began to be noted in English League grounds in the early 1970s, but English fans' passion for traveling to away matches meant that hooliganism was exported and earned clubs a bad name. Leeds United were barred from European football in the mid-1970s after their fans, angered by controversial refereeing in the 1975 Champions' Cup final against Bayern Munich, ripped out seats in the Parc des Princes in Paris.

A string of incidents occurred over the next decade and it was only after the Heysel disaster of 1985, when 39 Juventus fans died in Brussels after being charged by Liverpool followers, that both football and the law took action. The process was expanded after a crowd crush disaster at Hillsborough, Sheffield, in 1989. All-seater demands were imposed on all major sports venues, leading to the building of new grounds and total redevelopment of others. The pace of the stadia and security revolution persuaded UEFA to grant England hosting rights to the European Championship finals in 1996, which proved to be a huge success on and off the pitch.

English football has led the world game in many ways. In the late 1920s and early 1930s it was Arsenal, thanks to manager Herbert Chapman and forward Charlie Buchan, that conceived the "WM" system, a formation, that dominated the sport for four decades. In the early 1990s, England opened the way for foreign investors and owners, also creating the FA Premier League at a crucial time when satellite television was booming and clubs were turning to the London Stock Exchange.

Enormous controversy was generated by the purchase of Manchester United by the American Glazer family, although concerns about the club's debt and any loans were soon completely overshadowed by their remarkable continuing success on the pitch.

Chelsea emerged as United's major rivals after the remarkable takeover in 2003 by Russian oligarch Roman Abramovich, who invested seemingly limitless sums in paying off the club's debts and buying in some of the world's finest players. Abramovich's early rewards included Premier League titles in 2005 and 2006.

ABOVE David Beckham lines up England's winning penalty against Argentina in 2002

GREAT NATIONS
FRANCE

France's contribution to football goes far beyond its national team's significant achievements on the pitch. French administrator Jules Rimet was the brains behind the creation of the World Cup finals.

FOOTBALL FACTS

CHAMPIONS—LAST TEN YEARS
1999 Bordeaux
2000 Monaco
2001 Nantes
2002 Lyon
2003 Lyon
2004 Lyon
2005 Lyon
2006 Lyon
2007 Lyon
2008 Lyon

Another French administrator, Henri Delaunay, paved the way for the European Championship. Gabriel Hanot, editor of the daily sports newspaper *L'Equipe*, was the creative force behind the European Champions Clubs' Cup.

France's greatest achievement on the field was their World Cup victory, on home soil, in 1998. Inspired by midfielder Zinedine Zidane, they saw off Paraguay, Italy and Croatia in the knock-out stage before crushing Brazil 4-0 in the final.

Two years later, David Trezeguet scored the "golden goal" that beat Italy 2-1 in the 2000 European Championship final. Sylvain Wiltord had forced extra time with a last-gasp equalizer.

Zidane, who retired from international football after the 2004 European Championship, made an impressive comeback as France reached the final of the 2006 World Cup, but was sent off for head butting an opponent during defeat by Italy.

One of the greatest personalities in the modern French game has been Michel Platini. In 1984, he towered over the Euro finals—in France—scoring nine goals as the home team went on to beat Spain 2-0 in the final. Later, Platini progressed to become the country's national manager, President of the Organizing Committee of the 1998 World Cup and then a Counsellor to the FIFA President before being elected UEFA President in 2007.

French club football is often overshadowed by the national team, as so many home-grown players have moved abroad. One of the persisting problems for the league has been the lack of an established, successful club in the French capital, Paris. The power of the French game has resided largely in the provinces—the comparatively new team Paris Saint-Germain once reached the final of the now-defunct European Cup Winners' Cup, but are better known for a long series of boardroom and ownership battles.

RIGHT Raymond Kopa, the first French footballer to be hailed European Player of the Year

The first French club to make an international impression were Reims. Prompted by creative center forward Raymond Kopa, they reached the first European Champions' Cup final in 1956 and were losing finalists again three years later. Kopa was the playmaker for the France side that finished third in the 1958 World Cup finals and helped set up most of Just Fontaine's record tally of 13 goals. Fontaine had been brought into the team only at the last minute because of injury to Reims team-mate René Bliard.

No French club managed to reach the European Champions' Cup final again until the eruption of Olympique Marseille in the late 1980s and early 1990s. The team were bankrolled by the flamboyant businessman-turned-politician Bernard Tapie.

A team starring top-scoring French player Jean-Pierre Papin and England winger Chris Waddle finished as runner-up in the 1991 European Champions' Cup, losing on penalties to Red Stade Belgrade. Two years later, Olympique Marseille defeated AC Milan 1-0 with Papin playing for the Italian club. But that triumph was tarnished almost immediately as Marseilles were thrown out of European competition over a domestic match-fixing scandal that saw Tapie imprisoned.

Other French football clubs and their directors were punished, with sentences ranging from suspensions to fines for financial irregularities.

Lyon President Jean-Michel Aulas said: "What we need in the French game is greater financial freedom to run our own affairs. Then maybe we wouldn't have these other problems. Fans demand success and directors want to give that to them, for their own reasons."

Software millionaire Aulas knew his subject well. He had taken over Lyon when the club were in the second division, and supplied both financial and administrative resources to secure promotion and then a record run of seven successive league titles from 2002 to 2008.

Aulas even pressed successfully for a relaxation of laws barring sports clubs from obtaining outside, foreign investment. He claimed that, without new revenue streams, French clubs could not afford to buy the best players nor could they develop stadia to such an extent that the country could ever hope to host the finals of the World Cup or European Championship.

The factor that has continued to elude Aulas has been success in European competitions. Lyon have regularly reached the knock-out stage of the European Champions League without ever reaching even the semi-finals. Saint-Etienne (1976) and AS Monaco (2004) remain the only other French clubs aside from Reims and Marseille to have reached a European Champions League final. Saint-Etienne lost narrowly to Bayern Munich while AS Monaco crashed 3-0 to Porto.

BELOW Zinedine Zidane outplays Italy's Gennaro Gattuso in the 2006 World Cup final

GREAT NATIONS
GERMANY

"After the game is always before the next game."

SEPP HERBERGER

Germany have long been one of the most powerful countries in international football and their leading club, Bayern Munich, are one of the most famous, thanks to four European Champions' Cup victories.

FOOTBALL FACTS

CHAMPIONS—LAST TEN YEARS
- **1999** Bayern Munich
- **2000** Bayern Munich
- **2001** Bayern Munich
- **2002** Borussia Dortmund
- **2003** Bayern Munich
- **2004** Werder Bremen
- **2005** Bayern Munich
- **2006** Bayern Munich
- **2007** Stuttgart
- **2008** Bayern Munich

Football had difficulty establishing itself initially in Germany because of the social strength of the gymnastic movement. Attitudes changed gradually partly because of football's popularity among young people and, partly because toward the end of World War I, the Kaiser ascribed British strength of character on the battlefield to the morale and physical qualities developed through the team sports played at schools and universities.

Football clubs thrived in the inter-war years even though the domestic game was riven with tension over the issue of professionalism. Even under Hitler's National Socialist government in the 1930s, football was considered a recreation with payments to players prohibited. This did not prevent many clubs from bending the rules.

The leading club in the 1930s were FC Schalke, which came from the mining town of Gelsenkirchen in the Ruhr. All their players were paid as miners. Their star winger Ernst Kuzorra revealed years later: "The nearest we saw of a mine was the pithead in the distance."

The German game was organized in a regional championship, topped off by a play-off series to decide the national champions. The play-off final regularly drew crowds of 70,000–80,000. FC Schalke were crowned champions six times and won the domestic cup once in the 1930s. Their inside forward, Fritz Szepan, led Germany to third place in the 1934 World Cup. Kuzorra and Szepan both have roads named in their honor around the present FC Schalke stadium.

After the war, political reality saw Germany divided into west and east sectors. Ultimately, Soviet-supported East Germany, known as the German Democratic Republic, developed its own football federation and league. Although East Germany became a force in international swimming and athletics, it did not replicate this success in football. East Germany only ever qualified for the World Cup finals in 1974, and in the same year, Magdeburg won the nation's only European club trophy by taking the Cup Winners' Cup.

In contrast, football in West Germany went from strength to strength. Wily coach Sepp Herberger and captain Fritz Walter guided the West German team to a shock victory over hot favorites Hungary in the final of the 1954 World Cup. The victory was known as the "miracle of Berne." Hungary—as Olympic champions—had not been beaten for four years. Further World Cup triumphs followed in 1974 and in 1990.

In 1990, the collapse of the Berlin Wall led to the reunification of Germany and the integration of East German football into the German football federation, which had always styled itself as the "overall" Deutscher Fussball Bund.

Germany, whether West or unified, have also finished as World Cup runner-up four times (1966, 1982, 1986, and 2002) and third three times (1976, 1992, and 2008). They have also won the European Championship three times (1972, 1980, and 1996) and three times finished as runner-up (1976, 1992, and 2008).

A significant factor in the national team's success was the creation of the unified, fully professional Bundesliga in 1963. Bayern Munich, who have won 20 modern championships to add to their success in 1932, hold the record for the greatest number of domestic titles. The greatest personality to emerge from within Bayern Munich was Franz Beckenbauer, known as "Der Kaiser," who netted 68 goals in 62 games for his country, including the winning goal in the 1974 World Cup final against Holland.

As captain and sweeper, Beckenbauer led Bayern Munich to a European Champions' League hat-trick (1974, 1975, and 1976). He was ably supported by a host of stars that included goalkeeper "Sepp" Maier, full-back Paul Breitner, midfielder Uli Hoeness, and the greatest goal scorer of the modern era, Gerd Müller.

Beckenbauer later coached West Germany to 1990 World Cup victory over Argentina in Italy, having guided them to the final four years earlier. In the meantime, he coached Bayern Munich to UEFA Cup success in 1996 and became their club president in time to oversee their fourth European Champions' League victory in 2001.

Moving on up the political ladder, Beckenbauer led the German bid to win hosting rights to the 2006 World Cup finals for Germany and was then president of the FIFA Organizing Committee. As a vice-president of the German Football Federation he was also voted onto the executive committees of both FIFA and UEFA.

TOP Hosts West Germany await kick-off in the 1974 World Cup finals

BOTTOM Bayern's Gerd Müller pounces on a defensive slip

GREAT NATIONS
PORTUGAL

The Portuguese team are often known as the "Brazilians of Europe," thanks to the flamboyance of Eusébio in the 1960s, the "golden generation" of Luis Figo, João Pinto, and Rui Costa in the 1990s, and the country's latest idol, Cristiano Ronaldo.

FOOTBALL FACTS

CHAMPIONS—LAST TEN YEARS
1999 Porto
2000 Sporting Lisbon
2001 Boavista
2002 Sporting Lisbon
2003 Porto
2004 Porto
2005 Benfica
2006 Porto
2007 Porto
2008 Porto

Traditionally the power of the Portuguese game has been dominated by the three leading clubs of Benfica, Porto, and Sporting Lisbon. Only Belenenses in 1948 and Boavista in 2001 have broken their monopoly of the league since its formation in 1934. Benfica lead the way with 31 championships, with Porto picking up 16 of their 23 titles in the past 24 years.

Football was introduced to Portugal through the ports in the 19th century, but the relatively small size of the country meant the national team had little or no impact internationally. However, Portugal had a source of playing talent in their African territories, such as Angola and Mozambique. An increasing number of African players were imported by the clubs and, from the late 1950s, also selected for the national team. Such players included Benfica's goalkeeper Jose Alberto Costa Pereira, striker Jose Aguas, and the two inside forwards Joaquin Santana and Mario Coluna.

All four were members of Benfica's Champions' Cup-winning side that, in 1961, defeated favorites Barcelona 3-2 in Berne, Switzerland. Simultaneously, Benfica had also acquired the greatest African discovery of all in young striker Eusébio da Silva Ferreira. One year later he scored two thundering goals as Benfica defeated Real Madrid 5-3 to win their second Champions' Cup.

Eusébio would also lead Benfica to three more finals, albeit finishing on the losers' side against AC Milan (1963), Inter Milan (1965), and Manchester United (1968).

A mixture of Sporting Lisbon's defense, along with Benfica's midfield and attack, provided the backbone for the Portuguese national side that finished third in their first ever World Cup finals, Eusébio a nine-goal top scorer in England.

Like the country itself, Portuguese football suffered from economic decline in the following

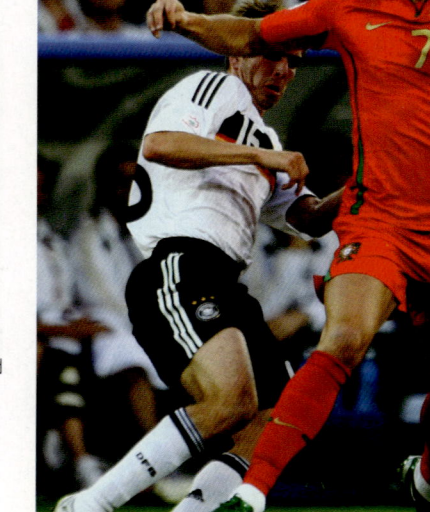

FAR RIGHT Eusébio floors Hungary's defence in the 1966 World Cup finals

RIGHT Cristiano Ronaldo escapes Germany's Philipp Lahm at Euro 2008.

168 GREAT NATIONS

decades but a new era dawned with triumphs in the 1989 and 1991 World Youth Cups. Ever since the emergence of the so-called "golden generation," Portugal became a potential threat at major tournaments.

Porto emerged as the dominant club under the controversial presidency of Jorge Nuno Pinto da Costa. He hired an equally controversial coach in Jose Mourinho and was rewarded with victory in the 2003 UEFA Cup and then, more impressively, in the European Champions League a year later—before Mourinho was lured away to Chelsea.

Portugal reached the semi-final stage of the 2000 European Championship in Belgium and Holland. The inability to compete in wages with the giants of England, Italy, and Spain meant the departure of stars such as Figo (Barcelona, Real Madrid, and Inter Milan), Simao Sabrosa (Barcelona and Atletico Madrid), Deco (Barcelona), and Cristiano Ronaldo (Manchester United). The national team gained from these players—technically and tactically—competing in better-quality leagues.

From 2003–08, the Portuguese Football Federation hired Luiz Felipe Scolari, Brazil's 2002 World Cup-winning coach, to bring the competitive best out of the country's depth of talent. Scolari succeeded to a qualified degree. Portugal finished as runner-up on home territory in the 2004 European Championship—losing to outsiders Greece in the final—and were fourth at the 2006 World Cup finals in Germany. Scolari conceded on leaving in 2008 to return to club football with Chelsea: "I did not win something big which is what I came to do."

Scolari's final game with Portugal was at the 2008 European Championship finals, when Portugal fell 3-2 to Germany in the quarter-finals. Critics in Libson claimed the team had been distracted by the mid-event announcement of Scolari's new job and by uncertainty over whether Ronaldo would be leaving Manchester United for Real Madrid.

GREAT NATIONS
SPAIN

No talented national side has underachieved quite as badly as Spain, who surprisingly have yet to win the World Cup. Yet their recent triumph at the 2008 European Championship could kick-off a new era.

FOOTBALL FACTS

CHAMPIONS—LAST TEN YEARS
1999 Barcelona
2000 Deportivo La Coruna
2001 Real Madrid
2002 Valencia
2003 Real Madrid
2004 Valencia
2005 Barcelona
2006 Barcelona
2007 Real Madrid
2008 Real Madrid

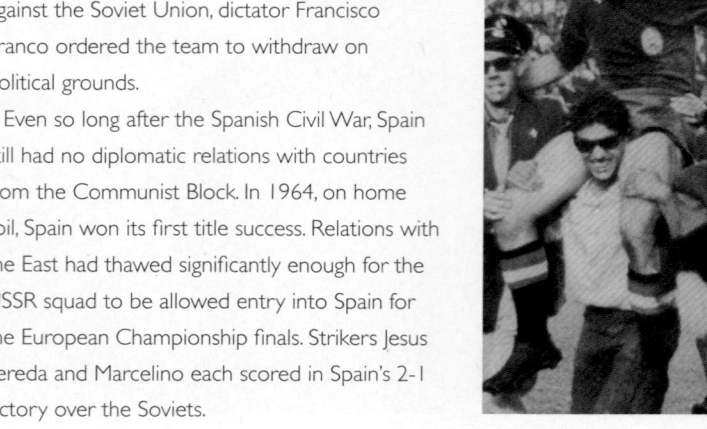

RIGHT Captain Fernando Olivella and coach Jose Villalonga, European winners in 1964

Spain have a history rich in great players and their 2008 European Championship victory means that their best players—goalkeeper and captain Iker Casillas, the midfielder trio of Cesc Fabregas, Xavi Hernandez and Andres Iniesta, and the strikeforce of Fernando Torres and David Villa—can claim equality of star billing in the hall of fame with older heroes. These included legends of the 1920s and 1930s, when goalkeeper Ricardo Zamora, defender Jacinto Quincoces, and inside forward Luis Regueiro helped Spain become the first foreign nation to beat England 4-3 in Madrid in 1929.

At the end of the 1950s, a team packed with stars such as Alfredo Di Stefano, Ladislav Kubala, and Luis Suarez saw Spain ranked as favorites to win the inaugural Nations Cup. However, when the 1960 quarter-final draw matched Spain against the Soviet Union, dictator Francisco Franco ordered the team to withdraw on political grounds.

Even so long after the Spanish Civil War, Spain still had no diplomatic relations with countries from the Communist Block. In 1964, on home soil, Spain won its first title success. Relations with the East had thawed significantly enough for the USSR squad to be allowed entry into Spain for the European Championship finals. Strikers Jesus Pereda and Marcelino each scored in Spain's 2-1 victory over the Soviets.

Spain's failure to achieve national team success in the succeeding four decades remains one of football's mysteries. The football federation has long run one of the most successful international youth sections and Juan Santisteban, once a European Cup-winning halfback with Real Madrid, has been perhaps the most respected age level coach in the world. But the best the seniors could point to was a runner-up spot at the 1984 European Championship finals and a

ABOVE Fernando Torres heads for glory against Germany in 2008

stunning 5-1 win over Denmark in the second round of the 1986 World Cup finals, when Emilio Butragueno, nicknamed "the vulture," scored four goals.

However, at club level the story could not be more different. Real Madrid were Europe's first club champions in 1956 and retained the trophy for the next four years, during a period of total domination in which the team enthralled with their victories in an entertaining manner. With nine European Champions' Cups, two UEFA Cups, and 31 domestic league titles, Real Madrid have their own special place in the history books.

They also led the way in European stadium development, which they owed to the vision of Santiago Bernabeu—a former player and coach, who became president in 1943. Bernabeu issued bonds to finance the building of a new stadium that was opened in 1947, and named the Bernabeu Stadium. Its capacity was increased in the late 1950s to 125,000, as fans flocked to watch their heroes and superstars at work.

In terms of power and ambition, however, the Catalan institution stands not far behind. With its motto of "More than a Club," Barcelona claims a unique loyalty on and off the field. Yet the club has never dominated the European Champions League Cup in the manner of their bitter rivals, Real Madrid. Barcelona were finalists in 1961 and 1986. But they have won twice, beating Sampdoria at Wembley Stadium in 1992 and seeing off Arsenal at the Stade de France in 2006.

SPAIN 171

GREAT NATIONS
RUSSIA

Europe's most populous nation has rarely punched its weight in international football. So far, its greatest days came in the early 1960s, while it was a part of the Soviet Union.

FOOTBALL FACTS

CHAMPIONS—LAST TEN YEARS
1998 Spartak Moscow
1999 Spartak Moscow
2000 Spartak Moscow
2001 Spartak Moscow
2002 Lokomotiv Moscow
2003 CSKA Moscow
2004 Lokomotiv Moscow
2005 CSKA Moscow
2006 CSKA Moscow
2007 Zenit St. Petersburg
Note: The Russian league runs spring-to-autumn

Moscow, the capital of the USSR, was the central force in its national football. It boasted all the major clubs—Dynamo, Spartak, Torpedo, Lokomotiv, and CSKA—and had all the finest players. The size of the country made it difficult for any other clubs to compete effectively until air travel was possible. Even that was a risk, with the entire first team squad of Pakhtakor Tashkent killed when their plane crashed in 1979.

By the mid-1960s, however, major powers were emerging in the club game in Georgia and Ukraine especially, and also in Armenia and Belarus. Dynamo Tbilisi, Dynamo Kiev, Dynamo Minsk, and Ararat Yerevan may have owed their creation to the Soviet model but all developed a style of football very different to the physical Moscow style. Tbilisi and Kiev played football with a Latin-style touch of flair. Kiev twice won in the European Cup Winners' Cup and Tbilisi won it once but their officials and coaches and players never co-exited happily with the Moscow factions.

The Soviet Communist attitude to sport brought other complications. The USSR ignored FIFA and would not compete internationally until after World War II. A tour of Britain by Moscow Dynamo in the winter of 1945 marked a slight thaw. Two years later the Soviet Union joined FIFA on condition that it could have a permanent vice-president.

By definition, Soviet footballers were amateurs, not paid for playing football though they were paid for their nominal roles in the armed services or other professions. The Soviet Union felt free to send its strongest possible team to the Olympics, while Western European rivals were weakened by the transparency of their own players' professional status. The Soviet national team competed internationally for the first time at the 1952 Olympic Games, which they duly won four years later in Melbourne, Australia. Their heroes were world-class footballers, goalkeeper Lev Yashin, and left-half skipper Igor Netto.

Yashin was a hero again when the Soviets won the inaugural 1960 European Championship. Milan Galic had given Yugoslavia the lead, right winger Slava Metreveli leveled, and journalist turned-

RIGHT Russia prepare for their Euro 2008 adventure

center forward Viktor Ponedelnik wrote his own page in history by scoring the extra time winner. The Soviet Union lost the 1964 final 2-1 to Spain and finished fourth in the 1966 World Cup finals.

The change in the balance of power is reflected in the league honors list when the Soviet Union was finally wiped off the map after the experiment with perestroika undermined the entire system. Kiev won 13 league titles in the Soviet era, Spartak Moscow 12, Dynamo Moscow 11, CSKA Moscow seven, and Lokomotiv Moscow three.

Yet not once in the Soviet era did a club from the Russian Republic win a European cup. That feat had to wait until 2005 when CSKA Moscow beat Sporting Lisbon 3-1 in the UEFA Cup final. Zenit St. Petersburg followed their example in 2008, when they also won the UEFA Cup, beating Rangers. Those achievements demonstrated how far Russian clubs have come since the break up of the Soviet Union and the formation of a Russian league—then virtually bankrupt—in 1992.

The collapse of central funding for football clubs from the various state organizations threw the domestic game into turmoil. Within a decade, only Lokomotiv were still in the controlling, supporting hands of the railway unions. All the other clubs had long since been cast adrift by the secret police (Dynamo), army (CSKA), and farms (Spartak).

The domestic game was rescued by the oligarchs who had taken massive financial advantage of the collapse of Communism and the bargain-basement sell-offs of the major utilities. Roman Abramovich's oil company Sibneft originally supported CSKA and the Russian energy giant Gazprom funded the 2007 champions Zenit. The outcome has been that Russian clubs now import star players from all over the world.

ABOVE Legendary goalkeeper Lev Yashin defies Portugal's Eusébio at the 1966 World Cup

GREAT NATIONS
REST OF THE WORLD

From small nations such as Luxembourg and San Marino to the array of African sides and former Soviet states, the status and power of world football is forever changing.

BELOW Bulgaria's Hristo Stoichkov (left) celebrates another goal for Barcelona

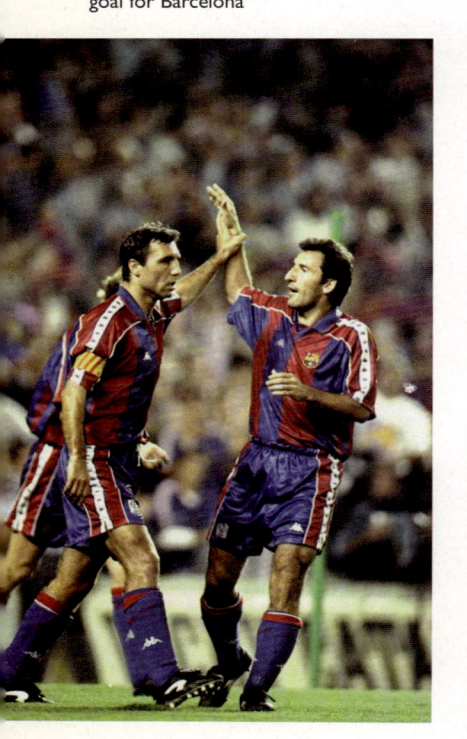

ALBANIA (Europe): Despite being among UEFA's founder members in 1954, Albanian football has been hampered by the country's poverty and isolation. They beat newly-crowned European champions Greece in the 2006 World Cup qualifiers, but are still waiting to reach their first tournament—though Albania's star midfielder Lorik Cana has proved outstanding at Marseille.

ALGERIA (Africa): Having broken away from France in 1958, Algeria's footballers beat eventual finalists West Germany at the 1982 World Cup thanks to Lakhdar Belloumi's goal but were eliminated in a convenient draw between the West Germans and Austria. Their finest moment came when Moussa Saïb captained the hosts to success at the 1990 African Cup of Nations. JS Kabylie are dominant at home, having won 13 league titles.

ANDORRA (Europe): Not too much can be expected of a country with a population of 72,000, squeezed between Spain and France. Andorra's team, largely made up of part-timers, only began playing international football in 1997. Ce Principat and FC Santa Coloma have won three league titles apiece since 1995.

ANGOLA (Africa): On the rise after years of being constrained by civil war and having their finest players poached by Portugal, Angola made an encouraging World Cup finals debut in 2006. Petro Atlético have been crowned as Angolan champions 13 times.

AUSTRALIA (Asia): After achieving nothing at the 1974 World Cup, the "Socceroos" did not bounce back until 2006, when Dutch manager Guus Hiddink made effective use of such talents as Tim Cahill, Harry Kewell, and Mark Viduka. The nation left the uncompetitive Oceania Football Federation for Asia later that year. The A-League kicked off in 2005–06, with one grand final triumph apiece for Melbourne Victory, Newcastle Jets, and Sydney FC.

AUSTRIA (Europe): The so-called "Wunderteam" of the 1930s, inspired by playmaker Matthias Sindelar and coach Hugo Meisl, finished fourth at the 1934 World Cup. Austrian coach Ernst Happel took Holland to the 1978 World Cup final; the Ernst Happel Stadium in Vienna is named after him. The stadium was also the venue for the Euro 2008 final. Rapid Vienna lead the way in home games, with an astonishing 31 league titles.

AZERBAIJAN (Europe): This former Soviet state has struggled since independence despite a spell in charge by World Cup-winning Brazil captain Carlos Alberto. The main stadium in Baku is named after linesman Tofik Bakhmarov, who decided England's third goal in the 1966 World Cup final really did cross the line. Neftchi Baku have won five league titles.

BELARUS (Europe): Midfielder Alexander Hleb put Belarus on the map with his club displays in Germany and England, but the former Soviet state narrowly missed out on a place at the 2002 World Cup finals after a last-gasp defeat to Wales. Dinamo Minsk have been the dominant side, with seven league crowns to their credit.

BELGIUM (Europe): Despite its small size, Belgium reached the 1980 European Championship final, beat holders Argentina in the opening game of the 1982 World Cup, and finished fourth in 1986 under Guy Thys. Goalkeeper Jean-Marie Pfaff, defender Eric Gerets, midfielder Jan Ceulemans, and forward Enzo Scifo formed the side's spine. Anderlecht have won not only a record 29 league titles but one UEFA Cup, a pair of European Super Cups, twice been crowned European Champions, and twice won the Cup Winners' Cup.

BOLIVIA (South America): The Hernando Siles Stadium in the capital of La Paz is one of the world's highest playing surfaces, at 3,637 meters above sea level. The national side have struggled, although they did win the 1963 Copa America courtesy of a 5-4 win over Brazil. Bolívar FC have won the domestic league 15 times.

BOSNIA-HERZEGOVINA (Europe): This former Yugoslav republic was accepted by UEFA in 1991, but promising players such as midfield schemer Zvjezdan Misimovic have not yet been able to reach a major tournament. Their football association has been under fire for its problems.

BULGARIA (Europe): This is one of Eastern Europe's most consistent producers of quality players. The national team's finest achievement was in reaching the World Cup semi-finals in 1994 with a team starring the legendary Hristo Stoichkov and Emil Kostadinov. The record domestic champions are CSKA Sofia with 31 league titles to their credit.

CAMEROON (Africa): Known as the "Indomitable Lions," they were the surprise package at the 1990 World Cup. They upset holders Argentina and pushed England hard in the quarter-finals, spearheaded by veteran striker Roger Milla. Barcelona's Samuel Eto'o holds the scoring record for the African Cup of Nations, a competition that Cameroon have won four times. Canon Yaoundé have won the African Championship three times to match their 11 domestic league titles.

CANADA (North America): Often overshadowed by CONCACAF rivals such as Mexico and the US, Canada failed to win the CONCACAF Gold Cup in 1990. This was despite spectacular saves from their former Premiership goalkeeper Craig Forrest and the goalscoring talents of Carlo Corazzin.

ABOVE Samuel Eto'o acknowledges the cheers greeting another of his goals for Cameroon

GREAT NATIONS
REST OF THE WORLD

CHILE (South America): Strike duo Marcelo Salas and Iván Zamorano helped guide Chile to the 1998 World Cup quarter-finals. But Chile's best run came when hosting the 1962 tournament, when they eventually lost to Brazil in a fiery semi-final. Colo-Colo have won 27 Chilean league titles, more than double the tally of their main rivals.

CHINA (Asia): The national team faced Manila in Asia's first international match in 1913, but made their World Cup finals debut only in 2002 when they lost all three matches. Versatile midfielder Zheng Zhi captained the side that hosted but lost the 2004 Asian Cup final to Japan.

COLOMBIA (South America): Carlos Valderrama, Faustino Asprilla and goalkeeper Rene Higuita (famous for his "scorpion kick") made Colombia one of the world's most entertaining sides in the 1990s. Iván Córdoba's goal beat Mexico in the 2001 Copa America final. Club Deportivo Los Millonarios, whose riches lured stars such as Alfredo Di Stefano in the 1940s and 1950s, have picked up 13 league titles.

CONGO DR (Africa): Under their former name of Zaire, they became the first black African side to reach the World Cup finals. But at the 1974 competition they were humiliated by eventual champions West Germany. They were crowned African champions in 1968 and 1974, but government support for the sport has dwindled since then, despite striker Lomana LuaLua's recent Premiership experience. AS Vita Club and DC Motema Pembe each have 11 league titles.

COSTA RICA (Central America): Consistent performers who reached their first World Cup in 1990 under charismatic coach Bora Milutinovic. They also appeared at the 2002 and 2006 tournaments. with striker Paolo Wanchope as the figurehead. They have won nine CONCACAF championships, though surprisingly none since 1989. Former CONCACAF club champions Deportivo Saprissa have a record 26 domestic league titles.

CROATIA (Europe): This Balkan country taught England a footballing lesson in qualifiers for the 2008 European Championship—just as they did to Germany on their way to third place at the 1998 World Cup. Back then they were inspired by the likes of Robert Prosinecki, Golden Boot winner Davor Šuker, and future national coach Slaven Bilic. More recently, Brazilian-born striker Eduardo and nimble midfielders Luka Modric and Ivan Rakitic have caught the eye. Dinamo Zagred have won the league 11 times since Croatia achieved independence from the former Yugoslavia.

CYPRUS (Europe): Small fry who were thrilled to pull off 1-1 draws against Italy, Czechoslovakia, and France in the 1990s. APOEL Nicosia and Omonia Nicosia have won the Cypriot league 19 times each.

CZECH REPUBLIC (Europe): The Czechs formed the larger part of the old Czechoslovakia, which reached the World Cup Final in 1934 and 1962—when Czech wing half Josef Masopust was voted European Footballer of the Year. Czechoslovakia won the European Championship

ABOVE Colombia's Carlos Valderrama has earned more than 100 caps playing for his country

in 1976. The "new" Czech Republic side lost the Euro 1996 final to Germany on a "golden goal." They also reached the semi-finals of Euro 2004. Sparta Prague have dominated domestic football, winning 11 championships since the Czechs and Slovaks split in 1993. But the best Czech players inevitably move to the big clubs in the West. Pavel Nedved of Juventus was voted European Footballer of the Year in 2003. Other stars have included Petr Cech (Chelsea), Tomas Rosicky (Dortmund and Arsenal), and Champions' Cup-winner Vladimir Smicer (Lens and Liverpool).

DENMARK (Europe): The Danes' greatest triumph came in 1992, when a goal by John Jensen beat Germany 1-0 to win the European Championship final. The Danes also reached the semi-finals of Euro 1984 and the last 16 of the 1986 World Cup. Denmark has produced many stars for rich Western clubs, such as the Laudrup brothers (Michael and Brian), Morten Olsen, and Manchester United great Peter Schmeichel.

ECUADOR (South America): Qualified for the last two World Cup finals tournaments and reached the last 16 in 2006.

EGYPT (Africa): Won the African Cup of Nations for a record sixth time in 2008, beating Cameroon 1-0 in the final.

EL SALVADOR (Central America): Reached the 1970 World Cup finals by beating local rivals Honduras. This stoked up an already tense situation between the two countries, culminating in a six-day conflict that became known as "the football war."

ESTONIA (Europe): Flora Tallinn have dominated the domestic championship since Estonia became a republic in 1992.

FAROE ISLANDS (Europe): The Faroes' best results have been a 1-0 win over Austria and a 2-2 draw with Scotland, both in European Championship qualifiers.

FINLAND (Europe): Noted for producing players for Europe's big clubs, such as Jari Litmanen (Ajax) and Sami Hyypia (Liverpool). The domestic championship has been dominated by HJK Helsinki, United Tampere, and Haka Valkeakoski.

GEORGIA (Europe): Their greatest moment came in 1981, when Dinamo Tbilisi, inspired by midfielder David Kipiani, beat Carl Zeiss Jena 2-1 in the European Cup Winners' Cup final.

GHANA (Africa): Ghana reached the last 16 of the 2006 World Cup finals with a team featuring Premier League stars such as Michael Essien and Sulley Muntari. They have won the African Cup of Nations four times.

ABOVE Theo Zagorakis, a European title-winning hero for Greece

GREAT NATIONS
REST OF THE WORLD

GREECE (Europe): Shock winners of the 2004 European Championship when Otto Rehhagel's side beat hosts Portugal 1-0 in the final with a goal from Angelos Charisteas. They then failed to qualify for the 2006 World Cup finals. Panathinaikos reached the 1971 European Cup final, losing to Ajax at Wembley. Olympiakos have dominated the domestic game, winning 11 of the last 12 championships. In 2008, they became the first Greek side to play in the last 16 of the Champions League.

HAITI (Central/North America): Haiti reached the World Cup finals in 1974 when Emmanuel Sanon scored a historic goal against Italy but have not been back since. They were CONCACAF champions in 1957 and 1973.

HONDURAS (Central/North America): Reaching the World Cup finals for the only time in 1982, they had been CONCACAF champions the previous year.

HUNGARY (Europe): The "Magnificent Magyars" were the finest team in the world in the early 1950s. Led by Ferenc Puskas, they included greats such as striker Sandor Kocsis, playmaker Nandor Hidegkuti, flying winger Zoltan Czibor, goalkeeper Gyula Grocis, and wing half Jozsef Boszik. But they were shocked by West Germany in the 1954 World Cup Final and the team broke up two years later after the Budapest uprising against Soviet control. A new side finished third in the 1964 European Championship and reached the 1966 World Cup quarter-finals after beating Brazil 3-1. Hungary have struggled at international level ever since.

ICELAND (Europe): Yet to make an impact in major competitions, they are, however, well known for exporting star players, such as former Chelsea and Barcelona forward Eidur Gudjohnsen.

INDIA (Asia): The team reached the World Cup finals once, in 1950, but withdrew after FIFA barred them from playing in bare feet.

IRAN (Asia): Although they have reached the World Cup finals three times, they have yet to reach the last 16. They have won the Asian Cup three times. Iran's best player Ali Daei has won 149 caps.

IRAQ (Asia): Iraq are the current Asian Cup holders after beating favorites Saudi Arabia 1-0 in the 2007 final.

ISRAEL (Asia): Israeli clubs dominated the early years of the Asian Club Championship, before political problems forced the country out into the cold and then into UEFA. The national team were World Cup finalists in 1970.

BELOW Haiti's Sanon runs with the ball in a 1974 World Cup match against Italy

LEFT The Ivory Coast team before their game against Ghana in the 2008

IVORY COAST (Africa): Winners of the African Cup of Nations in 1992, the national team reached the World Cup finals for the first time in 2006. The country is most famous for exporting star players such as Didier Drogba and Salomon Kalou (Chelsea), Kolo Toure (Arsenal), and Toure Yaya (Barcelona).

JAMAICA (Central America): Their best performance was reaching the 1998 World Cup finals with a team that included many England-based players.

JAPAN (Asia): Reaching the World Cup finals in 1998, Japan advanced to a best-yet place in the last 16 on home soil in 2002. They have won the Asian Cup three times.

KAZAKHSTAN (Europe): After gaining independence from the Soviet Union, the country switched from the Asian Confederation to UEFA in 2002. Arguably their greatest player was Oleg Litvinenko, who died tragically in November 2007, just four days short of his 34th birthday.

KUWAIT (Asia): The national team had one appearance in the World Cup finals in 1982. They managed a draw with Czechoslovakia but lost to both England and France. During the last of these, France famously "scored" while some of the Kuwaiti players had stopped playing, having heard a whistle. They walked off the pitch in protest and resumed only after the goal was disallowed.

LATVIA (Europe): Having regained their independence in 1991, they are the only Baltic team to have qualified for the European Championship finals when they upset Turkey in the qualifiers.

LIECHTENSTEIN (Europe): One of the whipping boys of European football, comprising mainly part-timers, the tiny principality improved in the Euro 2008 qualifiers when they upset Latvia 1-0 and followed that up with a 3-0 win over Iceland.

LITHUANIA (Europe): They came third in their group in both the Euro 96 and 1998 World Cup qualifying campaigns. Since then they have managed away draws with both Germany and Italy but, like many former Soviet states, they lack depth of quality as yet.

LUXEMBOURG (Europe): Historically one of Europe's minor teams, they once went 12 years without winning a competitive fixture.

REST OF THE WORLD

GREAT NATIONS
REST OF THE WORLD

ABOVE Mexico's Rafael Marquez and keeper Oswaldo Sanchez clear their lines at the 2006 World Cup

MACEDONIA (Europe): Only since the breakup of Yugoslavia have they had their own officially recognized team. The inaugural Macedonian side featured Darko Pancev, who won the Champions League with Red Star Belgrade in 1991. Away draws with England and Holland represent two of the country's modest high spots.

MALTA (Europe): With one of the oldest national associations in Europe, Malta owes much of its football fanaticism to the island's former British occupation. With a population of under 400,000, however, the national team draws from one of the smallest on the European continent.

MEXICO (Central and North America): Having qualified for no fewer than 13 World Cup finals, Mexico are hugely experienced. They reached the quarter-finals in 1970 and 1986, both times on home soil. Their 2-1 defeat by Argentina in the 2006 World Cup was regarded as one of the finest technical matches of recent tournaments.

MOLDOVA (Europe): Their two best-ever results came within a month of each other in the mid-1990s during the qualifiers for Euro 96, beating Georgia and Wales.

MONTENEGRO (Europe): Came into existence only after the 2006 World Cup after being politically tied to Serbia. The 2010 tournament is their first competitive opportunity.

MOROCCO (Africa): The first African team to win a group at the World Cup (1986), finishing ahead of Portugal, Poland, and England. Although always a contender, they have won the African Nations Cup only once, in 1976. Mustapha Hadji is arguably their best-known player having starred with both Benfica and Deportivo de La Coruna.

NEW ZEALAND (Oceania): In a country where rugby union is king, the New Zealand football league is semi-professional. They have reached the World Cup finals only once, in 1982, but lost all three games.

NIGERIA (Africa): With a rich footballing pedigree, Nigeria has exported a string of exceptional players to Europe. Current squad members include Obefemi Martins and Mikel John Obi. The "Super Eagles" usually reach the World Cup finals though they missed out in 2006 when Angola qualified instead.

NORTHERN IRELAND (Europe): Fans still talk nostalgically about their heyday when they qualified for the 1982 World Cup, reaching the quarter-finals, having beaten hosts Spain. Norman Whiteside became the youngest-ever player in the finals, at 17 years 41 days. Billy Bingham, a player in the team who had also reached the quarter-finals in 1958, was the manager and led his country to the finals again in 1986, the smallest European nation to qualify twice.

NORTH KOREA (Asia): The North Koreans' shining moment came in the 1966 World Cup when they upset Italy 1-0 to gain a spot in the quarter-finals. There, they went 3-0 up against Portugal, but the brilliance of Eusébio and his four goals stopped the fairytale and the match ended with the Koreans down 5-3. They have never threatened a repeat; political isolation has cost their football dear.

NORWAY (Europe): The greatest moment in Norwegian football, a 2-1 win over Brazil in the 1998 World Cup, sparked wild scenes back home. Rosenborg, the country's leading club, have perennially competed in the Champions League but almost all of Norway's top players go abroad even though the domestic league is now professional.

PARAGUAY (South America): Although they reached the second round of the World Cup in 1986, 1998, and 2002, they have never advanced beyond that stage. They Won the Copa América 1953 and 1979.

PERU (South America): Peru's "golden generation" in the 1970s and early 1980s was highlighted by the skills of Teofilo Cubillas, who scored five goals in two different World Cup finals. Defender Hector Chumputaz was one of the first South American players to have one hundred international appearances.

POLAND (Europe): They have twice finished third in the World Cup in 1974 and 1982, thanks to talents of outstanding players such as Zbigniew Boniek and Grzegorz Lato. Goalkeeper Jan Tomaszewski, whose performance at Wembley in 1973 prevented England reaching the World Cup finals in West Germany, remains an icon..

QATAR (Asia): Opening up the domestic league to foreign players turned Qatar into an attractive and lucrative new destination for veteran stars. But Qatar's wealth has also been invested in a sports academy to help develop home-grown talent.

REPUBLIC OF IRELAND (Europe): The Irish enjoyed their most euphoric era under the guidance of Jack Charlton and his successor Mick McCarthy. They qualified for Euro 88, reaching the quarter-finals of the 1990 World Cup and making the last 16 at both the 1994 and 2002 World Cups. The side gets its strength from the fact that most of the squad star in the English Premier League.

ROMANIA (Europe): The national side contested the first World Cup in 1930, and their "golden generation," led by Gheorghe Hagi, reached the 1994 World Cup quarter-finals. Steaua Bucharest became the first Eastern European side to win the European Champions Cup in 1985. The domestic scene is dominated by the clubs from Bucharest, with Steaua and Dinamo holding 41 titles between them.

SAUDI ARABIA (Asia): Three-time Asian Cup champions, their former goalkeeper Mohamed Al-Deayea is the most capped international male footballer, with 181 appearances. Al-Hilal have won the league title 11 times since it began in 1972.

SCOTLAND (Europe): The first-ever international game took place between Scotland and England in 1872. The fixture remains one of football's fiercest rivalries. Scotland have never reached the second stage of an international tournament, despite a famous victory over the Netherlands in 1978. The "Old Firm," Celtic and Rangers, enjoy a near-monopoly on the Scottish Premier League Championship. In 1967, Celtic became the first British team to win the European Champions Cup. Scottish players and managers have contributed enormously to the English League, including Kenny Daglish and Graeme Sounness at Liverpool and Sir Alex Ferguson at Manchester United.

SENEGAL (Africa): This nation's team stunned the world by beating defending title-holders France in the 2002 World Cup on their way to becoming only the second African team to reach the tournament's quarter-finals.

ABOVE Kenny Dalglish, hero of Scotland and Celtic

GREAT NATIONS
REST OF THE WORLD

SERBIA (Europe): They became a single footballing nation in 2006 after Montenegro gained independence. Serbia's most powerful clubs remain the ones that dominated within the original Yugoslavia—Partizan and Red Star, both from Belgrade.

SLOVAKIA (Europe): Originally a member of FIFA in 1907, Slovakia rejoined in 1994 after the break-up of Czechoslovakia. But they have yet to qualify for an international tournament's final stages.

SLOVENIA (Europe): A decade after gaining independence from Yugoslavia, Slovenia reached its first finals in the 2000 European Championship and the 2002 World Cup. NK Maribor, which beat Villarreal to win the 2006 Intertoto Cup, hold the most Slovenian league titles, with seven.

SOUTH AFRICA (Africa): They will become the first African nation to host the World Cup finals in 2010. Re-admitted to world footballing bodies in 1990 after the end of apartheid, the national team won the African Cup of Nations in 1996 after stepping in at the last minute as hosts. South African players Benni McCarthy, Mark Fish, Lucas Radebe, and Quinton Fortune have been successful at European club level.

SOUTH KOREA (Asia): With their semi-final appearance in 2002, South Korea recorded the best-ever performance by an Asian team in the World Cup. Traditionally strong in Asia, they won the first two Asian Cups. Manchester United's Park Ji-Sung is the most famous South Korean player in the world. Seongnam Ilhwa Chunma are the K-League's most successful team with seven championship trophies. Korean clubs have won the Asian Champions Cup seven times since 1985.

SWEDEN (Europe): World Cup runners-up as hosts in 1958, Sweden have also reached three other semi-finals, the most recent being third place in 1994. Swedish players have been successful across Europe, and Swede Sven-Göran Eriksson won the Italian title at Lazio before managing England to three successive quarter-finals. IFK Gothenburg are the leading domestic title-winners with 18, just ahead of Malmö on 15. IFK are also the only Swedish club to have won a European trophy, twice landing the UEFA Cup.

SWITZERLAND (Europe): One of Switzerland's major roles in the world game is off the pitch—hosting FIFA headquarters in Zurich and UEFA's headquarters near Geneva. Switzerland holds the dubious honor of being the only team to be eliminated from the World Cup (in 2006) in a penalty shoot-out without netting a single spot-kick. The domestic league is dominated by Grasshopper Club (27 titles) and the recently resurgent FC Zurich and FC Basel.

TOGO (Africa): Togo's first-ever appearance in the World Cup in 2006 was blighted by a dispute over player bonuses. The federation was subsequently fined by FIFA for "behavior unworthy of a participant in the World Cup." Tragedy struck in 2007, when 20 members of their delegation to the African Cup of Nations qualifier, including the Sports Minister but not any players, were killed in a helicopter crash. They have never gone past the first stage of the African Cup of Nations.

BELOW Trinidad's Dwight Yorke strikes for goal against Paraguay

TRINIDAD AND TOBAGO (Central and North America): Ex-Manchester United striker Dwight Yorke is such a hero in Tobago that the national stadium bears his name. Other notable players to have succeeded in England include goalkeeper Shaka Hislop, Stern John, and Kenwyne Jones. Trinidad and Tobago qualified for their first World Cup in 2006, where they were eliminated without scoring a goal.

TURKEY (Europe): Turkey's biggest footballing success came in the 2002 World Cup, where they finished third. Turkish teams have proved fearsome opposition in the UEFA Champions League, especially in their home legs, where an intimidating atmosphere is guaranteed. Hakan Sukur, scorer of the fastest-ever World Cup goal in 11 seconds in 2006, is Turkish football's top scorer. Only four clubs have won the Turkish top flight since 1959—Fenerbahce and Galatasaray (17 each), Besiktas (11), and Trabzonspor (six).

TUNISIA (Africa): Tunisia were the first African team to win a World Cup finals match, beating Mexico 3-1. They won the African Cup of Nations as host in 2004.

UKRAINE (Europe): Having provided some of the finest players to the Soviet Union national team for years, Ukraine reached the quarter-finals in their first World Cup as an independent nation, in 2006. Dynamo Kiev, the most successful Ukrainian team with 12 championships, were often the only challenger to Moscow clubs' domination during the Soviet era. Andriy Shevchenko and Sergei Rebrov spearheaded their European campaigns in the mid–late 1990s before the latter moved on to great success in Italy with AC Milan.

UNITED ARAB EMIRATES (Asia): The UAE has a lively and popular domestic league, dominated by Al-Ain FC, the first UAE winners of the Asian Champions Cup, in 2003. The national team's only appearance at a World Cup in 1990 ended in three defeats. Their one major international success was in winning the 2007 Gulf Cup of Nations.

UNITED STATES OF AMERICA (Central and North America): Though football struggles to compete with other American sports, the game is hugely popular with both young men and women. The US women's team are one of the most successful in the world, having won the inaugural Women's World Cup in 1991 and repeated the feat in 1999, thanks to key players such as Brandi Chastain and Mia Hamm. The men's professional domestic league, the MLS, has attracted European stars such as David Beckham.

URUGUAY (South America): The first hosts and first winners of the World Cup in 1930, Uruguay won the tournament again in 1950, but are no longer the international force they once were. Peñarol (36) and Nacional (30) have won the most national championships.

VENEZUELA (South America): Venezuela are the only member of the South American federation never to have qualified for the World Cup finals. Their best performance in the Copa America came when they reached the quarter-finals as hosts in 2007.

WALES (Europe): Few Welsh teams play in the English Football League. Cardiff City are the only non-English side to ever win the English FA Cup (in 1927) and they were runners-up to Portsmouth in 2008. Wales reached their only World Cup finals in 1958, with "Gentle Giant" John Carles, leading them to a quarter-final defeat against Brazil. Despite producing word-famous players in the 1980s and 1990s, they have failed to qualify for an international tournament since then.

ABOVE David Beckham turns on the style in the US for LA Galaxy

GREAT CLUBS

Club football provides the power base that keeps supporters mesmerized across the world, week-in and week-out. Initially, domestic leagues and cup competitions provided the staple diet for fans, but then the glamor of international competition provided icing on the cake from the 1950s onwards. Nowadays, international competition is crucial to the financial health of many clubs, and provides the funds that keep fans entertained with high-profile new signings.

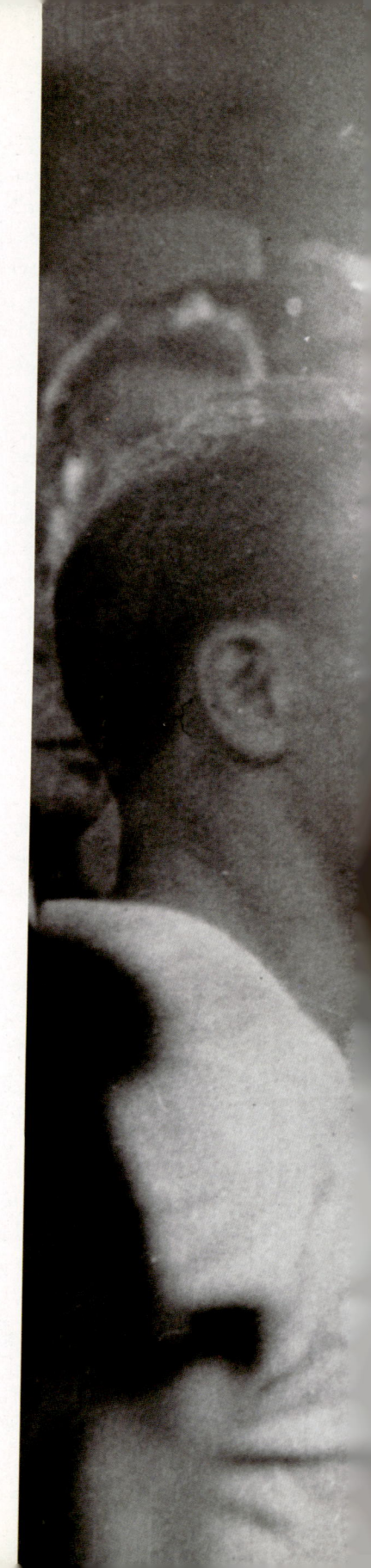

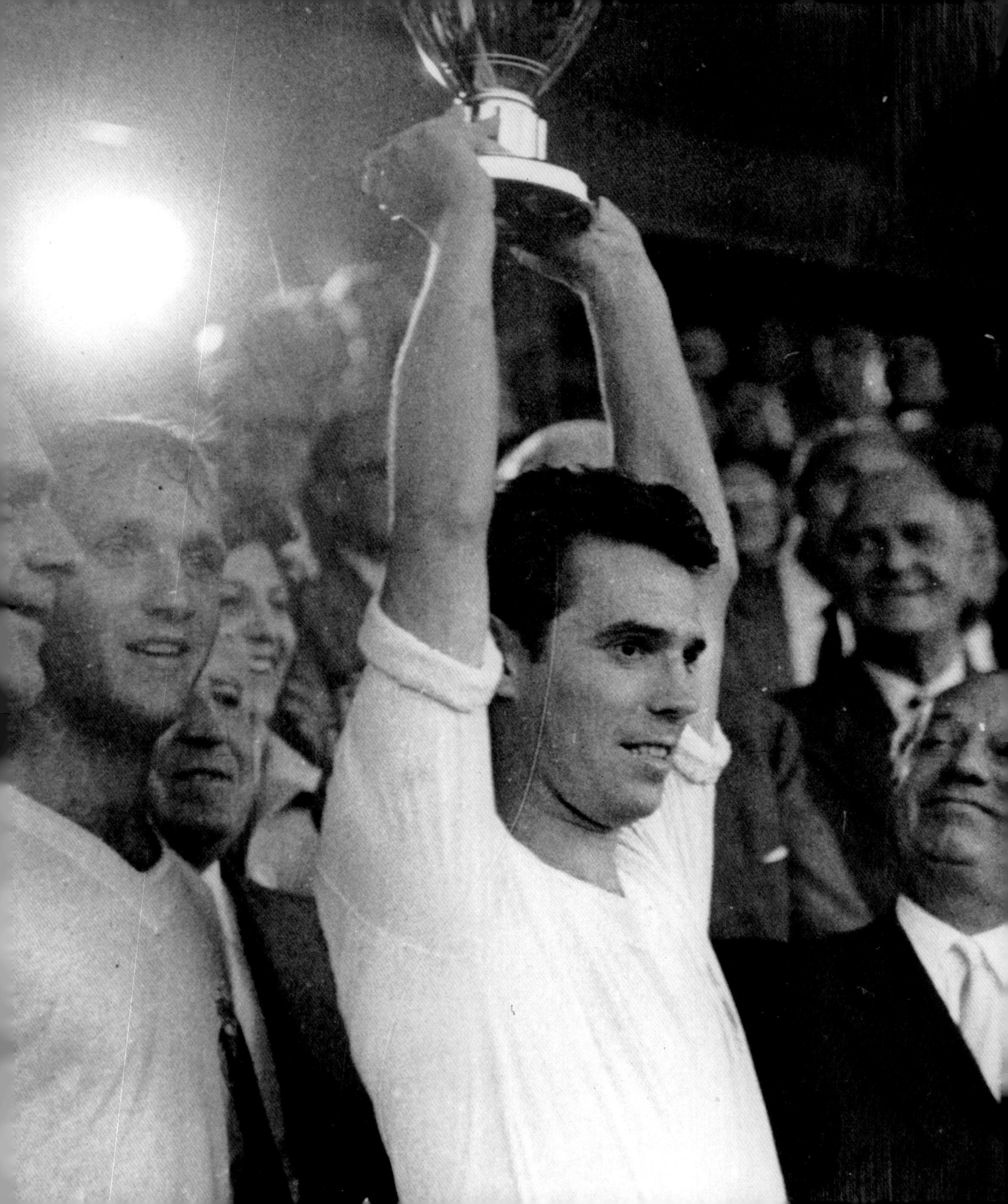

GREAT CLUBS EUROPE

TOP Johan Cruyff, three times a European champion with Ajax

ABOVE Arsenal celebrate their 1971 FA Cup final victory

PAGE 120 Liverpool celebrate a goal in 2005

PAGE 121 Zarrago, Real Madrid's captain, holds aloft the European cup

AJAX AMSTERDAM (Holland)
Ajax reached their peak in the early 1970s, when they pioneered the style known as "Total Football" and won the European Champion Clubs' Cup three times in a row. Coach Rinus Michels painstakingly built the side, led by the legendary Johann Cruyff, for five years before their victories from 1971 to 1973. Cruyff was the coach when Ajax lifted their next European trophy, the Cup Winners' Cup, in 1987. The club's renowned youth system cultured another European Cup-winning side in 1995, which finished as runner-up the following season. But the effects of the "Bosman Rule" have diminished Ajax's power, and now their stars inevitably move to richer clubs abroad.
Titles: World Club Cup 1972, 1995; European Champions League 1971, 1972, 1973, 1995; UEFA Cup 1992; Cup Winners' Club Cup 1987; Dutch champions 29 times; Dutch cup 17

ARSENAL (England)
Arsenal became the dominant force in England in the 1930s. Manager Herbert Chapman created their first truly great side, which won four league titles in five seasons, including three in a row between 1933 and 1935. After two post-war titles, Arsenal went through a barren spell. Victory over Anderlecht in the 1970 Fairs Cup final brought their first trophy for 17 years. They won the domestic "double" the following season and star player George Graham later delivered two more titles as coach with a host of home-grown players. Long-serving manager Arsène Wenger imported a host of foreign players with a French connection. His rewards include two league and cup "doubles."
Titles: UEFA/Fairs Cup 1970; Cup Winners' Cup: 1994; English champions 13 times; FA Cup 10; League Cup 2

ASTON VILLA (England)
Aston Villa were one of the 12 founding members of the Football League in 1888. They were a major force in its early years, winning five championships between 1894 and 1900 and the "double" in 1897. But after lifting the FA Cup in 1920, they went 37 years before gaining another major honor, beating Manchester United in the FA Cup final. Their most remarkable success was winning the European Cup in 1982. A quarter-final defeat by Juventus in 1983 signaled the start of a decline, and they were relegated in 1987. Aston Villa regained their elite status a season later. They finished league runner-up in both the 1988–89 and 1992–93 seasons.
Titles: European Cup 1982; English champions 7 times; FA Cup 7; League Cup 5

ATHLETIC MADRID (Spain)
Athletic Madrid have spent years playing second fiddle to neighbors Real Madrid, although they overshadowed their bitter rivals in the early 1950s, when master coach Helenio Herrera guided them to successive titles. Spanish champions in 1973, they came within a minute of winning the European Champion Clubs' Cup a year later. But were denied glory by a late equalizer that forced a replay, which Bayern Munich won 4-0. Athletic Madrid won the 1974 World Club Cup after Bayern Munich declined to compete. The club became synonymous with instability during the reign of president Jesus Gil, who hired and fired 23 different coaches between 1987 and 2003. They revived under Mexican coach Javier Aguirre, and in 2008 secured entry into the European Champions League for the first time in over a decade.
Titles: Intercontinental Cup 1974; Cup Winner's Cup 1962; Spanish champions 9 times; Spanish cup 9

BARCELONA (Spain)

Barcelona's motto is *"mas que un Clube,"* meaning "More than a Club," and they have long been a symbol for Catalonia's regional pride. Their bitter rivalry with Real Madrid is a key feature of Spanish football. Ronald Koeman's European Champion Clubs' Cup final winner against Sampdoria in 1992 healed Barcelona's wounded pride after so many disappointments in the competition, including defeats in the final to Benfica and Steaua Bucharest. Coach Johann Cruyff created the winning "Dream Team," featuring Koeman, Pep Guardiola, Hristo Stoichkov, and Michael Laudrup—which many regard as Barcelona's best-ever team. Frank Rijkaard, Cruyff's protege, later crafted the 2005–06 side that beat Arsenal 2-1 in the UEFA Champions League final and won La Liga. Ronaldinho and Samuel Eto'o were the stars. Rijkaard failed to win a trophy for two years, which cost him his job at the end of the 2007–08 season. Such are Barcelona's high expectations.

Titles: European Champions' Club Cup 1992, 2006; UEFA/Fairs Cup 1958, 1960, 1966; Cup Winner's Cup 1979, 1982, 1989, 1997; Spanish champions 18 times; Spanish cup 24

BAYERN MUNICH (Germany)

Bayern Munich succeeded Ajax as the dominant team in Europe in the mid-1970s, winning the UEFA Champions Club Cup three times in a row. The great Franz Beckenbauer was their conductor, supported by prolific striker Gerd Müller, and goalkeeper Sepp Maier. But Bayern came within a minute of losing the 1974 final to Athletic Madrid, before Georg Schwarzenbeck leveled. They won the replay 4-0. A year later they beat Leeds United 2-0 in the final and they completed their trio with a 1-0 win over Saint-Etienne. Bayern added a fourth Champions Club Cup triumph in 2001, when goalkeeper Oliver Kahn defied Valencia in a penalty shoot-out. Bayern have dominated the Bundesliga for nearly 40 years, winning 20 championships to add to their all-German title of 1932.

Titles: Intercontinental Cup 1976, 2001; European Champions League 1974, 1975, 1976, 2001; UEFA Cup Winners' Cup 1967; UEFA Cup 1996; German champions 21 times; German cup 14

BENFICA (Portugal)

Benfica fans look back on the 1960s as their club's golden years. They succeeded Real Madrid as European champions by beating Barcelona 3-2 in the 1961 final, then retained the European Champion Clubs' Cup with a 5-3 win over Real Madrid. Benfica also reached the final in 1963, 1965, and 1968 and supplied the bulk of the Portugal side that finished third in the 1966 World Cup finals. Benfica's hero was the great striker Eusébio. The team was packed with internationals, with Mario Coluna pulling the strings in midfield. Benfica lost in recent finals to PSV Eindhoven, on penalties in 1988, and AC Milan in 1990. They have since faded as a European power and been eclipsed at home by Porto and Sporting Lisbon.

Titles: European Champion Clubs' Cup 1961, 1962; Portuguese champions 31 times; Portuguese cup 24

BELOW Henrik Larsson, Carles Puyol and Ronaldinho take the Champions League Cup by tickertape storm in 2006

GREAT CLUBS EUROPE

BELOW Barcelona's Thierry Henry fails to breach Celtic's defense

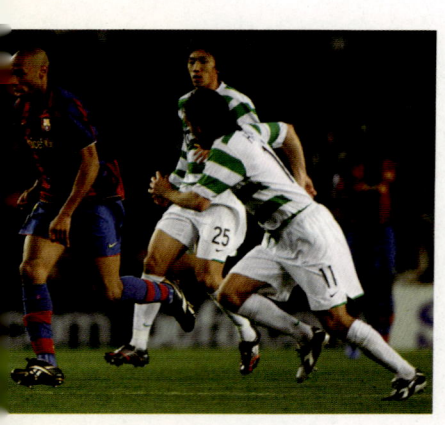

BORUSSIA DORTMUND (Germany)

Borussia Dortmund became the first West German team to lift a European trophy after they beat Liverpool in the 1966 Cup Winners' Cup final. But their greatest day came in 1997, when Ottmar Hitzfeld's side stunned Juventus 3-1 in the UEFA Champions League final. Hitzfeld had brought back Matthias Sammer, Andy Möller, Jürgen Koller, and Stefan Reuter from Italy to form the core of the team. Five years later, Borussia Dortmund won the Bundesliga and reached the UEFA Cup final, losing to Feyenoord Rotterdam. They came perilously close to bankruptcy in 2005.
Titles: Intercontinental Cup 1997; UEFA Champions League 1997; UEFA Cup Winners' Cup 1966; German champions 6 times; German cup 2

CELTIC (Scotland)

Celtic were the first British club to win the European Champion Clubs' Cup when they beat Internazionale 2-1 in the 1967 final at Lisbon. The team were then known as the "Lisbon Lions," and were all born within a 30-mile radius of Glasgow. Celtic also reached the final in 1970. They were managed by Jock Stein, and included outstanding figures such as Tommy Gemmell, Billy McNeill, Bobby Murdoch, and Jimmy Johnstone. That team began to break up after losing the 1974 European Cup semi-final to Athletic Madrid. But they still set a domestic record of nine consecutive championships. Celtic revived memories of those glory days with a run to the 2003 UEFA Cup final. Their fierce rivalry with Rangers dominates.
Titles: European Champions Clubs' Cup 1967; Scottish champions 41 times; Scottish Cup 31; League Cup 13

CHELSEA (England)

Chelsea's recent transformation into a European power has been bankrolled by Russian oil billionaire Roman Abramovich, the club's owner since 2003. His appointment of Portugal's Jose Mourinho as manager a year later galvanized the club. Mourinho spent heavily to win the Premier League and the League Cup, and delivered another league title in 2006. He left Chelsea in September 2007, despite guiding them to FA Cup and League Cup victories, after falling out with Abramovich. Israeli Avram Grant then took Chelsea to their first UEFA Champions League final, but was sacked after their shoot-out defeat by Manchester United. Chelsea, as 1955 league champions, had been the first English team invited to play in the European Cup but declined, following pressure from the Football League.
Titles: UEFA Cup Winners' Cup 1971, 1998; English champions 3 times; FA Cup 4; League Cup 4

DYNAMO KIEV (Ukraine)

Dynamo Kiev were the first club from the former Soviet Union to win a European trophy when they beat Hungary's Ferencváros in the 1975 European Cup Winners' Cup final. They saw off Athletic Madrid 3-0 to win the same competition 11 years later. The Ukrainians led non-Russian opposition to the Moscow clubs during the Soviet era, winning 13 championships and nine cup finals. They are seasoned UEFA Champions League competitors, despite normally needing to start in the qualifying stages, and reached the semi-final stage in 1999. Andriy Shevchenko was their inspiration with eight goals, earning him a lucrative move to AC Milan.
Titles: European Cup Winners Cup 1975, 1986; Soviet champions 13 times; Ukrainian champions 12 times; Soviet cup 9; Ukrainian cup 9

EVERTON (England)

Everton, formed in 1878, were founder members of the Football League, and one of its most successful clubs for many years. They reached their peak under Howard Kendall in the mid-1980s. They won the FA Cup in 1984, the league title (ahead of their great rivals, Liverpool) and the UEFA Cup Winners' Cup a year later, and added another title in 1987. In between, they finished as runner-up to Liverpool in the league and FA Cup. However, the ban on English clubs after the Heysel Stadium disaster denied Everton the chance to build on their European success, and eventually the team broke up. A string of managers struggled to rebuild the club in the years that followed, before David Moyes steered Everton to a UEFA Champions League qualifying place in 2005. The 2-0 win over Manchester United in the 1995 FA Cup remains their last major honor.
Titles: UEFA Cup Winners' Cup 1985; English champions 9 times; FA Cup 5

FEYENOORD ROTTERDAM (Holland)

Feyenoord Rotterdam became the first Dutch team to win the European Champions Club Cup when they beat Celtic 2-1 after extra time in 1970 in Milan. Four years later, they lifted the UEFA Cup after drawing with Tottenham in the first leg in London and winning the return 2-0. Three of that victorious side, Wim Rijsbergen, Wim Jansen, and Wim Van Hanegem, played for Holland in the 1974 World Cup final. Following almost 20 years without further European success, Feyenoord Rotterdam were surprise UEFA Cup winners in 2002, beating Borussia Dortmund 3-2. They have failed to make any impact in Europe since, and have not won the Dutch title since 1999. Instead, they have become a supplier of stars, including talents such as Robin van Persie, Dirk Kuyt, Salomon Kalou, and Royston Drenthe to clubs in richer leagues.
Titles: Intercontinental Cup 1970; European Champion Clubs' Cup 1970; UEFA Cup 1974, 2002; Dutch champions 14 times; Dutch cup 11

INTERNAZIONALE (Italy)

Internazionale were a dominant world power in the mid-1960s. They defeated Real Madrid 3-1 in the 1964 European Champion Clubs' Cup final and beat Benfica 1-0 a year later. But they lost the 1967 final against Celtic. However, coach Helenio Herrera was criticized for his defensive tactics and they were an unpopular side with neutral spectators, despite fielding greats such as full back Giacinto Facchetti, midfielder Luis Suarez, and attacker Sandro Mazzola. Internazionale reached another UEFA Champions Club Cup final in 1972, when they were swept aside by Ajax. They won only two domestic championships between 1972 and 2005, Internazionale have collected the past three Serie A titles, but have yet to reach the semi-final stage of the UEFA Champions League.
Titles: Intercontinental Cup 1964, 1965; European Champion Clubs' Cup 1964, 1965; UEFA Cup 1991, 1994, 1998; Italian champions 16 times; Italian cup 5

JUVENTUS (Italy)

Juventus boast an enviable record of appearing in the final of seven UEFA Champions League. The tragedy of the Heysel Stadium disaster dwarfed their first success, when Michel Platini's goal edged out Liverpool in the 1985 final. They won again in 1996, when Marcello Lippi's team beat Ajax Amsterdam on penalty kicks. Juventus have also lost finals to Ajax, Hamburg SV, Borussia Dortmund, Real Madrid, and AC Milan. They have amassed a record number of Italian titles, but recent successes have been dogged by controversy. Their three title wins between 1995 and 1998 were the subject of a doping enquiry. In 2006, Juventus were stripped of their 2005 and 2006 Serie A titles following a match-fixing scandal. The punishment included relegation, sending them to Serie B for the first time. Despite a 30-point deduction, they won promotion.
Titles: Intercontinental Cup 1985, 1996; European Champions Clubs' Cup 1985, 1996; Cup Winners' Cup 1984; UEFA/Fairs Cup 1977, 1990, 1993; Italian champions 27 times; Italian cup 9

ABOVE Alessandro Del Piero of Juventus celebrates a goal against Celtic in 2001

GREAT CLUBS EUROPE

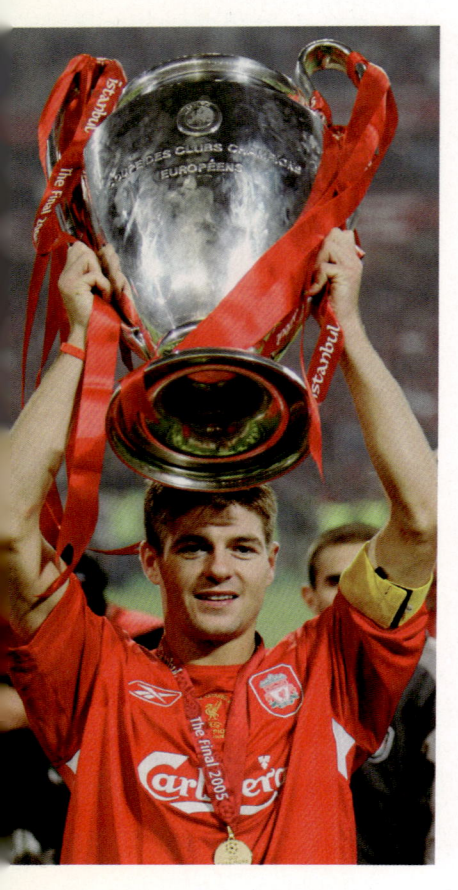

ABOVE Liverpool captain Steven Gerrard lifts the 2005 European Cup in Istanbul

LIVERPOOL (England)
Liverpool are the most successful English club in European competitions. They have won the European Cup Winners' Cup five times, the UEFA Cup three times, and have a hat-trick of European Super Cup prizes. Liverpool reached two other European Cup finals and may well have added more appearances to the list, but for the ban imposed on English clubs after the Heysel Stadium disaster. Liverpool changed their style in Europe after a home defeat by Red Star Belgrade and swiftly reaped the rewards from a more patient approach. Bob Paisley, who succeeded Bill Shankly, was the architect of their success. He steered Liverpool to a hat-trick of triumphs in the European Cup Winners' Cup—1977, 1978, and 1981—before handing over to Joe Fagan for their 1984 triumph. The Steven Gerrard-inspired comeback known as "the Miracle of Istanbul" brought Liverpool their fifth European Cup Winners' Cup in 2005. Paisley's team dominated in England as well as Europe. Such stars as Kenny Dalglish, Alan Hansen, Ian Rush, Graeme Souness, and Phil Thompson helped Liverpool to win a total of 18 championships—an English record. They have not won the league since 1990, and ending that run has become the club's priority.
Titles: European Champion Clubs' Cup 1977, 1978, 1981, 1984, 2005; UEFA Cup 1973, 1976, 2001; European Super Cup 1977, 2001, 2005; English champions 18 times; FA Cup 7; League Cup 7

LYON (France)
Lyon have monopolized French football since 2002. They have won the past seven championships, a domestic record. In 2008, they completed a league and cup "double." The 2002 title was Lyon's first, and a realization of the dreams of Jean-Michel Aulas, club president since 1987. Now Aulas, a computer software millionaire, is chasing an even bigger prize: the European Champions League. He has employed a succession of top French coaches—Jacques Santini, Paul Le Guen, Gerard Houllier, and Alain Perrin—who have all delivered championships. But Lyon have yet to advance beyond the quarter-final stage in European competitions except in the 1997 Intertoto Cup, which they won. One of their biggest problems is that they keep losing key players to UEFA Champions League rivals, such as Michael Essien to Chelsea and Mohamadou Diarra to Real Madrid. Striker Karim Benzema is the latest outstanding player off their production line.
Titles: Intertoto Cup 1997; French champions 7 times; French cup 4

MANCHESTER CITY (England)
Life has rarely been dull for fans at Maine Road or the new City of Manchester Stadium. Manchester City's recent history has seen them suffer the indignity of dropping into the second division before climbing back to the Premier League. They were relegated again, only for Kevin Keegan to lead them up again in 2002. Keegan, Stuart Pearce, Sven-Göran Eriksson, and Mark Hughes have each been in charge since their return to the big time. In the 1980s, they had seven bosses in ten years but Manchester City were at their best in the late 1960s. Manager Joe Mercer and assistant Malcolm Allison guided them to the championship in 1968, the FA Cup in 1969 and the European Cup Winners' Cup and League Cup the next season.
Titles: European Cup Winner's Cup 1970; English champions 2; FA Cup 4; League Cup 2

MANCHESTER UNITED (England)
Scottish managers have crafted Manchester United's post-war achievements. Sir Matt Busby built the team known as "the Busby Babes" who won two championships and reached the European Champion Clubs' Cup semi-finals twice, before being torn apart by the Munich air disaster in 1958. Busby went on to create another great side—featuring Bobby Charlton, Denis Law, and George Best—that won two more championships. They became the first English team to lift the European Champions' Club Cup, ten years after Munich. Sir Alex Ferguson then achieved greatness in his own style after delivering Manchester United's first league title for 26 years in 1993. His sides have dominated the lucrative Premier League era, claiming 10 of the 16 titles. They have added two UEFA Champions League triumphs—in 1999 and 2008. Manchester United's astonishing late rally, capped by Ole Gunnar Solskjaer's winner, pipped Bayern Munich in the 1999 final and gave the club a unique "treble", adding to the prizes of the Premier League and FA Cup. Nine years later, United keeper Edwin van der Sar held his nerve in the final shoot-out against Chelsea after Cristiano Ronaldo's goals had propelled Manchester United to another domestic league title.
Titles: Intercontinental Cup 1999; European Champion Clubs' Cup 1968, 1999, 2008; UEFA Cup Winners' Cup 1991; English champions 17 times; FA Cup 11; League Cup 2

AC MILAN (Italy)
AC Milan come second only to Real Madrid in terms of UEFA Champions League success, having captured the prize seven times and appeared in four other finals. They first lifted it in 1963 by deposing holders Benfica 2-1, and six years later crushed Ajax Amsterdam 4-1. They had to wait 20 years for their next victory, when the Dutch trio of Ruud Gullit, Frank Rijkaard, and Marco Van Basten inspired Arrigo Sacchi's cultured side to a 4-0 win over Steaua Bucharest. AC Milan triumphed again in 1994, tearing Barcelona apart 4-0. Defeat by Ajax Amsterdam the following year signaled the end of an era. The Dutchmen had already gone, but two defenders remained who would star in the next decade—Alessandro Costacurta and Paolo Maldini. AC Milan edged past Juventus on penalty kicks in 2003, then lost one of the most dramatic finals in 2005, after leading Liverpool 3-0 but were defeated on penalty kicks. They gained revenge on Liverpool two years later, when they won 2-1 and Maldini collected his fifth winners medal in the UEFA Champions League.
Titles: Intercontinental Cup 1969, 1989, 1990, 2007; European Champion Clubs' Cup 1963, 1969, 1989, 1990, 1994, 2003, 2007; European Cup Winners' Cup 1968, 1973; Italian champions 17 times; Italian cup 5

ABOVE Andrea Pirlo of AC Milan takes a free kick against Atalanta in 2008

OLYMPIQUE MARSEILLE (France)
Olympique Marseille's greatest achievement also led to their greatest crisis. They became the only French team to have won the UEFA Champions League, when they saw off AC Milan in the 1993 final. But Valenciennes defender Jacques Glassmann alleged that Marseille's Jean-Jacques Eydelie had tried to bribe him and two other

EUROPE 191

GREAT CLUBS MOMENTS

1960s

ABOVE Tottenham's Jimmy Greaves shoots for goal against Burnley

BELOW Celtic keeper Ronnie Simpson defies Internazionale in Lisbon

1970s

ABOVE Zico (left) is a legendary figure for Flamengo and Brazil

LEFT Benfica's Portugal hero Eusébio bears down on goal

BELOW Manchester United parade the Champions Cup in 1968

1980s   2000s

BELOW Carles Pujol and Ronaldinho raise the Champions Cup

RIGHT David Beckham takes to the wing for LA Galaxy

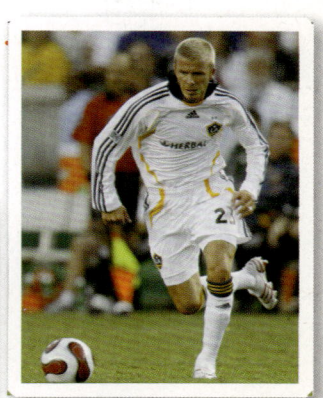

ABOVE Hugo Sanchez top-scored for Mexico, Real and Atletico Madrid

BELOW Alex (Santos) tackles Boca's Carlos Tevez

ABOVE Milan forward Kaka eludes Inter's Nelson Rivas

ABOVE RIGHT Etoile Sahel carry off the African Super Cup

MOMENTS 193

GREAT CLUBS
EUROPE

players to "go easy on them" in Marseille's last game before the final. The bribe attempt was traced back to Marseille's managing director Jean-Pierre Bernes and then to club president Bernard Tapie, who was jailed for his involvement. Olympique Marseille, who had won the previous five championships, were stripped of their 1993 crown and relegated to the second division. UEFA disqualified them from competing for a short period. The club reached the UEFA Cup final in 1999 and 2004, but the bribe scandal ended their recent glory days.

Titles: UEFA Champions League 1993; French champions 9 times; French cup 10

PORTO (Portugal)

Porto tasted glory under Jose Mourinho, as the new century unfolded. He steered them to the championship and a 2003 UEFA Cup final victory over Celtic. A year later, they were crowned champions of both Portugal and Europe. Mourinho's team destroyed AS Monaco 3-0 in the UEFA Champions League final, to deliver Porto's second such triumph. Mourinho then left for big-spending Chelsea, taking defensive duo Paulo Ferreira and Ricardo Carvalho with him. Porto have not advanced beyond the last 16 since. Their 2008 league title was their fifth in six seasons.

Titles: Intercontinental Cup 1987, 2004; European Champion Clubs' Cup 1987, 2004; UEFA Cup 2003; Portuguese champions 23 times; Portuguese cup 17

PSV EINDHOVEN (Holland)

PSV have overtaken Holland's former elite, Ajax Amsterdam and Feyenoord Rotterdam. They broke the dominance of the "Big Two" in the 1970s, when they won three championships in four seasons. They also snatched the UEFA/Fairs Cup in 1978 with a 3-0 aggregate win over Bastia. PSV Eindhoven's greatest moment came ten years later, when they beat Benfica on penalties in the European Champion Clubs' Cup final. The side have continued to challenge in the UEFA Champions League despite losing stars to England (Arjen Robben and Park Ji-Sung), Germany (Mark Van Bommel), and Spain (Arouna Kone). They lost on away goals to AC Milan in the 2005 semi-finals and reached the quarter-finals two years later.

Titles: European Champion Clubs' Cup 1988; UEFA Cup 1978; Dutch champions 21 times; Dutch cup 8

RANGERS (Scotland)

Rangers' run to the 2008 UEFA Cup final, which they lost 2-0 to Zenit St. Petersburg, marked the end of a 36-year gap since their last appearance in a European showpiece. In the previous final, they beat Dynamo Moscow 3-2 to lift the European

BELOW Jorge Costa and Vitor Baia lead Porto's European victory parade in 2004

Cup Winners' Cup—their only European prize. In 1961, Rangers had lost the first European Cup Winners' Cup final to Fiorentina. A year earlier, Rangers reached the UEFA Champions League semi-finals, but crashed 12-4 on aggregate to Eintracht Frankfurt. They made their biggest impact on the UEFA Champions League in 1993, when they finished a point behind winners Marseille in the last eight group stage. Rangers have won a record 51 Scottish League titles.
Titles: European Cup Winners' Cup 1972; Scottish champions 51 times; Scottish Cup 32; League Cup 25

REAL MADRID (Spain)
Real Madrid are the best known club in the world. They won each of the first five finals of the European Cup—defeating Reims twice, Fiorentina, AC Milan, and Eintracht Frankfurt—before the competition became known as the UEFA Champions League. The club was guided by visionary president Santiago Bernabeu, with the team ably led by the legendary Argentinian center forward Alfredo Di Stefano—who played in all five finals. The most renowned final was the 7-3 victory over Frankfurt in 1960, when Di Stefano hit a hat-trick and Hungary great Ferenc Puskás netted four goals. Winger Paco Gento was the only attacking link with that golden past when Real Madrid's new-look team edged Partizan Belgrade 2-1 to win the trophy again, six years later. They had to wait until 1998 for their next success, when Predrag Mijatovic scored the clincher against Juventus. Vicente Del Bosque revived past glories, steering Real Madrid to victories in 2000 and 2002. He was sacked after their 2003 semi-final, and club president Florentino Perez put together a star-studded side with the top players known as "Galacticos." Since Del Bosque's departure, Real Madrid reached the quarter-final stage just once.
Titles: Intercontinental Cup 1960, 1998, 2002; European Champion Clubs' Cup 1956, 1957, 1958, 1959, 1960, 1966, 1998, 2000, 2002; UEFA Cup 1985, 1986; Spanish champions 32 times; cup 17

AS ROMA (Italy)
AS Roma have enjoyed their most successful decade recently. They won Serie A in 2001 and have finished runner-up five times in the past seven years. They have also reached the UEFA Champions League quarter-finals in each of the past two campaigns. The fulcrum of AS Roma's success has been Francesco Totti, who holds the records for games and goals.
Titles: UEFA/Fairs Cup 1961; Italian champions 3 times; Italian cup 9

TOTTENHAM HOTSPUR (England)
Tottenham Hotspur became the first English club to win a European trophy when they beat Athletic Madrid 5-1 in the 1963 European Cup Winners' Cup final. The team, built by Bill Nicholson and skippered by Danny Blanchflower, are considered Tottenham's best ever. They won the first league and cup "double" of the 20th century in 1961, collecting the FA Cup again the following season, and reaching the European Champion Clubs' Cup semi-final Tottenham have added two UEFA Cup victories to their European honors.
Titles: European Cup Winner's Cup 1963; UEFA Cup 1972, 1984; English champions 2 times; FA Cup 8; League Cup 4

BELOW Tottenham Hotspurs' double-winning players enjoy their open-top bus parade in 1961

GREAT CLUBS SOUTH AMERICA

ABOVE Juan Román Riquelme, a latter-day hero for Boca Juniors

BOCA JUNIORS (Argentina)
No South American club has won more international titles than the Argentinian club from La Bombonera, the Buenos Aires stadium whose affectionate nickname translates as "The Chocolate Box." Their "*Superclásico*" rivalry with River Plate is one of the fiercest in the world, with Boca Juniors' supporters considering themselves as the city's working-class underdogs. Diego Maradona spent a title-winning season with the club before leaving for Spain in 1982, before coming back 13 years later. Juan Román Riquelme, was a modern-day heir whose return for a second spell led to Copa Libertadores glory in 2007.
Titles: World Club Cup 1977, 2000, 2003; Copa Libertadores 1977, 1978, 2000, 2001, 2003, 2007; Copa Sudamericana 2004, 2005; Argentine league 23 times

COLO COLO (Chile)
The "Snow Whites" of Santiago became the first, and so far only, Chilean club to win the Copa Libertadores—the South American equivalent of the UEFA Champions League—in 1991 when they beat Paraguay's Olimpia Asuncion 3-0 on aggregate. They are Chile's most successful club, with 41 domestic trophies and the only club to have contested every season without relegation since the league was founded in 1933.
Titles: Copa Libertadores 1991; Chilean league 24 times; cup 14

FLAMENGO (Brazil)
Flamengo began life in 1895 as a rowing club but embraced football 16 years later, after a breakaway by aggrieved members of neighboring Fluminense. They have since become Brazil's best-loved club, with an estimated fanbase of 40 million. Though, it was not until the late 1970s and early 1980s that they extended their domestic brilliance to the international arena. Zico was voted Man of the Match as Flamengo trounced Liverpool 3-0 in the 1981 Intercontinental Cup.
Titles: Intercontinental Cup 1981; Copa Libertadores 1981; Brazilian league 4 times, cup 2

INDEPENDIENTE (Argentina)
Years of decline and debts forced Independiente to sell wonder-kid Sergio Agüero to Athletic Madrid for $34m (£17m) in 2006, yet the club's history is perhaps as glorious as any in Argentina—including a record seven Copa Libertadores titles. These include four in a row between 1972 and 1975 that were inspired by midfielder Ricardo Bochini, who played for 20 years with the club. They have also been home to the World Cup-winning trio of Daniel Bertoni, Jorge Burruchaga and Oscar Ortiz.
Titles: Intercontinental Cup 1973, 1984; Copa Libertadores 1964, 1965, 1972, 1973, 1974, 1975, 1984; Argentine league 14 times

PENAROL (Uruguay)
Uruguay's most prestigious club provided the two scorers when Brazil were amazingly beaten in the 1950 World Cup finals, namely Alcides Ghigghia and Juan Schiaffino. At times in the 1960s, Peñarol could even outshine Pelé and Santos, including a 5-0 win in 1963, featuring a hat-trick by Alberto Spencer. He remains the all-time top scorer in the Copa Libertadores, leading the Montevideo club to three of their five triumphs. Peñarol have been crowned World Club champions three times.
Titles: Intercontinental Cup 1961, 1966, 1982;

Copa Libertadores 1960, 1961, 1966, 1982, 1987; Uruguayan league 36 times

RIVER PLATE (Argentina)

Along with Buenos Aires arch rivals Boca Juniors, River Plate remain one of Argentina's biggest, best-supported teams. Their formidable five-man forward line of the early 1940s was dubbed "*La Máquina*" (The Machine) but a sixth striker that decade was perhaps their greatest of all, Alfredo Di Stefano. Argentina's 1978 World Cup-winning captain Daniel Passarella spearheaded a club revival in the 1970s, before boyhood fan Hernan Crespo shot to fame at the Estadio Monumental in the 1990s. 1986 was a perfect year for River hinchas, not only were Argentina crowned World Champions, but River captured the league, the Copa Libertadores and the World Club Cup, beating Steaua Bucharest.
Titles: World Club Cup 1986; Copa Libertadores 1986, 1996; Supercopa Sudamericana 1997; Copa Interamericana 1987; Argentine league 32 times

SANTOS (Brazil)

For much of the 1960s, Santos were the side the whole world wanted to see—largely thanks to their iconic No10, Pelé. As well as clinching two world club titles beating Benfica and AC Milan, and several state championships, the Brazilian entertainers toured the world almost non-stop to play money-making exhibition matches for huge crowds. Pelé's departure in 1972 inevitably signaled an end to the glory days, and they had to wait until 2002 for their next Brazilian league title. In recent years the club has produced such young stars as Robinho, Elano, and Diego.
Titles: World Club Cup 1962, 1963; Copa Libertadores 1962, 1963; Copa CONMEBOL 1998; Brazilian champions 2 times

SÃO PAULO (Brazil)

Brasilia is the country's capital, Rio's clubs have the most fervent support, and neighbors Santos boasted Pelé, but São Paulo can claim to be Brazil's most successful club. Leonidas da Silva in the 1940s, Gerson in the 1970s, Careca in the 1980s and more recently Kaka have contributed to their collection of domestic and world titles. Their Copa Libertadores win in 2005 made them the first Brazilian club to claim a hat trick of titles, and the first team to beat a side from the same country in the final, Atletico Paranaense.
Titles: World Club Cup 1992, 1993, 2005; Copa Libertadores 1992, 1993, 2005; Copa CONMEBOL 1994; Recopa Sudamericana 1993, 1994; Supercopa Sudamericana 1993; Brazilian champions 5 times

VASCO DA GAMA (Brazil)

Vasco da Gama was founded in 1898 by Portuguese immigrants, they take their name from the revered Portuguese explorer of the 14th and 15th centuries, and call for much of their support on Rio's Portuguese communities. World Cup-winning striker Romario started his career at Vasco in 1985 and retired in 2008 after his fourth term at the club, which included the goal he claimed was the 1,000th of his career. But his 316 goals for Vasco da Gama were less than half the tally of their leading goalscorer, Roberto Dinamite. He scored 698 in 1,110 games between 1971 and 1993. Vasco has not won the league since 2000.
Titles: Copa Libertadores 1998; Brazilian champions 4 times

BELOW Pelé takes aim for Santos in 1973

GREAT CLUBS
REST OF THE WORLD

ABOVE Jaime Moreno of DC United looks for an opening against the New York Red Bulls

AL-AHLY (Egypt)
Little wonder the Cairo side were named in 2000 as the Confederation of African Football's club of the century. Egypt's so-called "People's Club" has won a record five African club championships, and a major haul of domestic titles. They even managed to remain unbeaten from 1974 to 1977. The "Red Devils," whose former players include Egypt's record scorer Hossam Hassan, have a ferocious rivalry with city rivals Zamalek. Foreign referees are often asked to handle their turbulent derby games.
Titles: African Champions League 1982, 1987, 2001, 2005, 2006; African Cup Winners' Cup 1984, 1985, 1986, 1993; African Super Cup 2005; Arab Champions Cup 1996; Arab Cup Winners' Cup 1994; Arab Super Cup 1997, 1998; Egyptian league 33 times, Egyptian cup 35

CLUB AMERICA (Mexico)
Club America have been Mexico's big spenders since a 1959 takeover by television giant Televisa. Until recent years at least, such power guaranteed success, including a record five crowns as CONCACAF Champions (the same number won by rivals Cruz Azul) and ten league titles (Chivas have won 11 championships). Big-name foreign imports have included Argentina's Oscar Ruggeri, Chilean Ivan Zamorano, and Romania's Ilie Dumitrescu. But they have also developed home-grown talent such as Mexican playmaker Cuauhtemoc Blanco. Club America play at the 114,465-capacity Azteca in Mexico City, the only stadium to have hosted two World Cup finals.
Titles: CONCACAF Champions Cup 1978, 1987, 1991, 1993, 2006; CONCACAF Cup Winners' Cup 2001; Copa Interamericana 1978, 1991; Mexican league 10 times, Mexican cup 5

DC UNITED (United States)
Captain John Harkes, returning home from the English Premier League, and coach Bruce Arena led the Washington DC-based club to the first two MLS titles in 1996 and 1997. They also became the first US club to win the CONCACAF Champions' Cup in 1998. But trophies have proved harder to come by since Arena left to become national coach in 1998, despite high-profile signings such as iconic Hristo Stoichkov and Freddy Adu—who made his debut aged 14.
Titles: CONCACAF Champions Cup 1998; Copa Interamericana 1998; US MLS Cup four times; US Open Cup 1

ETOILE SAHEL (Tunisia)
Tunisia may have underachieved internationally, with only one African Cup of Nations triumph. But their oldest club has proved the pride of a nation, with impressive performances in all CAF competitions. Dynamic young striker Armine Chermiti helped them achieve surprise Champions League glory in 2007. Victory over holders Al-Ahly, made them the first club to have, won each of the African Federation's Club trophies.
Titles: African Champions League 2007; CAF Cup 2006; African Cup Winners' Cup 1997, 2003; African Super Cup 1998, 2008; Tunisian league 8; President's Cup 7; League Cup 1

LOS ANGELES GALAXY (United States)
LA Galaxy pulled off the most high-profile signing in MLS history when world superstar and England's iconic David Beckham joined from Real Madrid in 2007. Another great, Holland's Ruud Gullit, was then appointed LA Galaxy coach after a disappointing first season for Beckham. The midfielder's arrival helped the club sell 700 times

as many replica shirts as before, and inspire hope among directors and fans that they might win the CONCACAF Champions League Cup for a second time. Long-serving Cobi Jones was among the scorers when they won in 2000.
Titles: CONCACAF Champions Cup 2000; US Open Cup 2

KAIZER CHIEFS (South Africa)
Kaizer Chiefs, one of South Africa's first professional clubs, take their name from the former international midfielder, Kaizer Motaung. He co-founded the club in 1970 after returning from a spell in the US. He has since served them as a player, in three separate stints as coach, and now as club president. The Chiefs passionately contest the Soweto derby with Orlando Pirates, another of Motaung's old teams. Their home at Johannesburg's FNB Stadium is being rebuilt as Soccer City to host the 2010 World Cup final.
Titles: African Cup Winners' Cup 2001; South African league 2

POHANG STEELERS (South Korea)
Pohang Steelers dominated in the 1970s and 1980s, then suffered a 15-year barren spell in the K-League until their 2007 title triumph. In 1997, they became the third South Korean team to win the Asian Champions League by beating compatriots and defending champions Seongham Ilhwa Chunma. They retained the trophy the following year against China's Dalian Wanda. Crucial to their success in the 1990s was reliable center back Hong-Myung Bo, who went on to become his country's most-capped player.
Titles: Asian Champions League 1997, 1998; South Korean league 3; South Korean cup 1

UNAM PUMAS (Mexico)
UNAM Pumas, the club affiliated to Latin America's largest university, has long put a useful emphasis on youth and proudly produced Mexican legends such as Luis Garcia, Jorge Campos, and Hugo Sanchez.

The inspirational striker scored 96 goals for UNAM Pumas from 1976 to 1981, then returned as coach 19 years later, guiding the club to four trophies in 2004. Characterful goalkeeper Campos loved to roam upfield but also occasionally played in attack with 35 goals to his credit in 199 games. UNAM Pumas' home in Mexico City was the main venue for the 1968 Olympics Games.
Titles: CONCACAF Champions Cup 1980, 1982, 1989; Copa Interamericana 1981; Mexican league 5, Mexican cup 1

URAWA RED DIAMONDS (Japan)
Urawa Red Diamonds, won four league titles and four Emperor's Cups before the Japanese game turned professional in 1993. They made a bad start in the J.League, finishing bottom in the first two seasons. The team nicknamed "The Nearly Men" lived up to their image by just missing out on the 2004 and 2005 titles. But they finally sparkled, to become J.League champions in 2006 and win the Asian Champions League in 2007. Star players have included Japanese midfielder Shinji Ono and Brazilian striker Edmundo.
Titles: Asian Champions League 2007; Japanese league 5; Emperor's Cup 6; J.League Cup 1

BELOW Urawa Reds Diamonds take the glory after their Asian Champions League triumph in 2007

GREAT PLAYERS & MANAGERS

Match and trophy-winning performances depend on a combination of teamwork and spirit from both the players and their managers. Even the stars that shine like no other—such as Stanley Matthews, Diego Maradona, Ronaldo, Pelé, and Zinedine Zidane—would have been unable to express their genius without a manager to guide them. Nowadays, players are not only chasing the ball but also the opportunities to earn fame, fortune, and even notoriety for their successes and failures, goals and gaffes.

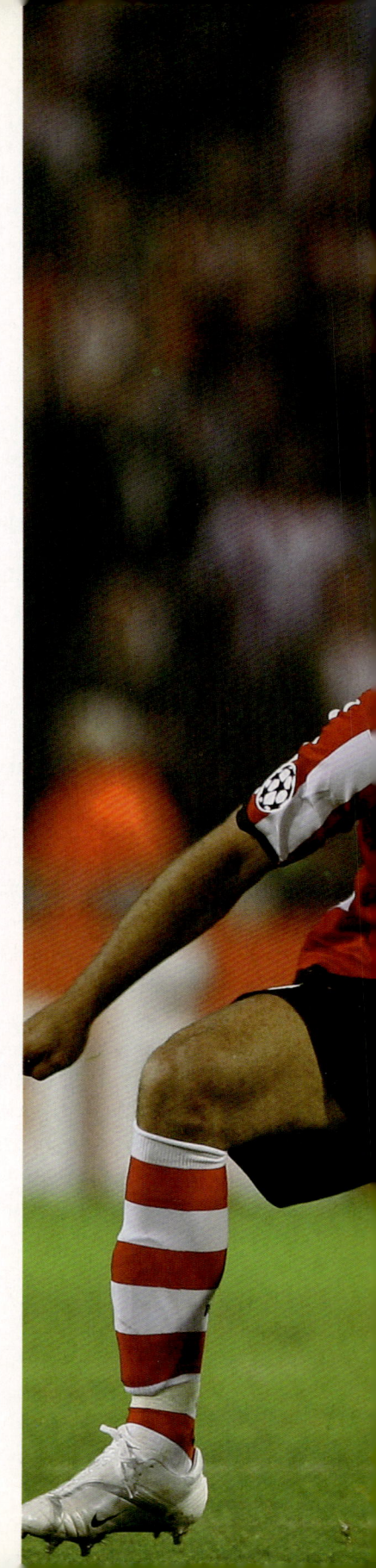

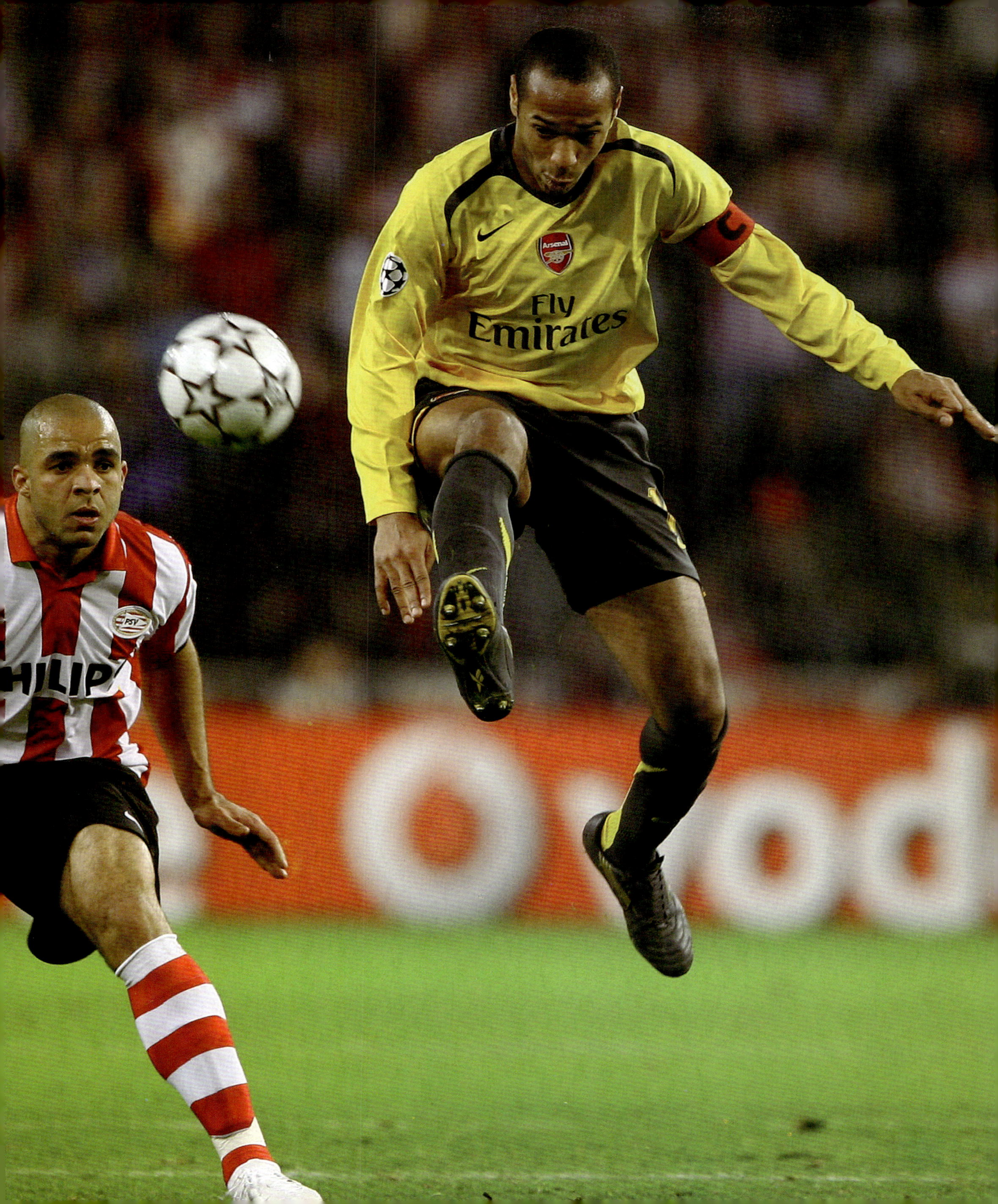
Arsenal
Fly
Emirates
PSV

GREAT PLAYERS & MANAGERS
MANAGERS

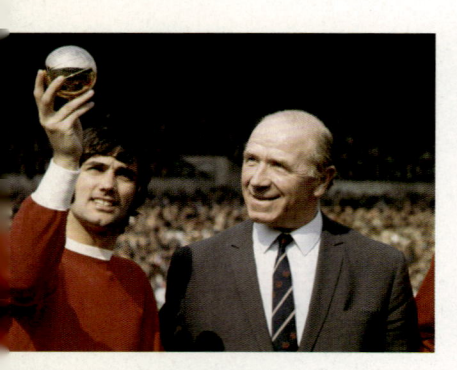

TOP Sir Matt Busby (right) admires George Best's European footballer prize

ABOVE Fabio Capello, star midfielder turned star manager

PAGE 136 Guus Hiddink trains his team in preparation for the 2008 UEFA European Championship.

PAGE 137 Thierry Henry playing for Arsenal against PSV Eindhoven

SIR MATT BUSBY (born 26 May 1909, died 20 January 1994)
Greatest success: European Champion Clubs' Cup 1968 (Manchester Utd)
Busby managed Manchester United between 1945 and 1969 and again for the 1970–71 season. He was responsible for creating the "Busby Babes" who won the league in both 1956 and 1957. After the 1958 Munich air crash in which 23 people died, including eight players, he built a new side with the survivors and new players such as George Best. Busby's crowning glory was the emphatic 4-1 defeat of Benfica in the European Champion Clubs' Cup final at Wembley in 1968.

FABIO CAPELLO (born 18 June 1946)
Greatest success: 1994 European Champions League (AC Milan)
The Italian was appointed England's coach in December 2007. He had previously won the league title with every club he had managed: AC Milan, Real Madrid, Roma, and Juventus. He also coached AC Milan to their masterful 4-0 thrashing of Johan Cruyff's Barcelona in the 1994 Champions League final.

BRIAN CLOUGH (born 21 March 1935, died 20 September 2004)
Greatest successes: 1979 and 1980 European Champion Clubs' Cups (Nottingham Forest)
Clough was the first manager since Herbert Chapman to win the Championship in England with two different clubs (Derby County and Nottingham Forest). He was an iconic if idiosyncratic manager who could draw the best out of problematic players. His outspoken manner did not always endear himself to players—he lasted only 44 days at Leeds United in 1974.

HERBERT CHAPMAN (born 19 January 1878, died 6 January 1934)
Greatest successes: 1924, 1925, 1931, and 1933 English league titles (Huddersfield Town and Arsenal)
Chapman is associated indelibly with Arsenal in the 1930s, but he made his name as a manager of Huddersfield Town in the 1920s. He laid out a five-year plan for success for Arsenal, which came to fruition exactly on schedule when his team won the 1930 FA Cup at the expense of his former club, Huddersfield Town. The victory laid the foundations for a decade in which Arsenal dominated English football.

VINCENTE FEOLA (born 1 November 1909, died 6 November 1975)
Greatest success: 1958 World Cup (Brazil)
Feola famously guided Brazil to their first World Cup triumph in Sweden, although he took some persuading from senior players to pick both Garrincha and Pelé in the middle of the tournament when they appeared to be floundering. Because of illness, Feola missed their successful defense of the World Cup in 1962. He returned for the luckless 1966 finals in England, when his side went out in the group stage. Feola finished with an outstanding career record of only losing six matches out of the 74 his team played.

SIR ALEX FERGUSON (born 31 December 1941)
Greatest successes: 1999 and 2008 European Champions League Club Cups (Manchester Utd)
Ferguson has become the most successful manager in the history of English football since he succeeded Ron Atkinson at Manchester United in 1986. Ferguson was lured south from Aberdeen, which

he had famously guided to victory at the expense of Real Madrid in the European Cup Winners' Cup final. His success at United began with an FA Cup win in 1990, and included an incredible treble of winning the Champions League, Premier League, and FA Cup in 1999. Ferguson came close to a repeat of this feat in 2008, winning the Premier League title and the Champions League in the 50th anniversary year of the Munich air crash.

JOSEF "SEPP" HERBERGER (born 28 March 1897, died 20 April 1977)
Greatest success: 1954 World Cup (West Germany)
Herberger became manager of Germany in 1938 and used all his sports and political influence to try to keep his players away from the battle fronts during World War II. He returned as national manager after the war and won West Germany's first World Cup in 1954. The final was aptly labeled the "Miracle of Berne" after his team beat hot favorites Hungary 3-2.

HELENIO HERRERA (born 17 April 1910, died 9 November 1997)
Greatest successes: 1964 World and European Champion Clubs' Cups (Internazionale)
Herrera, known widely in his heyday simply as "HH," managed a number of top clubs and national teams (including Italy and Spain), winning 16 major trophies. Born in Morocco but brought up in Argentina, he played in France before concentrating on coaching in France, Spain, and Italy. Herrera pioneered the use of psychological motivational ploys and, more controversially, artificial substances.

GUUS HIDDINK (born 8 November 1946)
Greatest success: 1988 European Champion Clubs' Cup (PSV Eindhoven)
Hiddink, a former central defender who wound down his career in the North American Soccer League, sprang to prominence at PSV in the late 1980s as a manager. He enjoyed success in Spain with Real Madrid and Valencia before leading South Korea to a fourth place finish in the 2002 World Cup. Hiddink had previously managed the Dutch national team at Euro '96 and led Australia to the finals of the 2006 World Cup for their first appearance in the tournament for 32 years. He then revitalized the Russian national team, guiding them to the semi-final stage of Euro 2008.

VALERI LOBANOVSKI (born 6 January 1939, died 13 May 2002)
Greatest successes: 1975 and 1986 European Cup Winners' Cups (Dynamo Kiev)
Lobanovski was a hero in the Ukraine before the collapse of the Soviet Union. He was the Dynamo Kiev manager for 15 years, twice winning the Cup Winners' Cup and also beating Bayern Munich to take the 1975 European Supercup. Lobanovski spent three spells managing the Soviet Union and also managed the Ukraine.

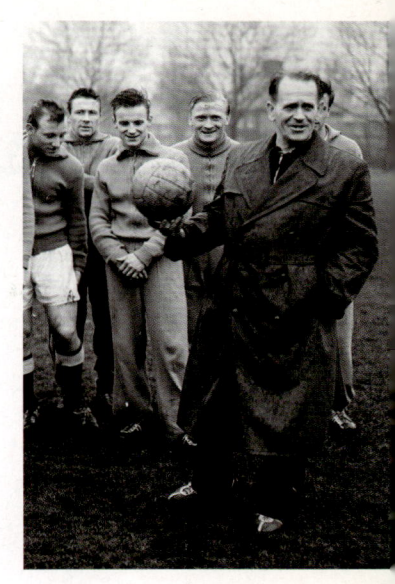

CÉSAR LUIS MENOTTI (born 5 November 1938)
Greatest success: 1978 World Cup (Argentina)
In 1978, the left-leaning César Luis Menotti made himself immune from action by the ruling military junta because he was busy leading Argentina to their first-ever World Cup success. Menotti believed in positive, attacking football, which set him at odds with other top Argentinian coaches of the era such as Juan Carlos Lorenzo and Osvaldo Zubeldía. Menotti quit after Argentina's shock second round group exit at the 1982 finals in Spain, suffering defeat at the hands of Brazil and Italy.

BOB PAISLEY (born 23 January 1919, died 14 February 1996)
Greatest successes: 1977, 1978, and 1980 European Champion Clubs' Cups (Liverpool)
Paisley stepped up, virtually unknown outside Anfield, from the role of assistant when Bill Shankly retired unexpectedly in 1974. During his nine years in charge, Paisley guided Liverpool to six league titles. Paisley remains the only man to have managed one club to three European Cups. He won 19 major titles in all.

ABOVE Sepp Herberger plots the "Miracle of Bern"

BELOW Sir Alex Ferguson makes a winning point in training

GREAT PLAYERS & MANAGERS
MANAGERS

VITTORIO POZZO (born 12 March 1886, died 21 December 1968)
Greatest successes: 1934 and 1938 World Cups, 1936 Olympic Games (Italy)
Pozzo, who was also a journalist, learned to love football during a period of study in England. In 1934 he had no doubts about using former Argentina internationals, such as Luis Monti and Raimundo Orsi, to strengthen his first World Cup-winning side. Ruthlessly, he then scrapped almost the entire team to build a new side for the 1938 competition. In between these triumphs, Pozzo guided Italy to gold medal success at the 1936 Olympic Games. Sadly, Pozzo retired in 1949 after the Superga air disaster wiped out the entire playing staff of Torino, around whom he was planning to build a team for the 1950 World Cup.

SIR ALF RAMSEY (born 22 January 1920, died 28 April 1999)
Greatest success: 1966 World Cup (England)
Ramsey shall always hold a special place in the hearts of England fans as the only manager to have brought the country success in a major competition. A year after his achievement, he was knighted. However, Ramsey was forced out in early 1974 because of England's unexpected failure to qualify for the World Cup finals in West Germany.

SIR BOBBY ROBSON (born 18 February 1933)
Greatest successes: 1978 FA Cup, 1981 UEFA Cup (Ipswich Town)
Robson was a managerial legend at Ipswich Town, where he remained for 13 years before his England call-up. At club level, Robson's side twice finished as runner-up in the league, but made amends by capturing the FA Cup in 1978 and lifting the UEFA Cup in 1981. Robson moved abroad to win league championships in both Holland and Portugal. He later took England to the brink of the 1990 World Cup final—they fell only in a penalty shoot-out to West Germany—before returning to club management.

ARRIGO SACCHI (born 1 April 1946)
Greatest successes: 1989 and 1990 European Champions League (AC Milan)
Sacchi never played football professionally but more than made up for that as a coach. "You don't need to have been a horse to become a successful jockey" was arguably one of his best quotes. He had been plucked from Serie B obscurity by Silvio Berlusconi, the new AC Milan owner, in the mid 1980s, and swiftly introduced a new, positive, and—most importantly—winning approach to the Italian game. AC Milan's squad was bursting with talent, including the trio of Dutchmen Ruud Gullit, Marco Van Basten, and Frank Rijkaard. His AC Milan successes led to an appointment as coach of Italy, who finished as runner-up to Brazil in the 1994 World Cup.

HELMUT SCHÖN (born 15 September 1915, died 23 February 1996)
Greatest success: 1974 World Cup (West Germany)
Under Schön's 14-year-leadership, West Germany won the World Cup on home territory in 1974, after finishing third at Mexico in 1970 and runner-up to England in 1966. West Germany hosted the World Cup finals as worthy winners of the 1972 European Championship under Schön. He is the only manager to have won both the World Cup and European Championship and the sole manager to hold the titles simultaneously.

BELOW Sir Alf Ramsey in training in 1974

BILL SHANKLY (born 2 September 1913, died 29 September 1981)
Greatest success: 1966 and 1973 English league titles, 1973 UEFA Cup (Liverpool)
Shankly is remembered by Liverpool fans as their greatest ever manager, his legend embellished by a string of witty one-liners such as: "some people believe football is a matter of life and death. I'm very disappointed with that attitude. I can assure you it is much, much more important than that." Liverpool had been a club stuck in the second division doldrums when Shankly took over in 1959, but he soon transformed it on and off the field, and developed a unique team spirit and identity that lives on to this day. He secured Liverpool's inaugural European trophy in 1973, courtesy of a UEFA Cup final victory over Borussia Mönchengladbach.

JOCK STEIN (born 5 October 1922, died 10 September 1985)
Greatest success: 1967 European Champion Clubs' Cup (Celtic)
Jock Stein was one of the most successful Scottish managers ever. Between 1965 and 1978, his Celtic side lifted the European Champion Clubs' Cup, ten Scottish League titles, eight Scottish Cups, and six Scottish League Cups. Stein's Celtic became the first British club to win the European Champion Clubs' Cup as a result of his "Lisbon Lions" defeating Internazionale in 1967 in Portugal. He took over the position of Scotland's manager in 1978, where he remained until he died of a heart attack just after his Scottish side had equalized against Wales and earned a place in the 1986 World Cup finals.

GIOVANNI TRAPATTONI
(born 17 March 1939)
Greatest success: 1985 European Champion Clubs' Cup (Juventus)
Giovanni Trapattoni is Italy's most successful club manager, winning seven Serie A titles and the European Cup. He and Germany's Udo Lattek are the only managers to have won all three major European club titles. He had a glittering career as an AC Milan defender, where he twice won the European Cup. Trapattoni has a wealth of experience, having coached both Milan clubs, Fiorentina, Juventus, Bayern Munich (twice), Benfica, Stuttgart, and Red Bull Salzburg, with an impressive record of ten domestic titles in four countries. He was also in charge of the Azzurri from 2000 to 2004, but his side struggled in both the 2002 World Cup finals and 2004 European Championship. In May 2008, he took over the reins of the Republic of Ireland.

ARSÈNE WENGER (born 22 October 1949)
Greatest successes: 1998 and 2002 English league and FA Cup doubles (Arsenal)
Arsène Wenger made a major contribution in transforming the English game after being brought in by Arsenal in 1996. He was comparatively unknown in England when he first arrived, despite being both successful and respected in France and Japan. Since then, Wenger has guided Arsenal to three league titles and four FA Cup triumphs, including league and cup doubles in 1998 and 2002. Remarkably, the 2003–04 season saw Wenger became the first manager in the English league to complete an entire league campaign unbeaten. He is the club's most successful and long-serving manager.

MARIO ZAGALLO (born 9 August 1931)
Greatest success: 1970 World Cup (Brazil)
Mario Zagallo is a Brazilian icon, having enjoyed a magnificent career in football, both as a player and a coach. He played as an industrious left winger in the World Cup-winning sides in 1958 and 1962, then graduated to manage the side in 1970, winning the 1970 finals in Mexico. With this victory, he became the first person to win the World Cup as both a player and a coach. His career with Brazil has continued in various roles, including the post of technical director at the 2006 World Cup finals. His Brazilian team won the World Cup in 1994 but finished as runner-up to France in the 1998 World Cup finals.

ABOVE Bill Shankly laid the foundations for the Liverpool revival

BELOW Arsène Wenger guided Arsenal to two domestic doubles

GREAT PLAYERS & MANAGERS
EUROPEAN PLAYERS

MARCO VAN BASTEN (born 31 October 1964)
Holland: 58 games, 24 goals
Marco Van Basten scored one of the finest goals in international history when he volleyed home Holland's second in their victory over the Soviet Union in the final of the 1988 European Championship. The goal sealed Van Basten's reputation as one of the finest center forwards to grace European football, not only with Holland but also with top club sides Ajax Amsterdam and Milan. Injury forced his premature retirement.

FRANZ BECKENBAUER (born 11 September 1945)
West Germany: 103 games, 14 goals
Franz Beckenbauer is one of the few defenders guaranteed a place in any football hall of fame. Initially a playmaker, "The Kaiser" was converted into a creative sweeper by Yugoslavian coach Tschik Cajkovski at Bayern Munich in the 1960s. He won every honor at domestic level and lifted the World Cup as the West German captain in 1974 and again as national coach in 1990. In recent years he has served as president of Bayern, as a member of the FIFA executive, and has chaired the organizing committee for the 2006 World Cup.

DAVID BECKHAM (born 2 May 1975)
England: 102 games, 17 goals
A boyhood Manchester United fan, David Beckham went on to win a historic treble with the club in 1999. He was subsequently sold to Real Madrid in 2003, winning the Spanish league in the last of his four seasons with the club, then joined LA Galaxy. Beckham played in three World Cup finals for England, which included a controversial sending off against Argentina in 1998.

GEORGE BEST (born 22 May 1946, died 25 November 2005)
Northern Ireland: 37 games, 9 goals
Best was arguably the greatest player never to have made an appearance in the World Cup finals. A magical talent, one of the most exciting to grace English football, he made his Manchester United debut as a winger aged 17 in 1963 and went on to win the European Champion Clubs' Cup in 1968 and two league titles, before being driven out of the British game by the pressures of his own fame. His greatest exploit was in United's 5-1 thrashing of Benfica in Lisbon in a European Champion Clubs Cup quarter-final in 1966. He was voted European Footballer of the Year in 1968.

LIAM BRADY (born 13 February 1956)
Republic of Ireland: 72 games, 9 goals.
Liam Brady was the commanding heart of Arsenal's midfield in the 1970s and won the FA Cup three times in a row. Regularly voted as Footballer of the Year in both England and the Republic of Ireland, he emigrated to Italy for a much-admired league title-winning stint with Juventus and further spells with Ascoli, Internazionale, and Sampdoria. He returned to

RIGHT George Best, both European Champion and European Footballer of the Year in 1968

England with West Ham United before retiring and later rejoining Arsenal as youth boss. Brady has joined his former boss at Juventus, Giovani Trapattoni, on the backroom staff of the rejuvenated Republic of Ireland squad.

SIR BOBBY CHARLTON
(born 11 October 1937)

England: 106 games, 49 goals

Bobby Charlton had just established himself in the Manchester United side when the squad was tragically torn apart by the 1958 Munich air crash—eight players died in the disaster. Charlton survived and helped lead the reconstruction of the devastated Manchester United side. Ten years later, he captained them to victory in the European Champion Clubs' Cup. He scored two goals in the 4-1 victory over Benfica in the final at Wembley Stadium. Two years earlier, Charlton's unerring shooting had helped fire England to their sole success as World Cup champions. He was briefly manager of Preston but returned to his beloved Manchester United as a director. He was knighted in 1994.

JOHAN CRUYFF (born 25 April 1947)

Holland: 48 games, 33 goals

Johan Cruyff, son of a cleaner at the Ajax Amsterdam offices, grew up to be the epitome of Holland's "Total Football" revolution, as well as being voted European Footballer of the Year three times in the 1970s. Ajax's unique style of play brought the club—and Cruyff—three successive victories in the European Champion Clubs' Cup. Cruyff, despite being the club's captain, was sold to Barcelona for the then world record of $1.85 million (£922,000) prior to the 1974 World Cup finals, where hosts West Germany edged past the Dutch 2-1 in the final. Cruyff controversially refused to play in the 1978 World Cup finals in Argentina, because of the kidnap threats made to him and his family. Holland reached the semi-final stage, but critics believe that with his presence they could have returned from South America with the coveted Jules Rimet trophy. When he returned to Ajax as technical director, the side went on to win the 1987 European Cup Winners' Cup. He later managed Barcelona, who he guided to victory in the 1992 European Cup.

KENNY DALGLISH (born 4 March 1951)

Scotland: 102 games, 30 goals

Kenny Dalglish achieved a remarkable feat by winning league titles as both a player and a manager in England with Liverpool and in Scotland with Celtic. A nimble, quick-thinking forward, Dalglish moved from Glasgow to Anfield in 1978 as replacement at Liverpool for the legendary Kevin Keegan. He duly proved that he could fill the boots of the Kop hero—he was the club's leading scorer in his first season. After a glittering playing career for Liverpool, he successfully made the transition to managing the club in 1985, and became the only player-manager in modern times to steer his club to a domestic double in both league and FA Cup. His glittering career saw him equal the scoring record with Denis Law for Scotland, but he stands alone with the record for most appearances.

DIXIE DEAN (born 22 January 1907, died 1 March 1980)

England: 16 games, 18 goals

Dixie Dean remains the most prolific striker of English football after rattling home 60 goals in just 39 matches for Everton in the 1927–28 season. His record is virtually untouchable, but the center forward was merely taking advantage of a recent change to the offside law. Dean's incredible career total of 349 goals in 399 games helped Everton collect two league titles and one FA Cup. However, Dean only played 16 times for England, despite scoring 18 goals in those games.

BELOW Johan Cruyff, a club champion of Europe as both player and coach

GREAT PLAYERS & MANAGERS
EUROPEAN PLAYERS

ABOVE Just Fontaine in triumph after scoring four goals against West Germany in the 1958 World Cup

EUSÉBIO (born 25 January 1942)
Portugal: 64 games, 41 goals
Eusébio da Silva Ferreira, a Mozambican-born Portugese striker, was nicknamed the "Black Panther" for his valuable goals. He inspired Benifica to a 5-3 victory over Real Madrid in the Champion Clubs' Cup with Benfica in 1962, although his team could only finish as the runner-up in the same competition in 1963, 1965, and 1968. Over the 15 years Eusébio spent at Benfica, he won the Portuguese league title ten times. In the 1966 World Cup finals in England, he guided Portugal to third place and won the Golden Boot as top scorer in the competition with nine goals. His finest performance was in the memorable quarter-final against North Korea. The Koreans raced to a 3-0 lead before Eusébio came on and scored four goals to give his country a 5-3 victory.

JUST FONTAINE (born 18 August 1933)
France: 21 games, 30 goals
Just Fontaine was a fast, brave center forward who wrote his name into World Cup history by scoring 13 goals for third-placed France in the 1958 finals—Fontaine scored in all six games. Fontaine, born in Morocco, was brought to France to play for Nice, with whom he won the French League title in 1956. He was then sold to the great Reims side that dominated French football at the time. In the 1957–58 season, his goals helped secure the double of the French League and cup for Reims. Fontaine only got his chance in the 1958 World Cup finals because Reims team-mate Rene Bliard was ruled out with an ankle injury. Fontaine's career was ended prematurely in 1961, because of two serious leg fractures. He won the domestic league four times and the French Cup twice.

FRANCISCO GENTO
(born 21 October 1933)
Spain: 43 games, 5 goals
"Paco" Gento set a record in 1966 when, as captain of Real Madrid, he collected a sixth European Champion Clubs' Cup Winner's medal. Gento, from Santander in northern Spain, was nicknamed "El Supersonico" for his electric pace on the left wing. His distracting effect created valuable extra space to assist the goal-scoring exploits of team-mates such as Alfredo Di Stefano and Ferenc Puskás. Gento was a key figure in Real Madrid's triumphs of the 1950s and 1960s, scoring 126 goals in 428 games over 18 years. He won the domestic league title 12 times, represented Spain in the 1962 and 1966 World Cup finals, and played a key role in the side that dominated the first five European Champion Clubs' Cup finals with successive victories in the late 1950s.

RUUD GULLIT (born 1 September 1962)
Holland: 66 games, 17 goals
Ruud Gullit was hailed as Europe's finest player in the late 1980s, when he moved from Dutch football to help inspire a revival at AC Milan. Gullit, World Player of the Year in 1987 and 1989, was a favorite of AC Milan owner Silvio Berlusconi, winning two European Champion Clubs' Cups and three Italian league titles. He captained Holland in the 1988 European Championship, heading home the opening goal in the 2-0 victory over Russia in the final. He moved to Chelsea as a player and later became their coach—he was the first non-British manager to win the FA Cup. He subsequently had brief spells as manager of Newcastle United and Dutch giants Feyenoord.

GHEORGHE HAGI (born 5 February 1965)
Romania: 125 games, 35 goals
Gheorghe Hagi was nicknamed the "Maradona of the Carpathians" during the late 1980s because of his cultured left foot and silky skills. His huge self-confidence helped him to push forward from midfield to score goals, but his main strength lay in his skill and vision as a playmaker. Such outstanding talent earned special permission, in a restrictive political era, to move abroad to ply his trade. He played for Real Madrid, moved to Brescia in Italy, and then on to Barcelona before ending his career at Turkish side Galatasaray. Hagi was the fulcrum of the Romanian side that reached the quarter-final stage of the 1994 World Cup.

THIERRY HENRY (born 17 August 1977)
France: 100 games, 44 goals
Thierry Henry set a scoring record for Arsenal over eight seasons, proving to be a bargain signing even at $21 million (£10.5 million) when he was bought from Juventus in 1999. At Arsenal he was converted from a winger to a striker, and went on to win a slew of honors, with the club. He also won World Cup and European Championship medals with France and was named in the 2006 FIFPro World XI team. In 2007 he was sold to Barcelona.

GEOFF HURST (born 8 December 1941)
England: 49 games, 24 goals
Sir Geoff Hurst remains the only player to have scored a hat-trick in a World Cup Final, an achievement which ultimately earned him a belated knighthood. Hurst only came into the England side because Jimmy Greaves was injured. As well as his match-winning performance in the final, Hurst scored what proved to be the decisive goal in the quarter-final against Argentina.

RAYMOND KOPA (born 13 October 1931),
France: 45 games, 18 goals
Raymond Kopa was the son of a Polish mining family from northern France. His talent was first spotted by Angers, who then sold him on to Reims in 1950. He was sold to Real Madrid after the Spanish club defeated Reims in the European Champion Clubs' Cup final in 1956. At Real Madrid he won the European Champion Clubs Cup three times and was crowned 1958 European Footballer of the Year. Kopa won four French and two Spanish league titles.

ABOVE Thierry Henry, a record marksman with both Arsenal and France

EUROPEAN PLAYERS 209

GREAT PLAYERS & MANAGERS MOMENTS

1930s

ABOVE Herbert Chapman, Arsenal's first great manager

BELOW Jimmy Hogan staging a coaching lesson for troops

1940s

ABOVE Alfredo Di Stefano scores for Real Madrid against Eintracht

RIGHT England boss Sir Alf Ramsey (right) with Bobby Charlton

BELOW Bobby Charlton shoots for goal against France at Wembley

1960s

1970s

ABOVE Nottingham Forest's Brian Clough in trademark green jumper

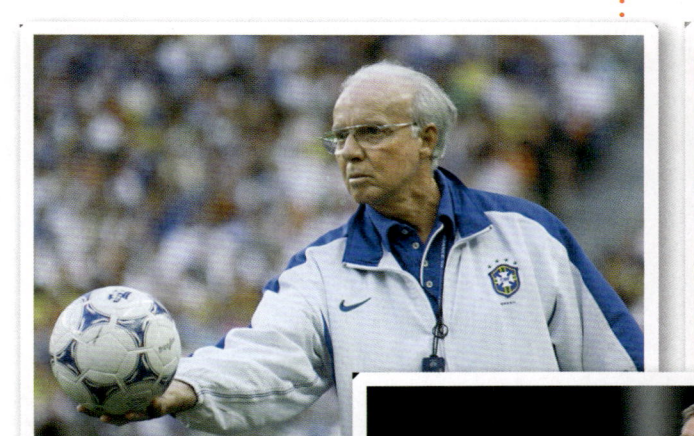

ABOVE Mario Zagallo, a World Cup winner as player and manager

1990s

ABOVE Sir Bobby Robson points the way for Newcastle

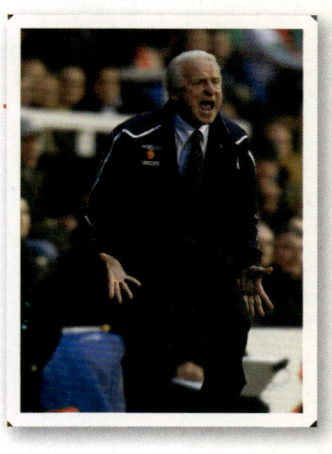

2000s

ABOVE Giovanni Trapattoni brings the winning touch to Ireland

ABOVE Arsène Wenger took Arsenal to the double in his first full season

LEFT Sir Alex Ferguson lifted Manchester United to new glory

MOMENTS 211

GREAT PLAYERS & MANAGERS
EUROPEAN PLAYERS

HANS KRANKL (born 14 February 1953)
Austria: 69 games, 34 goals
Hans Krankl was one of the great Austrian center forwards. In 1978 he scored 41 goals for Rapid Vienna, winning the Golden Boot as Europe's leading league scorer. He starred for Austria at the World Cup finals in Argentina, where he netted the winning goal against West Germany—Austria's first victory over their neighbors for 37 years. He went on to play for Barcelona, where he won the 1979 European Cup Winners' Cup.

MICHAEL LAUDRUP (born 15 June 1964)
Denmark: 104 games, 37 goals
Michael Laudrup stood out in Denmark's outstanding team that reached the semi-finals of the 1984 European Championship and the second round at the 1986 World Cup finals. He achieved club success with Juventus before moving to Lazio, and he was part of Johan Cryuff's "Dream Team" at Barcelona where he won four league titles. He also played for for Real Madrid and Ajax.

DENIS LAW (born 24 February 1940)
Scotland: 55 games, 30 goals
Denis Law, whatever the competing talents of Bobby Charlton and George Best, was the king of Old Trafford in the 1960s. His ebullient personality, and his ability to create chances and goals out of nothing, earned him the adulation of Manchester United fans. Law started at Huddersfield Town, and had brief spells at Manchester City and Torino before being brought to Manchester United in 1962. He repaid the club's financial investment with 171 goals in 309 league games. He won the European Footballer of the Year prize in 1964.

GARY LINEKER (born 30 November 1960)
England: 80 games, 48 goals
Gary Lineker made his name with home town Leicester City, but his career took off after his transfer to Everton in 1985. Lineker moved on to Barcelona, winning the European Cup Winners' Cup, and in the 1986 World Cup finals Lineker won the Golden Boot as the leading scorer with six goals. The prolific striker returned to England for a successful spell with Tottenham before ending his career in Japan.

JOSEF MASOPUST (born 9 February 1931)
Czechoslovakia: 63 games, 10 goals
Josef Masopust was a midfield heir in the 1950s and early 1960s to the great pre-war traditions of Czechoslovak football. An attacking midfielder, he played the majority of his career with the army club Dukla Prague before moving to Belgium

BELOW Denis Law takes the high road for Manchester United at Old Trafford

and turning out for Crossing Molenbeek. He reached his peak at the 1962 World Cup in Chile, where he helped to inspire his side all the way to the final. Although he opened the scoring against Brazil for an unexpected lead, the holders fought back to triumph 3-1. Masopust won the 1962 Footballer of the Year award following his outstanding displays in Chile, where he was nicknamed "the Czech Knight."

STANLEY MATTHEWS (born 1 February 1915, died 23 February 2000)
England: 54 games, 11 goals
Sir Stanley Matthews was the first active player to be knighted as reward for extraordinary service to the game both before and after World War II. He was an outside right whose mesmerizing talent earned him the nickname the "Wizard of Dribble." Matthews achieved his ambition to win the FA Cup with Blackpool in 1953, when, aged 38 he famously rescued his side from a 3-1 deficit by setting up three goals. In 1956, he received the inaugural European Player of the Year. His fitness and enthusiasm saw him play at the 1954 World Cup finals and then lead his original club, Stoke City, to promotion back into the old first division in 1962.

GIUSEPPE MEAZZA
(born 23 August 1910, died 21 August 1979)
Italy: 53 game, 33 goals
Giuseppe Meazza was one of only two Italian players—Giovanni Ferrari was the other—to have won the World Cup for the Azzurri both at home and also away from Italy. Meazza was a powerful, goal-scoring inside forward with Internazionale in the 1930s, scoring 287 goals in 408 games for the club. He was a World Cup winner at home in 1934 and was the captain in France when Italy triumphed in 1938. He won three league titles and finished as top scorer in Serie A three times. He played briefly for AC Milan and guested for Juventus and Varese during World War II. He finished his playing career at Atalanta before managing Internazionale.

BOBBY MOORE (born 12 April 1941, died 24 February 1993)
England: 108 games, 2 goals
Bobby Moore proved to be an ideal captain for England, leading them to glory at the 1966 World Cup and also during their unsuccessful defense of the trophy in 1970. He played for the majority of his career with West Ham United, initially as an attacking wing half before moving to the heart of defense. Respected by his team-mates for his tough tackling and silky skills, Moore achieved a remarkable hat-trick at Wembley Stadium by winning the FA Cup in 1964, the European Cup Winners' Cup in 1965, and the World Cup in 1966. A bronze statue of Moore stands outside the new Wembley Stadium. He finished his career with Fulham, San Antonio, and finally Seattle.

ABOVE Stanley Matthews teasing Manchester United's Roger Byrne in an international training session

EUROPEAN PLAYERS 213

GREAT PLAYERS & MANAGERS
EUROPEAN PLAYERS

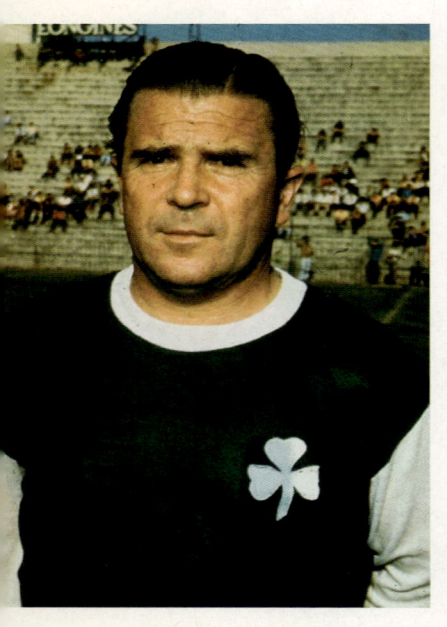

ABOVE Ferenc Puskás, legendary No 10 for Honved and Real Madrid

GERD MÜLLER (born 3 November 1945)
West Germany: 62 games, 68 goals
Gerd Müller was the most prolific goal scorer in modern German football and the all-time top scorer at the World Cup finals. He was voted European Player of the Year in 1970, having scored ten times at that year's World Cup finals in Mexico—he hit successive hat-tricks against Bulgaria and Peru—to finish as the highest scorer and win the Golden Boot. He notched an incredible 398 goals for Bayern Munich, where he was a key figure during the mid-1970s, when they won the European Champion Clubs' Cup three times in succession. He also scored the winning goal for West Germany in the 1974 World Cup final victory over Holland.

FERENC PUSKÁS (born 2 April 1927, died 17 November 2006)
Hungary: 85 games, 84 goals
Spain: 4 games, no goals
Ferenc Puskás is one of the game's all-time greats, famed for his goals, his leadership, and the way that he reconstructed his career after the 1956 Hungarian Revolution. Puskás and Hungary were unbeaten for four years, going into the 1954 World Cup finals as Olympic champions, but fell 3-2 to West Germany in the final. He defected to the West, where he rebuilt his career with Real Madrid and won the league title five times and the European Cup three times.

CRISTIANO RONALDO
(born 5 February 1985)
Portugal: 55 games, 20 goals
Cristiano Ronaldo became Britain's most expensive teenager when, aged 18, he cost Manchester United the remarkable sum of $25 million (£12.4 million) in 2003. At first, the self-indulgence of his trickery on the right wing frustrated fans and team-mates alike, but once he adapted to the difficult demands of the English game, he proved to be equally dangerous on the left wing and a real handful to deal with in the air. In the 2007–08 season, he scored 42 goals in all competitions, which helped guide Manchester United to a double of the English league title and the Champions League.

PAOLO ROSSI (born 23 September 1956)
Italy: 48 games, 20 goals
Paolo Rossi looked a great prospect after the 1978 World Cup finals, but he was banned for two years over a match-fixing scandal. The striker only returned to top-class action weeks before the 1982 World Cup finals kicked off, yet he finished as the top scorer with six goals to his credit. These strikes included a hat-trick to deliver the knock-out blow to Brazil in the quarter-final. Rossi continued to score, helping guide Italy to world champions and himself to the coveted Golden Boot.

MATTHIAS SINDELAR (born 10 February 1903, died 23 January 1939)
Austria: 43 games, 27 goals
Matthias Sindelar was the inspirational center forward of the Austrian "Wunderteam" that ruled European football in the late 1920s and early 1930s. Sindelar, nicknamed the "Man of Paper" because of his delicate build, won a league title, twice triumphed in the Mitropa Cup, and scored five Austrian Cup successes with Austria Vienna. A World Cup semi-finalist in 1934, five years later he died of carbon monoxide poisoning in his Viennese apartment in unexplained circumstances.

HRISTO STOICHKOV
(born 8 February 1966)
Bulgaria: 83 games, 37 goals
Hristo Stoichkov, once banned for life from the sport but reinstated on appeal, was a huge success at club and national team level. In 1994, Stoichkov picked up the European Player of the Year prize and won the Golden Boot as joint highest scorer at the World Cup finals as he inspired Bulgaria to reach the semi-finals. His move to Barcelona in 1990 saw him collect four Spanish league titles and the Spanish cup once.

FRITZ WALTER (born 31 October 1920, died 17 June 2002)
West Germany: 61 games, 33 goals
Fritz Walter owed his life to national manager Sepp Herberger and repaid him in glory. Walter, an inside forward from Kaiserslautern who made his international debut just before World War II, was kept away from the front by Herberger's string-pulling before finally being drafted in 1942. He was captured and eventually repatriated by the Soviet army. He relaunched his football career and captained Herberger's West Germany to their unexpected World Cup final victory over the mighty Hungary in 1954.

LEV YASHIN (born 22 October 1929, died 20 March 1990)
Soviet Union: 78 games, no goals.
Lev Yashin, nicknamed the "Black Spider," ranks as arguably the greatest ever goalkeeper. Originally an ice hockey star, he succeeded "Tiger" Khomich between the posts at Dynamo Moscow in the early 1950s. Yashin won a gold medal in the 1956 Olympics, followed by victory at the 1960 European Championship. In 1963 he became the first goalkeeper to capture the European Player of the Year prize. Yashin played in three World Cup finals, reaching the semi-finals in his last appearance in 1966. He was awarded the Order of Lenin in 1967 and he retired in 1971. He is immortalized in the form of a statue at the entrance to the Dynamo Stadium in Moscow.

ZINEDINE ZIDANE (born June 23, 1972)
France: 108 games, 31 goals
Zidane was the outstanding French playmaker of the late 1990s and early 2000s. He was making headlines until the very last moment of his career—he was sent off in extra time in the 2006 World Cup Final, his last game, for headbutting Italy's Marco Materazzi. He scored twice in France's 1998 World Cup final win over Brazil and also starred for Bordeaux, Juventus, and Real Madrid.

DINO ZOFF (born 28 February 1942)
Italy: 112 games, no goals
Dino Zoff made his name with Udinese and Mantova before making the big time, first with Napoli and later with Juventus. He set numerous records at Juventus and picked up almost every title possible—initially as player and then as coach. Zoff was Italy's goalkeeper captain when they swept past all opponents at the 1982 World Cup finals. Aged 40, Zoff was the oldest player to win the World Cup after the Azzurri thumped West Germany 3-1 in the final. After retiring as Italy's most capped player, he coached Juventus, Lazio, and Fiorentina, as well as the national team, which he guided to the final of the 2000 European Championship.

BELOW Dino Zoff saves against Brazil in the 1978 World Cup

GREAT PLAYERS & MANAGERS
AMERICAS' PLAYERS

ABOVE Alfredo Di Stefano scores for Real Madrid against Manchester United

ANTONIO CARBAJAL (born 7 June 1929)
Mexico: 48 games, no goals
Antonio Carbajal became the first player to appear in the finals of five World Cup competitions, but ended up on the winning side only once. The Leon goalkeeper's debut in the finals was against Brazil in 1950, when he conceded four goals. He played in the 1954, 1958, and 1962 World Cup finals before bowing out after a scoreless draw against Uruguay in the 1966 finals. Carbajal kicked off his career at Mexico City, but played at Leon for the majority of his career.

JOSÉ LUIS CHILAVERT (born 27 July 1965)
Paraguay: 74 games, eight goals
José Luis Chilavert was renowned for his scoring achievements despite being a goalkeeper. He claimed 62 goals from penalties and free kicks in a 22-year career with clubs in Argentina, France, Paraguay, Spain, and Uruguay (Spain was the only country where he did not win at least one league title.) Chilavert's ultimate ambition was to score a goal in the World Cup finals, but he failed, despite having scored four in qualifying matches for the 2002 tournament. He was voted the world's top goalkeeper three times.

ROBERTO CARLOS (born 10 April 1973)
Brazil: 125 games, 11 goals
Roberto Carlos da Silva Rocha proved to be one of Brazil's most popular exports to Europe because of the power of his shooting and the exuberance of his attacking play from left back. In 2002, he won the World Cup with Brazil and the European Champions League with Real Madrid. Roberto Carlos played more games for Real Madrid than any other foreigner, before moving to Turkey with Fenerbahce.

TEÓFILO CUBILLAS (born 8 March 1949)
Peru: 81 games, 26 goals
Teófilo Cubillas shot to stardom as an inside forward in the outstanding Peru team that reached the 1970 World Cup quarter-finals and the second round at the 1978 World Cup finals. Cubillas was voted South American Player of the Year in 1972, and won the Copa America with Peru in 1975. He began his career with Alianza of Lima, then played in Switzerland, Portugal, and the United States.

DIDI (born 8 October 1929, died 12 May 2001)
Brazil: 68 games, 20 goals
Didi, full name Valdir Pereira, won the World Cup twice with Brazil in 1958 and 1962. Brazil might not have even been at the finals in 1958 at all, but for a remarkable free-kick from Didi that bent in the air and flew into the net against Peru in a qualifying tie. The "Falling Leaf" became Didi's trademark and has been copied by players all over the world ever since. He played most of his career with Botafogo of Rio de Janeiro either side of a short, unhappy spell in 1959–60 with Real Madrid.

ALFREDO DI STEFANO
(born 4 July 1926)
Argentina: six games, six goals
Spain: 31 games, 23 goals
Alfredo Di Stefano remains, for many experts, the greatest ever player because of his all-action performances as a pitch-roaming, high-scoring center forward. He starred for Argentina's River Plate and Colombia's Millonarios, before inspiring Real Madrid to victory in the first five European Champion Clubs' Cup competitions. Di Stefano scored in all five finals, and totalled 216 league goals for Real Madrid over 11 years.

216 GREAT PLAYERS & MANAGERS

LANDON DONOVAN (born 4 March 1982)
United States: 100 games, 35 goals

Landon Donovan promises to be the long-serving, outstanding international that US football has long been waiting for. By the age of 26 the midfielder had already reached a century of international appearances and starred in two World Cup finals. Donovan had two spells with Bayer Leverkusen, but has preferred to play in the United States, latterly for Los Angeles Galaxy.

ENZO FRANCESCOLI
(born 12 November 1961)
Uruguay: 72 games, 15 goals

Enzo Francescoli, nicknamed "The Prince", is arguably the last great Uruguayan player. However, he played the majority of his club career in Argentina, France, and Italy. He played the 1989–90 season with Olympique Marseille, where he was the footballing hero and inspiration for the teenage Zinedine Zidane. A tall, graceful inside forward, Francescoli was a three-times winner of the Copa America with Uruguay and played twice at the World Cup finals. He was voted South American Player of the Year in both 1984 and 1995.

GARRINCHA (born 28 October 1933, died 20 January 1983)
Brazil: 50 games, 12 goals

Garrincha, full name Manoel dos Santos Francisco, lived a life that was a tale of triumph and tragedy. Nicknamed "the Little Bird," he won the World Cup in 1958 and 1962, with his goals proving to be decisive. He was at Rio's Botafogo for 12 years, scoring 232 goals in 581 games. Yet his love of the good life meant he was also his own worst enemy and a nightmare for coaches. He tragically died of alcohol poisoning.

JAIRZINHO (born 25 December 1944)
Brazil: 81 games, 33 goals

Jairzinho, full name Jair Ventura Filho, was the free-scoring successor to the Brazilian tradition of great outside rights, from Julinho in the mid-1950s to Garrincha in the late 1950s and 1960s. He played, like his hero Garrincha, for Rio's Botafogo. In 1970, he recovered twice from a broken right leg and became the only player to score in every round of the World Cup finals in Mexico, scoring seven goals overall. Jairzinho, nicknamed "God," also played in the World Cup finals of 1966 and 1974. He famously discovered an outstanding 12-year-old in Rio de Janerio, a talent called Ronaldo.

KAKÁ (born 22 April 1982)
Brazil: 59 games, 22 goals

Kaká, full name Ricardo Izecson dos Santos Leite, was generally hailed as having established himself as the world's top player in 2007. During 2007, he set up AC Milan's victory in the European Champions League and was voted both FIFA Player of the Year and European Player of the Year. The supremely gifted Brazilian forward originally made his name with São Paulo, following a remarkable recovery from a swimming pool accident that left him temporarily paralysed. AC Milan paid a comparatively low $10 million (£5 million) for him in 2003.

MARIO KEMPES (born 15 July 1954)
Argentina: 43 games, 20 goals

Mario Kempes emerged with Rosario Central in the early 1970s and was one of the finest prospects on view when he played for Argentina at the 1974 World Cup finals. Valencia snapped up Kempes, who twice finished leading scorer in Spain and was one of only two foreign-based players called up by Argentina boss César Luis Menotti for the 1978 World Cup. Kempes was an inspiration, scoring six goals for the hosts, including two in the extra time victory over Holland.

DIEGO MARADONA
(born 30 October 1960)
Argentina: 91 games, 34 goals

Diego Maradona ranks among the greatest ever players, despite controversy over his off-

BELOW Argentina captain Diego Maradona had a big hand in winning the 1986 World Cup

AMERICAS PLAYERS

GREAT PLAYERS & MANAGERS
AMERICAS' PLAYERS

the-pitch antics and the "Hand of God" goal against England in the 1986 World Cup quarter-finals. Discovered by Argentinos Juniors, he starred for Boca Juniors before moving for world record fees to Barcelona and then Napoli. Captain and inspiration in the 1986 World Cup finals, his second strike against England is considered to be one of the greatest ever goals. A runner-up in the 1990 World Cup, he was suspended from the sport in 1991 after failing a drugs test, and three years later failed a World Cup finals' doping test.

PELÉ (born 23 October 1940)
Brazil: 92 games, 77 goals
Pelé, full name Edson Arantes do Nascimento, made his league debut for Santos aged 15. One of only a few who could realistically claim to be the greatest footballer who ever played, he was a World Cup winner at 17—scoring twice in the 5-2 victory over Sweden in the 1958 final. Injury prevented Pelé playing in the 1962 World Cup final and he endured an unhappy tournament in 1966, but he was back at his best for the 1970 final and scored in the 4-1 win over Italy. He came out of retirement in 1975 to help New York Cosmos spearhead the North American Soccer League revolution before hanging up his boots in 1977, having amassed over 1,000 goals.

RONALDINHO (born 21 March 1980)
Brazil: 80 games, 32 goals
Ronaldinho, full name Ronaldo de Assis Moreira, was the attacking midfielder who inspired Barcelona to two league titles and also victory in the 2006 Champions League. He joined Barcelona after spells with Grêmio in Brazil and Paris Saint-Germain. A key figure in Brazil's 2002 World Cup win, Ronaldinho was voted FIFA World Player of the Year in 2004 and 2005.

RONALDO (born 22 September 1976)
Brazil: 97 games, 62 goals
Ronaldo Luis Nazário de Lima was discovered as a 12-year-old by World Cup-winning hero Jairzinho. Five years later, he was at the 1994 World Cup, albeit a non-playing member of the Brazilian squad. In 1998, he was a runner-up amid controversy—playing despite having been taken ill shortly before Brazil's listless final defeat by France. Ronaldo made amends by scoring twice in the 2002 World Cup final win over Germany and scored a record 15th goal at the 2006 World Cup finals. Knee injuries have marred much of his senior career with PSV Eindoven, Barcelona, Internazionale, Real Madrid, and AC Milan.

HUGO SÁNCHEZ (born 11 July 1958)
Mexico: 58 games, 29 goals
Hugo Sánchez numbers among the most prolific scorers in the history of Mexican football and as one of its greatest personalities. He led the attack in three World Cup finals, and ranks as the second-highest overall scorer in Spain's La Liga, with 234 goals amassed at Athletic Madrid and Real Madrid. He was the international manager of Mexico for 16 months until March 2008.

HECTOR SCARONE (born 1 January 1900, died 4 April 1967)
Uruguay: 51 games, 31 goals
Héctor Scarone, nicknamed "the Magician," was the original star of the World Cup after leading Uruguay to victory over Argentina in the inaugural finals in 1930. He played briefly in Europe with Barcelona and Internazionale, and for two seasons with Palermo. He won eight Uruguayan league titles and scored 301 goals in 369 games with Nacional Montevideo.

ABOVE Bobby Moore with Pelé at the 1970 World Cup

ALBERTO PEDRO SPENCER

(born 6 December 1937, died 3 November 2006)
Ecuador: 11 games, four goals (four games, one goal for Uruguay)

Alberto Pedro Spencer is record scorer in the history of the Copa Libertadores. He scored 54 goals in 12 years, mostly for Uruguay's Peñarol, and was the first world-famous Ecuadorian player. Spencer had been recommended to Peñarol, with whom he went on to win two World Club Cups and eight league titles, by Juan Lopez—Uruguay's manager for the 1950 World Cup win in Brazil.

CARLOS VALDERRAMA

(born 2 September 1961)
Colombia: 111 games, 11 goals

Carlos Valderrama, nicknamed "The Kid," was a colorful character who led Colombia from midfield at the World Cup finals of 1990, 1994, and 1998. He was renowned almost as much for his outrageous, long blond hair as for his supreme talent. He was voted South American Player of the Year and represented Colombia a record 111 times. Valderrama spent most of his 22-year career in Colombia, although he played for Montpellier in France and Real Valladolid in Spain before a six-year career in the United States' MLS.

OBDULIO VARELA

(born 20 September 1917, died 2 August 1996)
Uruguay: 49 games, 10 goals

Obdulio Varela was the attacking center half who captained Uruguay to World Cup victory in 1950. Varela apparently told the team to ignore their manager's talk and follow his orders—they bounced back with two goals to spring one of the World Cup's greatest shocks: a 2-1 win over Brazil.

IVAN ZAMORANO

(born 18 January 1967)
Chile: 69 games, 34 goals

Ivan Zamorano was Chile's iconic hero in the 1990s, when he led the national team's World Cup attack and starred in European football. Zamorano was brought to Europe by the Swiss club Saint Gallen. After three terms he moved to the Spanish La Liga for six seasons. In 1995 he was the league's top scorer, with 27 goals for Real Madrid. He went on to win the 1998 UEFA Cup with Internazionale before returning to Chile with Colo Colo via a two-year stint in Mexico.

ZICO

(born 3 March 1953)
Brazil: 88 games, 66 goals

Zico, full name Artur Antunes Coimbra, shot to stardom with Rio de Janerio's Flamengo in the mid-1970s. He followed his 16-year career in Brazil with a two-year spell with Udinese in Italy before returning to Flamengo. However, despite being a legendary Brazil forward, he failed to win a World Cup and missed a crucial World Cup quarter-final penalty against France in 1986. He won the 1990 World Club Cup, inspiring Flamengo's victory over Liverpool, then coached with success in Japan and Turkey.

ABOVE Zico takes on Argentina's Jorge Olguín in the 1982 World Cup finals

GREAT PLAYERS & MANAGERS MOMENTS: 1970s

ABOVE Gerd Müller, triple European champion with Bayern Munich

BELOW Franz Beckenbauer (left) closes in on England's Colin Bell

ABOVE Sepp Maier in training in Munich's Olympic stadium

LEFT Franz Beckenbauer hoists aloft the World Cup in 1974

BELOW Uli Hoeness finds space in the World Cup final

1980s

1990s

2000s

ABOVE France winger Didier Six (right) takes on the Czech defense

BELOW Ossie Ardiles in English action for Tottenham

ABOVE Eric Cantona making his debut for Manchester United

ABOVE David Beckham strikes a winning penalty against Argentina

ABOVE Steve Gerrard celebrates another of his England goals

LEFT Cristiano Ronaldo top-scored with 31 goals in the 2008 Premier League

GREAT PLAYERS & MANAGERS
REST OF THE WORLD

ABOVE Hong Myung-Bo is challenged by Mexican forward Cuauhtemoc Blanco in 1998

DIDIER DROGBA (born 11 March 1978)
Ivory Coast: 52 games, 33 goals
Didier Drogba was a late starter, not making his professional breakthrough until he was 20 with French club Le Mans. He moved on to Guingamp in the French first division at the age of 24 before being bought by Marseille, who he led to the 2004 UEFA Cup final. His next step was a transfer to newly-enriched Chelsea for a then club record $48 million (£24 million). He has scored over 70 goals in four seasons for the club and has won the Premier League, FA Cup, and League Cup. He was named African Player of the Year in 2007.

SAMUEL ETO'O (born 10 March 1981)
Cameroon: 76 games, 31 goals
Samuel Eto'o is an explosive Cameroon striker who was brought to Europe by Real Madrid. However, he failed to impress the club and was sold. He has made them regret it with four wonderful seasons each at Mallorca and then Barcelona. In 2006, Eto'o won the Golden Boot as Europe's leading league scorer with 26 goals, helping to fire Barcelona to their Champions League success over Arsenal as well as winning the Spanish Super Cup.

HONG MYUNG-BO
(born 12 February 1969)
South Korea: 135 games, nine goals
Hong Myung-Bo was the first Asian player to appear in four World Cup finals tournaments. Originally a powerful defensive midfielder, he was soon switched to central defense. He made his international debut in 1990 and was chosen to be part of the South Korean World Cup squad in Italy later that year. He earned international admiration for his displays in the 1994 and 1998 World Cup finals, despite the first round exits. He was a national hero long before he captained South Korea to the final four on home territory at the 2002 World Cup finals.

HOSSAM HASSAN (born 10 August 1966)
Egypt: 170 games, 69 goals
Hossam Hassan is the world's second most capped player with 170 appearances for the Pharaohs, just behind Mohammed Al Deayea's 181 games for Saudi Arabia. He has yet to announce retirement and continues to break Egyptian records: winning 41 titles as a player, playing 21 matches over seven African Nations' Cup competitions, and being the oldest scorer in an Egyptian national shirt. Hossam has also played for Paok Saloniki in Greece, Neuchatel Xamax in Switzerland, and El-Ain in the UAE.

ROGER MILLA (born 20 May 1952)
Cameroon: 102 games, 28 goals
Roger Milla had long been an African hero before his goal-celebrating dance around the corner flags brought him global fame at the 1990 World Cup. Milla scored four times at those finals, making him the oldest ever World Cup goal scorer at the age of 38. He returned to the World Cup finals four years later, before retiring with an impressive career record: he twice picked up the African Player of the Year award (1976 and 1990), and in 2007 was voted the best African Player of the last 50 years by the Confederation of Africa (CAF).

HIDETOSHI NAKATA
(born 22 January 1977)
Japan: 77 games, 11 goals
Hidetoshi Nakata was the first Japanese player to make a major impact in Europe. Nakata had been hailed Asian Player of the Year before his 1998 World Cup finals debut. He played in the next two World Cup finals, announcing his shock retirement immediately after the 2006 World Cup match against Brazil in Germany. Nakata played seven seasons for various sides in Italy's Serie A and had a short spell in England's Premier League with Bolton Wanderers.

JAY-JAY OKOCHA (born 14 August 1973)
Nigeria: 74 games, 14 goals
Augustine "Jay-Jay" Okocha provided the midfield command that lifted Nigeria's "Super Eagles" out of the nearly-rans of Africa to near-regular appearances at the World Cup finals. He played in the 1994, 1998, and 2002 finals, but the "Super Eagles" somehow failed to qualify for the 2006 World Cup finals. Okocha helped Nigeria win the 1996 Olympic gold medal and was a recipient of the African Player of the Year award. He played for a variety of clubs in Germany, Turkey, France, and England. At the end of the 2007–08 season, after helping Hull City to attain Premier League status, he was released from his contract.

SAEED AL-OWAIRAN
(born 19 August 1967)
Saudi Arabia: 50 games, 24 goals
Saeed Al-Owairan won the accolade of the Asian Player of the Year in 1994, largely thanks to his memorable solo strike against Belgium in that year's World Cup finals. His goal for Saudi Arabia was comparable with Diego Maradona's sensational strike against England in 1986. Saeed Al-Owairan had only played as a professional for two years before his famous goal.

ABOVE Roger Milla's World Cup exploits earned him a string of international awards

ABOVE Samuel Eto'o celebrates yet another goal for Barcelona in 2008

INDEX

African Champions League 148
African Nations Cup 116, 118, 119, 180, 222
Ajax Amsterdam 50, 128, 131-3, 139, 158-9, 186, 189, 191, 194, 206-7, 212
Al-Ahly 123, 148, 198
Al-Owairan, Saeed 223
Albania 53, 62, 102, 174
Algeria 58, 81, 119, 174
Altidore, Jozy 56-7
America
Central/North American Club Cup 149
  CONCACAF Gold Cup 56, 90, 121, 175
  COPA América 216-7
  great clubs 198
  great players 216-7
  World Cup 26-7, 56-7, 90
America (Mexican club) 123, 198
Andorra 42, 43, 99, 174
Anelka, Nicolas 44-5, 141
Angola 71, 116, 118, 168, 174, 180
Aquilani, Alberto 48-9
Argentina
  Copa America 91, 116-7, 155
  Copa Libertadores 122, 144, 146-8, 154-5, 196, 197
  great clubs 196-7
  great players/managers 91, 203, 216-7
  World Cup 17, 21-4, 27, 31, 33-4, 38-9, 80
Armenia 54, 55, 172
Arsenal 9, 29, 42, 43, 62, 69, 78, 95, 96, 97, 99, 136-7, 140-2, 163, 171, 186, 202, 205, 209-11
Asian Club Cup 148
Asian Cup 121, 176, 178-9, 181, 182
Aston Villa 135, 186
Australia 59, 67, 70, 81, 84, 98, 120-1, 123, 148-9, 174
Austria 9, 13, 15, 44, 45, 58, 73, 113, 137, 174, 177, 212, 214
Azerbaijan 46-7, 94, 174

Ballack, Michael 31, 46-7, 92
Barcelona 66, 91, 96-7, 123, 125, 130, 135, 137-43, 168, 171, 174, 187, 188, 223
Basten, Marco van 50, 95, 107, 110, 135, 158-9, 191, 204, 206
Bayern Munich 78, 86, 90, 94, 104, 123, 132-3, 135, 138-40, 163, 165-7, 187, 220
Beckenbauer, Franz 17, 19, 21, 23-4, 104, 132, 160, 167, 187, 206, 220
Beckham, David 28, 29, 31, 35, 42, 145, 148, 163, 183, 193, 198, 206, 221
Belarus 42-3, 99, 172, 175
Belgium 8, 9, 22, 23, 54-5, 80, 104, 106-7, 175, 212, 223
Benfica 130-1, 136, 144, 158, 163, 168, 187, 192
Bergkamp, Dennis 29, 35
Best, George 122, 131, 136, 191, 202, 206, 212
Boca Juniors 38, 122-3, 144, 146-7, 154-5, 196-7, 218
Bolivia 26, 38-41, 61, 72, 79, 79-80, 117, 146, 175
Bosingwa, José 52
Bosnia-Herzegovina 175
Brady, Liam 206-7
Brazil
  Copa America 40, 116, 117
  Copa Libertadores 153, 196
  great clubs 196-7
  great players/managers 89, 202, 205, 216-9
  World Cup 13-16, 18-24, 26–31, 33, 39–41, 61, 72, 76, 79, 80
Brehme, Andy 23-5, 35
Buffon, Gianluigi 32-3, 48, 87
Bulgaria 26, 48, 49, 174-5, 214-5
Busby, Sir Matt 130, 191, 202

Cahill, Tim 59, 67, 98, 174
Cameroon 24, 60, 96, 119, 174, 222-3
Canada 121, 152, 175
Capello, Fabio 42-3, 139, 160, 202
Carbajal, Antonio 216
Carlos, Roberto 28, 216
Casillas, Iker 88, 113, 170
Celtic 122, 124-5, 132-3, 137, 158, 181, 188-9, 192, 205, 207
Chapman, Herbert 163, 186, 202, 210
Charlton, Sir Bobby 17, 131, 162, 191, 207, 210, 212
Chelsea 43, 73, 83, 91, 93, 113, 136, 140-1, 143, 145, 162-3, 169, 188, 209, 222
Chile 8, 16, 27, 38-41, 61, 72, 79, 114, 117, 146, 176, 196, 219
China 6, 8, 59, 114, 176
Clough, Brian 133, 202
Club World Championships 122-3, 148-9
Colo-Colo 146-7, 176, 196
Colombia 26-8, 38, 61, 65, 72, 79, 91, 128, 146, 219
CONCACAF Gold Cup 90, 121, 175
Congo, DR 176
Copa América 155, 175-6, 181, 183, 216-7
Copa Interamericana 148, 197-9
Copa Libertadores 122, 146-7, 154-5, 196-7, 219
Costa Rica 32, 57, 65, 69, 79, 84, 89, 121, 148, 149, 176
Croatia 28-9, 42-3, 80, 99, 176
Cruyff, Johan 21, 105, 107, 132, 139, 158-60, 186-7, 202, 207
Cubillas, Teofilo 181, 216
Cyprus 49, 176
Czech Republic 74-5, 113, 176

Dalglish, Kenny 133, 181, 190, 207
DC United 198
Dean, Dixie 207
Denmark 8-9, 31, 52-3, 62, 102, 107, 109-10, 170, 177, 212
Didi 153, 216
Di Stefano, Alfredo 122, 129-30, 136, 154-5, 170, 176, 195, 197, 208, 210, 216
Donovan, Landon 56-7, 90, 217
Dortmund, Borussia 78, 122, 138, 143, 166, 188-9
Drogba, Didier 66, 83, 118-9, 179, 222

Ecuador 38-9, 40, 61, 72, 79, 146, 177, 219
Egypt 49, 58, 81, 89, 118-9, 148, 177, 198, 222
Eindhoven 24, 107, 135, 158, 187, 194, 202
El Salvador 57, 65, 69
England
  European Championship 103-4, 106-7, 109-12
  great clubs 186, 188-91, 195,
  great players/managers 99, 202-7, 210-13
  World Cup 13-14, 17, 19-21, 23-5, 28-31, 33, 35, 42-3, 80
Eriksson, Sven-Goran 31, 33, 69, 143, 182, 190
Essien, Michael 63, 93, 118, 177, 190
Estonia 54-5, 177
Etoile Sahel 123, 148-9, 193
Eto'o, Samuel 60, 96, 116, 118-9, 175, 186, 222-3
European Champions Club Cup 126, 128-9, 187, 189, 191
European Champions' League 165, 167, 169, 171, 186-7, 190
European Championship 135, 141, 143, 156, 158-9, 163-5, 169-70, 172, 175-9, 182, 202, 204-6, 209, 212, 215
European Cup Winners' Cup 165, 172, 177, 188, 190-1, 195, 203, 207, 212-3
Eusébio 17-8, 108, 118, 130, 144, 168-9, 173, 180, 187, 192, 208
Everton 76, 98-9, 189, 207, 212

Fabiano, Luis 40-1, 80
Fabregas, Cesc 54-5
Faroe Islands 44-5, 73, 176
Feola, Vincente 15, 153, 202
Ferguson, Sir Alex 52, 82, 163, 181, 191, 202-3, 211
Fernandez, Matias 41, 61
Feyenoord 50, 95, 132-3, 135, 158, 188-9, 194, 209
FIFA 6, 8-9, 12-3, 24-8, 30, 45, 48, 54-5, 66, 69, 74, 76, 89-91, 93, 98, 100, 102, 120-21, 123, 128, 147, 164, 167, 172, 178, 182, 206
Finland 46-7, 177
Flamengo 153, 192, 196, 219
Fontaine, Just 15, 18, 118, 165, 208
Football Association (FA) 7, 8
Forlan, Diego 79, 84
France
  European Championship 107-9, 112
  great clubs 190-1
  great players/managers 86, 97, 209
  World Cup 12, 17-18, 23, 28-33, 44-5

Garrincha 15, 16, 152-3, 202, 217
Gento, Francisco "Paco" 195, 208
Georgia 48-9, 177, 180
Germany
  European Championship 104-7, 110-11, 113
  great clubs 187-8
  great players/managers 92, 94, 203-4, 206, 208, 214-5
  World Cup 13-14, 16-26, 31-3, 35, 46-7
Ghana 63, 93, 119, 177, 179
Greece 6, 27, 45, 64, 78, 82, 97, 102, 112-3, 132, 169, 177, 178, 222
Gullit, Ruud 106-7, 135, 159, 191, 198, 204, 209

Hagi, Gheorghe 26, 181, 209
Haiti 178
Hassan, Hossam 198, 222
Henry, Thierry 44-5, 97, 188, 202, 209
Herberger, Josef "Sepp" 14, 166, 203, 215
Herrera, Helenio 130, 186, 189, 203
Hiddink, Guus 31, 59, 158-9, 174, 202-3
Hogan, Jimmy 9, 210
Holland
  European Championship 105-7, 109-11, 113
  great clubs 186, 189, 194
  great players/managers 202-3, 206-7, 209
  World Cup 21, 25, 29, 34-5, 50-1
Honduras 57, 65, 69, 81, 90, 178
Hungary 9, 13-5, 53, 62, 102, 104, 129, 166, 168, 178, 214
Hurst, Geoff 16-8, 162, 209

Iceland 50-1, 178
Independiente 84, 154-5, 196
India 178
Intercontinental Cup 122-3, 155
Internazionale 28, 130, 132, 138, 141-3, 189, 192, 213
Iran 68, 77, 149, 178
Iraq 59, 76, 178
Ireland
  Northern 22, 74-5, 120, 206
  Republic of 27, 45, 48-9, 80, 86, 88, 97, 181, 206
Israel 64, 78, 141, 148, 178
Italy
  European Championship 103-4, 112-3,
  great clubs 189, 191, 193, 195
  great players/managers 87, 202-5, 213-5
  World Cup 13, 17, 22, 25, 27, 32-3, 48-9
Ivory Coast 66, 81, 83, 95, 119, 179

Jairzinho 19-20, 153, 217, 218
Jamaica 179
Japan 30-1, 59, 67, 98, 123, 148, 179, 199, 223
Juventus 22, 29, 32, 63, 87, 97, 132, 134-5, 137, 139-43, 156-7, 163, 189, 191, 195

Kahn, Oliver 31, 47, 144, 187
Kaizer Chiefs 148, 199
Kaka 40-1, 89, 117, 128, 140, 153, 193, 217
Kazakhstan 42-3, 99, 179
Kempes, Mario 21, 154, 217
Kiev, Dynamo 172, 183, 188, 203
Klose, Miroslav 33, 46-7, 94, 102
Kopa, Raymond 164-5, 209
Korea, North 17, 18, 68, 156, 160, 180, 208
Korea, South 30-1, 68, 77, 81, 87-90, 92, 123, 148, 182, 199, 222
Krol, Ruud 34, 132, 158
Kuwait 179
Kuyt, Dirk 50-1, 189

Lampard, Frank 80
Latvia 64, 78, 179,
Laudrup, Michael 110, 177, 187, 212
Law, Denis 131, 191, 207, 212
Liechtenstein 46-7, 179
Lineker, Gary 23, 24, 34, 161, 162, 212
Lithuania 44, 45, 73, 86, 179
Liverpool 85, 123-5, 133-5, 137-8, 140-3, 145, 186, 188-91, 196, 203, 205, 207
Los Angeles Galaxy 148, 198, 217
Luxembourg 64, 78, 174, 179
Lyon 63, 164-5, 190

Macedonia 50, 51, 99, 180
Madrid
  Atletico de 50, 85, 122, 132-3, 143-4, 193
  Real 28, 82, 88-9, 96, 102, 122, 128-31, 135-6, 138-44, 146, 154, 168, 170-71, 186-7, 195, 208, 210
Malta 52-3, 62, 180
Manchester City 40, 124, 190
Manchester United 33, 51-2, 77, 82, 84, 91, 96, 98-9, 122-3, 128, 131, 138-41, 145, 163, 168, 186, 188-9, 191-2, 202, 206-7, 211-14, 216, 221
Maradona, Diego 22-5, 34, 38-9, 45, 80, 91, 154-5, 196, 200, 217, 223
Marseille 83, 86, 139, 165, 191, 194-5, 222
Masopust, Josef 16, 176, 212-3
Materazzi, Marco 32-3, 215
Matthews, Stanley 200, 213
Mazzola, Sandro 131, 156, 189
Meazza, Giuseppe 13, 156, 213
Menotti, Cesar Luis 21, 154-5, 203, 217
Messi, Lionel 38, 91
Mexico 12, 26-7, 56-7, 65, 69, 90-1, 121, 145, 147, 161, 176, 180, 193, 216, 218-9
Milan 64, 73, 89, 117, 122-4, 128, 130-1, 135, 137-41, 144-5, 156, 158, 165, 168, 191, 193
Milla, Roger 24, 96, 175, 223
Mitropa Cup 121, 124, 138, 156, 214
Moldova 64, 78, 180
Montenegro 33, 48-9, 73, 91, 180-1
Moore, Bobby 17, 104, 162, 213, 218
Morocco 23, 60, 96, 119,
Müller, Gerd 19, 21, 104-5, 132-3, 167, 187, 214, 220

Netherlands see Holland
New Zealand 70, 76, 85, 121, 149, 180
Nigeria 27, 71, 76, 91, 93, 118-9, 180, 223
Norway 27, 50-1, 181

Oceania Club Championship 149
Oceania Nations Cup 121
Okocha, Jay-Jay 118, 223
Olympique Marseille see Marseille
origins of game 6 – 9

Paisley, Bob 133, 190, 203
Paraguay 8, 23, 38-41, 61, 72, 79, 146, 164, 182
Pelé 14-17, 20, 26, 31, 146, 152-3, 160, 197, 200, 202, 218
Peñarol 122, 146, 196, 219
Peru 21, 39-41, 61, 72, 79, 146, 181, 216
Platini, Michel 97, 107-8, 110, 129, 134, 164, 189
Pohang Steelers 199
Poland 13, 21, 23, 74-5, 181
Porto 123, 125, 135, 141, 165, 168-9, 187, 194
Portugal 17-8, 30, 32-3, 44-5, 52-3, 62, 64, 82, 85, 95, 99, 107, 108, 112-3, 141, 160, 161, 168-9, 192
Pozzo, Vittorio 13, 156, 204
PSV Eindhoven see Eindhoven
Pumas 199
Puskas, Ferenc 14-5, 122, 129, 130, 136, 178, 195, 208, 214

Qatar 59, 67, 98, 181

Ramsey, Sir Alf 17, 20, 102, 104, 162, 204, 210
Rangers 58, 60, 143, 173, 181, 188, 194-5
Ribery, Franck 44, 86
Riquelme, Juan Roman 38-9, 116, 144, 196
River Plate 154-5, 196-7, 216
Robson, Sir Bobby 24, 162, 204, 211
Roma 41, 135, 142-3, 157, 195, 202
Romania 19, 25, 27-8, 38, 44-5, 73, 107, 135, 154, 209
Ronaldinho 31, 40, 117, 187, 193, 218
Ronaldo 28-9, 31, 152, 200, 217, 218
Ronaldo, Cristiano 33, 52-3, 82, 112-13, 141, 145, 168-9, 191, 214, 221
Rooney, Wayne 33, 42-3, 99
Rossi, Paolo 22, 156-7, 214
rules of game 7, 9
Russia 45-7, 75, 94-5, 172-3, 209

Sacchi, Arrigo 191, 204
San Marino 74-5, 174
Sanchez, Hugo 193, 199, 218
Santos 15, 145-7, 153, 155, 193, 197, 217-8
São Paulo 89, 122-3, 147, 153, 197, 217
Saudi Arabia 68, 77, 84, 94, 96, 178, 181, 223
Schiaffino, Juan 14, 196
Schön, Helmut 104-5, 204
Scotland 21, 34, 51, 92, 110-11, 120-1, 177, 181, 188, 194, 207, 212
Senegal 30, 58, 84, 119, 181
Serbia 32, 44-5, 73, 91, 97, 181
Shankly, Bill 133, 190, 203, 205
Sindelar, Matthias 174, 214
Slovakia 74-5, 182
Slovenia 74-5, 182
South Africa 38, 76
South America
  Copa America 40, 84, 91, 116-7, 155, 176, 181, 216-7
  Copa Libertadore 122, 146-8, 153-5
  great clubs 196-7
  great players/managers 202-3, 216-219
Soviet Union 15, 16, 25, 102, 104-5, 107, 159-60, 170, 172-3, 206, 215
Spain
  European Championship 103, 107-9, 113
  great clubs 186-9, 195
  great players 85, 88, 208
  world cup 16, 22, 32, 54-5, 80
Spencer, Alberto Pedro 146, 196, 219
Stein, Jock 131, 188, 205
Stoichkov, Hristo 174-5, 187, 198, 215
Sweden 13, 15, 30, 33, 52-3, 62, 82, 85, 182, 218
Switzerland 15, 26, 64, 78, 99, 182

Togo 60, 182
Torres, Fernando 54-5, 85, 113, 170-1
Tottenham Hotspur 24, 65, 195
Trapattoni, Giovanni 130, 205, 207, 211
Trinidad and Tobago 183
Tunisia 28, 71, 183
Turkey 30-1, 55, 102, 113, 183

UEFA Cup 87, 124, 126, 129, 142-3, 158, 167, 169, 171, 173
  International Club Competitions 130-45
Ukraine 42-3, 64, 78, 92, 183
United Arab Emirates 68, 77, 183
United States 14, 26-7, 55, 56-7, 65, 69, 76, 81, 85, 91, 116, 121, 183
Urawa Red Diamonds 148, 199
Uruguay 10, 12, 14, 17, 19, 38-41, 61, 72, 79, 84, 97, 116-7, 152, 154, 183

Valderrama, Carlos 26, 176, 219
Van Persie, Robin 50, 95, 189
Vasco da Gama 76, 123, 146, 197
Venezuela 38-41, 61, 72, 79, 147, 183

Wales 46-7, 152, 183
Walter, Fritz 14-5, 166, 215
Wenger, Arsene 97, 205, 211

Yashin, Lev 16, 102, 172-3, 215
Yugoslavia 25, 102-3, 105, 107, 110

Zagallo, Mario 20, 24, 27-8, 153, 205, 211
Zaire 119, 176
Zamora, Ricardo 13, 170
Zamorano, Ivan 176, 198, 219
Zico 22, 67, 192, 196, 219
Zidane, Zinedine 28-30, 32-3, 35, 86, 139, 141, 157, 164-5, 200, 215, 217
Zoff, Dino 22, 103, 112, 156-7, 215

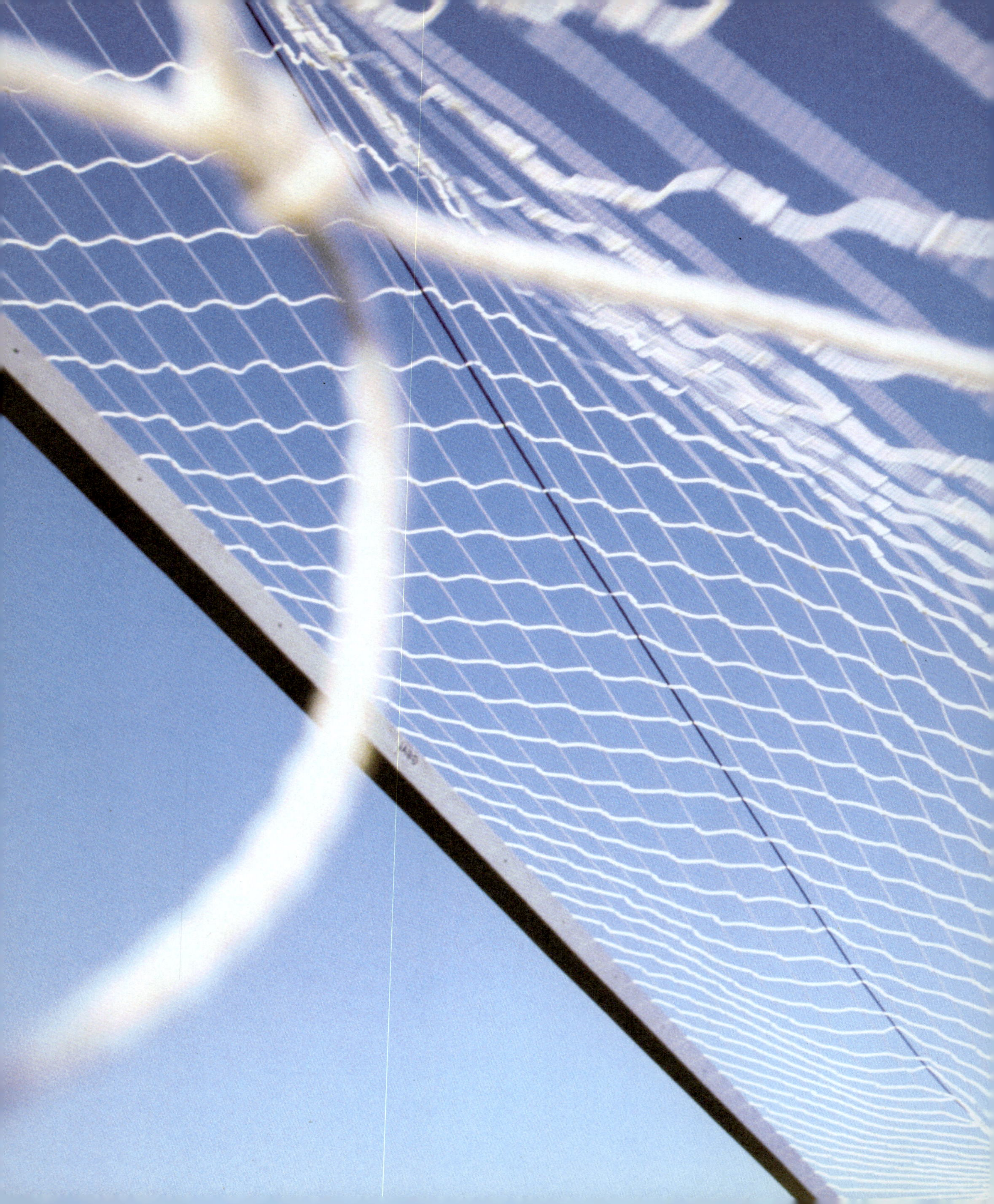